From the Shadows of
Coyote Mountain

From the Shadows of Coyote Mountain

TO THE BASE OF MOUNT DIABLO

The journey through life of a child raised
by Nellie Mac Pherson of "Deep Stuff"

David K. Mc Arthur

Author and Illustrator

From the Shadows of Coyote Mountain
to the Base of Mount Diablo

Text, photographs and Illustrations copyright by
David K. Mc Arthur
Cover Design by Janette Stuart and David K. Mc Arthur
Research Compiled by Celeste Rush, Lyn Winer and David Mc Arthur

Toll Gate Publishing, Danville, CA
IBSN-13 9781530517039 (CreateSpace-Assigned)
ISBN-10 1530517036
Library of Congress Number: 2016904865
CreateSpace Independent Publishing Platform
North Charleston, South Carolina

1 Title
2014

Table of Contents

Acknowledgements

~~~

I WISH TO GRATEFULLY ACKNOWLEDGE the inspiration and help of the following people, without whom this book could not have come to fruition.

First and foremost, to my wife, Nelda Mc Arthur, who has accompanied me on many trips to Idaho and borne with me as we walked many of the old paths and roads of my younger days while I relived the times and places in my mind. Also for the past several years that I have spent many an hour before the computer, tuned out to the needs of everyday living to get this written down. She has never complained.

To Celeste Rush and Lyn Winer who have been my inspiration to actually tackle this effort. Without them nothing would have happened with my story other than my sharing with family and friends orally. They inspired me to write it all down and taught me the perseverance to see it through.

To the Ourada's who have been links to my past in so many ways. They have always made us welcome at their gatherings and provided us with transportation to the Toll Gate. They have shared memories, letters and pictures. Most of all, they have been our friends.

To the Echanove's who have shared their memories of my youth.

To the Bicandi's; who were like family to us at the Toll Gate providing a link to the world outside of our immediate surroundings.

To the Mac Leod's who have let me live on their land, bought me food and allowed me to return to the Toll Gate on many occasions since I first left it. I wish I had been more expressive in what that has meant to me while the three Colin's still lived.

To Emily Gonzales for many hours of editing and correcting my errors.

To my Aunt Nellie and Uncle Angus, without whom I may well have no memories worth writing. Though they had nothing much in the way of worldly goods we never felt poor or left out. I have never felt that I missed out on the good things in life.

These are memories as I remember them occurring. Others may remember things differently. If you have any comments, questions, concerns, or just want to share your memories, please feel free to email me at my home, daveymc29@sbcglobal.net. I am looking for early pictures of the Healy Toll Gate. Also if you wish information on buying Deep Stuff send me an email. I will try to assist you.

A special thanks to my favorite daughters. Janette Stuart, who has borne with me as I tried to make this book as easy to read and appealing as possible. She also helped design the covers. Also Darlene Mc Bride, , who really did nothing but come in with the baton at the finish line of editing this book (and also wrote this in).

Glenn Oakley of Bogus Basin Rd, Boise, Idaho for his professional picture of Coyote Mountain and the ruins of the Shearer House featured on the front cover of this book.

My Dentist, Paul Cannariato for his picture of Mount Diablo featured on the back cover of this book.

To Richard L. Wren. He is the author of many books including, booklets on publishing which have been most helpful. Also he took the time to meet with us privately and explain things we didn't quite understand.

I purposely haven't written much about other family members as my hope is the living will eventually write their own stories, and descendants will for those gone ahead of me.

Introduction

THIS IS THE STORY OF a different type of early life. One not typically lived by modern day Americans. We were not born wealthy, privileged or powerful. We lived in poverty, in squalor, more or less. We had dried animal hides for carpeting, unpainted buildings without concrete foundations, no electricity and no indoor plumbing. No car, no radio and no telephones. The walkways were dirt paths. The front lawn was full of animals and their droppings. Often the entire income for the year was derived from the sale of a cow, sheep or horse. We grew up to be self sufficient, mostly well educated and productive members of society, not victims. I don't want anyone to feel sorry for me, or my siblings who had a share in this early life. We lived in the middle of a 55 thousand acre sheep ranch of which we owned not one square foot. Yet we could grab a rifle, walk for a day in most any direction, climb over any fence and go anywhere we wished, and no one yelled at us to get off their lawn, or any of their property.

Now I live in a beautiful home on a half-acre lot, which I own outright. It is walking distance to the stores, restaurants, the post office and town hall. The neighborhood is very peaceful and quiet. We have phones throughout, televisions, computers, FAX, a cell phone, and yet I cannot cut down a tree, build a fence, dig a pool or put up any building, without prior permission from some bureaucrat from our city. I can't build a fire because we have "no burn" days. I can't play outside late at night because our noise laws prevent it and heaven help us if I ever fired a gun. So am I better off? You will have to be the judge.

CHAPTER 1

Nellie Mc Arthur

SINCE ALL STORIES MUST START somewhere, let me begin this one with my Aunt Nellie. Nellie along with her husband, Angus Mac Pherson, raised me. They took me in shortly after I was born until a month before my fourteenth birthday. I say Mac Pherson, but Mc Pherson is written everywhere except in the minds of the true Scottish people who love the Mac as much as my Aunt Nellie and Uncle Angus did.

Nellie Mc Arthur was born September 24, 1890. She was raised in a fairly typical Mormon farm family near Mount Pleasant, San Pete County, Utah. This family goes back in history to Glen Lyon in Scotland. In the year 1772, John Mc Arthur, Nellie's great-great-grandfather, came to America. In 1838 his son, Duncan Mc Arthur and family, became followers of Joseph Smith, the founder of the Mormon Church. That alienated them from the rest of the family line and most of their friends. With the murder of Joseph Smith on June 27, 1844, in a Carthage, Illinois jail, Duncan and family then followed Brigham Young. Eventually they settled in Utah. My aunt had a pretty strong background in the Mormon Church and was brought up in that good family-oriented environment that the Mormon Church is known for.

Nellie attended good schools in Utah and received a teaching degree. She started doing some teaching at the school from which she graduated, the University of Utah. The Utah Democratic Senator, William King's first wife had died leaving him with two small children. After about two years, Senator King married Vera Sjodahl, and before long she was having children. At the same time his career was growing by leaps and bounds. He and his new young wife eventually hired Nellie as a nanny. My aunt travelled to Washington D.C. with the Kings and they became a part of the Washington elite scene.

Vera King and Nellie were close to the same age and got along very well. They were more like sisters than employer and employee. They attended parties and balls together, saw all the sights of Washington D.C., traveled to New York, and visited many other historical sites near D.C. They attended all the high society things such as plays, operas, ballets and parties with the celebrities of the time. Nellie loved the parties and the fast life of the Washington crowd. My aunt met rich, famous and powerful people and enjoyed being part of that group.

Nellie Mc Arthur

Nellie eventually met a young lady named Tallulah Bankhead. Tallulah's father was a member of the Alabama House of Representatives. He was a widower who let his daughter run her own life pretty much as she pleased.

TALLULAH BANKHEAD

Nellie liked Tallulah and though she was but fifteen, while Nellie was about twelve years older, Nellie learned a lot from Tallulah. The learning included, but was not limited to, smoking, drinking, doing drugs and avoiding pregnancy while enjoying the men they met. Of course she also learned to not flaunt any of that in such a way as to embarrass the Senator or Vera. It was best the Kings not know of the drinking, carousing and good times the girls enjoyed. Coffee, cigarettes and drugs weren't something good Mormon girls got involved with. Sex? Well maybe that was not so frowned upon if the gentleman was mature enough. ("Old Buzzards, or Bastards"), was how Nellie would have explained it.) She and Tallulah certainly did agree on many things, some being that they both liked well-endowed men and a fast and carefree lifestyle while being surrounded by wealthy and powerful people.

Nellie also went to London and Paris with the Kings and eventually did more traveling on her own around Europe, learning some bits of the languages wherever she went. She was clever and picked up phrases quickly and gave the impression she knew more of the languages than she actually really did. She did learn to read, write and speak French quite well. Later in life she and Senator King's son David, who also became a Senator, would exchange letters in French.

She also once went to Cuba, with Tallulah Bankhead, but she doesn't remember how she got there or what happened while there. She had awakened in a hotel room in Havana some days later; alone, feeling sick, and not knowing how long she had been there. Tallulah came back after a day or two, and they returned to D.C. Tallulah never did explain any of what had taken place while they had been in Cuba nor did she explain why Nellie could not remember any of the details.

Now with the power of the Internet it is possible to look up some of the people Nellie met and knew. Some of them she knew more than to just shake hands with. Some of these people were; Albert Roper, Habib Lotfallah, Tallulah Bankhead, both Senators King, and Ester Blenda Nordstrom. I have letters or personal cards from all of the above, with the exception of Tallulah. Nellie and Tallulah did exchange letters for years but a lot of things were lost or perhaps given away when she and Angus later moved to the Stack Rock School house from their Healy Toll Gate home. After Angus died the schoolhouse building and contents were moved to the Dry Creek ranch of Dick Smith. Nellie's steamer trunk with furs, gowns and many other keepsakes including letters were lost or given away. Somehow they disappeared along with some White House silver service that I saw when I lived with her at the Toll Gate. She told me she had been given these pieces as keepsakes. Nellie told me there were always extras at the parties to offset those stolen by hired help or guests.

While in Europe, my aunt met a writer, Ester Blenda Nordstrom, a free-spirited lady from Sweden. They immediately became fast friends and remained so until Ester Blenda passed away in the mid forties. They wrote to each other often and Ester Blenda was often telling Nellie to get off her butt and write something. She even suggestied the title, "Deep Stuff. This was to be Nellie's life story, telling what she knew of the workings of the powerful folks in our government and the shenanigans they were prone to pull in order to stay in power.

Nellie eventually left the employment of Senator King and returned to Idaho where in 1919, her father had purchased a farm just west of Melba. She worked for an insurance man and later for her cousin Rex Jensen. There she met an old country Scotsman, Angus Mac Pherson, who also had a job with Rex Jensen. They married in May of 1936. Angus by then owned a few head of cattle, some horses and had homesteaded 640 acres below Stack Rock, which is north of Boise. Nellie was forty-six and he was fifty-five. Neither had been married before nor did they subsequently have any children of their own. Nellie's father had died a couple of years prior and his 100 acres west of Melba were sold and split among his second wife and Nellie's six siblings.

Angus Mac Pherson

My own thoughts on this marriage are that Nellie and Angus both gave the other the impression of being much better off than they were. She was living at the farm in Melba and I'm sure gave the appearance of being the sole owner. He gave the impression of being a landowner and stockman of some renown. I doubt either was quite honest with the other about the truth of their individual plights. Nellie had to share her father's assets and Angus' 640 acres were mostly a few dry hillsides with a bit of timber in the middle of a vast sheep ranch owned by his cousin. The stock Angus owned couldn't survive on just his acreage alone. He must have been aware that he would be forced by circumstances to sell his homestead. The fact was that it couldn't produce a living. Also he couldn't get enough work locally to keep himself and his stock fed and cared for. I believe they each realized the situation they were in however neglected to share those thoughts with each other until after the marriage took place.

CHAPTER 2

Toll Gate Sheep Company
and Spring Valley Ranch

ANGUS HAD TWO BROTHERS, DONALD and William, who had come to the USA around the turn of the century. They reached to the area of the Toll Gate by about 1900. I believe they left from Scotland in 1899. They worked around the Healy Toll Gate area raising sheep and eventually bought the Healy Toll Gate property and started the Toll Gate Sheep Company. They were modestly successful in raising sheep and maintaining their holdings until a brother, William Mac Pherson, was killed in a driving accident in 1910.

He had taken his wagon to town and was returning to a ranch on Jump Creek, where he had been working, as a carpenter, for his cousin, Colin Mac Leod. There was a horrible blizzard at the time he had chosen to go back to Jump Creek. His team ran away, his wagon overturned and he was dragged for three days behind the broken bits of wagon. Eventually most of the wagon fell apart and the team went back to Jump Creek with only the tongue and double tree of the wagon. Hands were sent out to look for William and found him barely alive, badly frozen and hanging upside down from a leg caught in a wheel of the broken wagon. He was taken to the ranch and medical help summoned. He was so frozen that when they applied lukewarm water to his stomach, it also froze. He died a couple of days later.

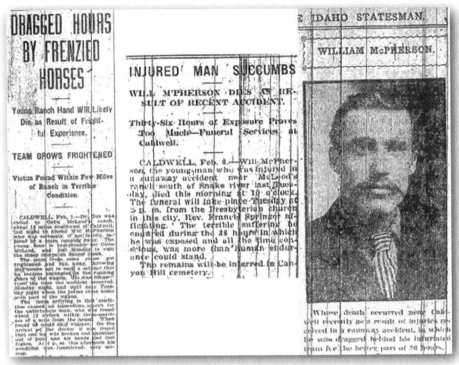

William Mc Pherson*

Angus's cousin, Colin Mac Leod had come from Ardgay, Scotland in 1899, at the age of 19. He went to work near Rockville, Idaho*[1] for Finley Mac Kenzie, whom he worked for six years before buying a sheep ranch with Johnny Bruce. The ranch was west of Marsing and was the Jump Creek Ranch. The date was about 1905. John Bruce died in 1906 and Colin married his widow in 1907. By 1910 Colin and his wife were living in Caldwell and doing well raising sheep at Jump Creek. Colin also bought the Spring Valley ranch around 1910, with a partner as he was trying to expand his land and his herds of sheep. The economy took a turn for the worse and that put stress on the Spring Valley Ranch.

The loss of William and the financial problems of the times were enough to have both, Spring Valley Ranch, and the Toll Gate Sheep Company

1 Some sources say he worked near Jordan Valley, OR

thrown into financial troubles. The banks holding the mortgages forced the two ranches to join together under the Spring Valley name. Donald Mc Pherson held 10% and Colin Mac Leod held 90%. Colin had bought out his partner. One can foresee the outcome of that arrangement. As I'm sure we could all guess, Colin made an offer to Donald that he couldn't refuse. Around 1916, Colin bought Donald out, though at a fair price.

After William's death, His mother sent another son, Angus, over to the States to take over William's share and oversee operations. Since Angus was five years older than Donald she thought that would be best. However by the time Angus finally got to the States, the die had been cast and the two ranching operations were merged, under pressure exerted by the banks. Soon Angus and Donald were both homesteading property that would eventually be bought by Colin Mac Leod. As time passed Angus ended up living on the Toll Gate property, though owning none of it. Donald Mc Pherson, after being bought out by his cousin, moved to Boise. Later he bought a ranch in Payette from Andy Little and became a successful sheep man on his own.

So there we have two success stories and Angus. I believe that Angus never had the drive to prosper like his brother Donald did. Nor did he have the will to succeed that his cousin Colin Mac Leod had. He just plodded along, worked where he could, made no gambles and took no chances. He was happy to have a roof overhead and a warm bed to lie in. Colin Mac Leod let him live at the Toll Gate, which had become part of the Spring Valley Ranch. Angus could raise his own stock and in return he kept up the Toll Gate fields; fences, irrigation system and anything else Colin asked. Colin must have also paid off some of our grocery bills when things got financially bad for us.

CHAPTER 3

I Enter the Picture

NELLIE AND ANGUS MARRIED ON April 14, 1936. I was born on June 30, 1936. Nellie was present at my parents' home when I was born. My father was her youngest brother Perry Walter Mc Arthur. My parents rented a house on Laurel Avenue and California St., In Oakland, California. My mother had five kids already and was not in good health after my birth. My parents decided I should go to Idaho with Nellie and live at the farm in Melba until it was sold and the money divided. This money would permit my parents to buy a home of their own and bring me back to Oakland. I believe they thought this their last and best hope for a normal family life. Shortly after that decision was made, Nellie and I were on a train to Ogden, Utah then another train to Nampa, Idaho. From there we went to the farm out west of Melba where Angus, Nellie and I started living our lives together. At that point in time, there were just the three of us living at my grandfather's farm.

I don't have memories of living at that farm. I do recall being there later on visiting the new owner, Ray Mc Claren, and his family. Ray's son had made a little vehicle out of a large wooden box and a few small tires and wheels. This vehicle was powered by a small gasoline engine, which had been taken from a Maytag washing machine. I loved that thing and he drove me around quite a bit on it. There was a long dirt driveway from the highway to the farmhouse. We would cruise up and down that driveway for what seemed like hours of joyous time together. That began a life-long fascination with automotive power, old cars and such, which hasn't abated yet.

Rex Jensen lived close by on Hwy 45, a couple of miles west and north of Melba. He owned several farms in the area. His daughter Marion and her husband, Dean Jesse James, lived next to Rex in a small bunkhouse. I was told by Dean later on in life, that he had heard of Nellie's living at her father's old place and that she had brought a young boy to live with them. This had to have been after I had been living in Melba for several months. I believe that Dean and Marion had just gotten married about that time. He remembered coming over to visit and as he walked up to the house he noted a small stream of water coming through the front screen door. To his amusement I was the source of that stream, and he thought it hilarious.

Nellie also told me of going to a stage play in Nampa with Roxie Jensen. She left me home with Angus and her brother, Roy. They were playing cards with some friends and I was in my crib, so I'd be no trouble and certainly be safely taken care of. When she came home the men were still at their card game. I was wet and standing in the crib with strange looking eyes. She changed me and got the bottle to give me some milk. She found it had been filled with beer. I guess I had cried and the men knew how to make me happy and quiet. I still like the flavor of beer though it doesn't always make me quiet.

CHAPTER 4

Angus' Homestead

Angus's Homestead
CABIN
Door faced east

AFTER THE MELBA FARM WAS sold, there came a time that we had to vacate that property. I believe that we moved to Angus' homestead cabin. Nellie told me of my laughing at the squirrels and birds around the homestead cabin and how she loved it there during the summer. It was out in the open, just a few hundred yards from the timber and there was a pretty creek that ran by, between the house and the timber. There was no well, so they had to fetch water from that creek. There was no electrical power, paved road or a phone within 10 miles. I remember from later trips there that it was beautiful and quiet, except for the breeze through the forest in the evenings. Sometimes the quiet was broken by the screech of an owl or the melody of the howling of coyotes on distant hills. Other times the scolding of the grey squirrels would be the only sound.

This homestead was east approximately three miles and upstream from the Toll Gate. It was close to 4500 feet above sea level. The snow in the winter was a real problem for anyone living there and for any livestock that they may own. I do think that we moved there in the spring or early summer, after we left Melba. I doubt that we ever spent the winter there. It is quite possible that we never really lived there, just spent a week or two during the good weather and then moved to the upper house on Coyote Mountain.

CHAPTER 5

The Upper House on Coyote Mountain

THERE WAS A HOUSE THAT had been a bunkhouse for field workers at the Toll Gate, situated on the north end of Coyote Mountain about one quarter mile east of the Toll Gate itself. We referred to it as the "Upper House" on Coyote Mountain. I believe that we moved there before the first snow of winter fell so that we didn't have to remain in Angus' tiny homestead cabin through the winter. That cabin must have been about ten by ten feet and I know it was cold. Years later. when Perry and I would go there to get out of the weather while deer hunting nearby, or while gathering firewood in the winter, we found that it protected us from the wind but not the cold. It was of single wall construction with no type of covering over the studs inside and offered only minimal protection from the wind-chill. There had been a stove, but it had been removed and brought to the Toll Gate.

My first memories are of living in the upper house. It stood pretty much by itself, no real barn or out buildings. It must have had an outhouse and I am sure it was located west of the house by a small wash that separated the yard of the upper house from the hayfield of the Toll Gate. There were some shade trees nearby but they weren't close enough to provide shade for the house. There was a sort of stockade enclosure built right against, and maybe even dug a bit into, the mountain. There was a spring nearby and two hundred feet below the house there was a creek that flowed

15

year round. Guessing, I would put this house at 4,000 feet elevation. It did get a little more snow than the Toll Gate, (3800 ft. elev.) but not nearly as much as the homestead cabin. On each floor there were two windows, one in each end east and west. The west end off the second floor also had a door added and some bare stairs that Angus brought over from the Shearer house.

Upper House on Coyote Mountain

For clarification you may have noticed that I use the "Toll Gate" and the "Healy Toll Gate" interchangeably. That is the way it was referred to when I lived there. If we were talking to strangers about where we lived we called it the Healy Toll Gate. If we were discussing it with friends and neighbors "Toll Gate" explained everything. There was no other Toll Gate for miles around that any of us had ever heard of. Also "Spring Valley" was the home place of Spring Valley Ranch, which had been the location of the town of Howell. It was that portion located along Hwy 55, which had been the original ranch. We knew that we lived on Spring Valley Ranch property but Toll Gate meant a specific place on the ranch just as Stack Rock did. they were all part of the Spring Valley Ranch.

There were alfalfa fields at the Toll Gate, which covered the area between the Toll Gate and that upper house. Angus had built ditches that carried water to the highest fields at the Toll Gate. One of those ditches started just a quarter of a mile downstream from his homestead and wound southerly around the hillside, picking up another small stream and continued south out over a plain that was known to us as the Russell*[2] place. That house was a ruin the first time I remember being there in about 1942. The ditch flowed across a plain for about a half-mile and then fed into Spring Creek. Angus also dammed Spring Creek and made a ditch skirting the north end of Coyote Mountain to a point about 100 feet above that upper house. From that spot he could direct water over about half of the Toll Gate fields.

The north sides of most of the hills near the Toll Gate were quite steep. As a little kid, I could face many spots on these hills and reach out and touch them without bending forward much. To climb them, I would grasp the sagebrush that grew there and use it to pull myself forward as I walked. Imagine the amount of skill it took to run a plow along those steep hillsides with a team of horses pulling it, no survey marks to follow, just a natural ability to guide two horses and at the same time keeping the plow in the ground and traveling in a straight line. Of course that line had to have a little fall to it to bring the water to the fields, but not so much fall as to

---

2 This was another abandoned homestead that had become a part of the Spring Valley Ranch by 1940's.

have the water moving very rapidly. That would have caused erosion and washout of the ditches.

I know that Nellie and Angus had a Ford Coupe when they were first together. She would put me in the package rack while she tooled about Melba and Nampa. We had no functional automobile at the homestead, the upper house or at the Toll Gate. There was an old Hupmobile sedan, about a 1925, parked at the west end of the upper house, but I never knew it to run. Nellie let me play in it and I doubt that was a good thing for either the car or for me. I do remember sucking on a fuse for a long time then chewing the glass part into a fine powder and swallowing most of it. I remember the upholstery being all ragged and springs coming through the material on the seats. It also had that distinctive musty smell of old uphol-stery that has been wet often. Apparently the fabric roof must have leaked.

By this time I was getting old enough to wander a bit and so Nellie would put me down with a bottle while she was out milking the cow. I would be in a lean-to, made of poles and covered with sagebrush and hay, called a Wiki-up. This structure was close to where she milked the cow and therefore she could know if something went wrong with me. One day I let the baby hog taste the bottle and the little rascal liked it so well he clamped onto it and took off running. I bawled my head off and Nellie came running to see what had happened. I told her, "Hoggy got my bottle." With that she chased him into some corner, retrieved the bottle and plopped it back in my mouth, problem solved. Pig slobber would never hurt anyone, according to Nellie

We had a small bulldog. I can't remember the name but it was a very little black and white thing that liked me and followed me constantly. It was a guardian and companion when I was outside, which was often dur-ing the good weather of spring and summer. At some point a big bull was around. It got curious about me toddling about and came over to investi-gate. The little dog jumped between us and the bull put his head down as if to charge. The dog clamped onto the bulls nostrils and hung on for dear life. The bull shook its head and ran away across the hay field. I went to get

Nellie, who had seen the whole thing and was petrified for fear I'd be gored or trampled by the bull. She scooped me up and ran me into the house and then called for Angus to rescue the dog. He went out to look and the dog was coming back to the house but the bull was still going away at a trot. I don't recall the bull ever coming near the house again nor near that dog.

Four crotched posts were set into the ground, desribing the corners of the Wikiup. The two in the front were about eight feet tall, those in the rear only two or three feet tall. (From the ground to the Wye. Then two rails were lashed into place securely. Next three beams were placed fore and aft on top of the cross beams. All were then lashed tightly together and then small branches were thrown on top of the framework and poked into the ground at the rear and some times at the sides and a portion of the front. Sagebrush then was piled on top of the framework and you now had a shaded area for livestock to get out of the weather, heat or cold , wind or rain. Angus made a couple, one was small and as pictured, the other was larger and served as a makeshift barn at that Upper House. The smaller one was for small animals to use. That is where Nellie put me to have my bottle while she milked the cow. My problem was I shared with a small pig and he didn;t share back. He took off with the milk and I bellered my head off until Nellie got it back for me.

As a little boy I didn't know a lot about Colin Mac Leod, just that he was the nice man that owned everything around us and that he was Angus' cousin. One day he came to our place in his pickup truck. When he was about to leave he asked if I wished to join him in going down to the north hay field of the Toll Gate. He would be there for a while pulling cockle burr plants out of the creek and I could pile them up for him to haul away and burn. I thought that would be great fun as I would get to ride in the seat of his pickup truck something I had never done before. So off we went and he began pulling the plants and I took them up the bank to his pickup. He had been at that for probably twenty minutes which time seemed like twenty hours to me, I got the urge to go home, so I did. He kept pulling weeds and then after a time he noticed that I was gone. He got a bit worried and called after me but I didn't hear. Then he really started to look for me and had visions of me face down in some pool of water, of which there were plenty in that creek. He retraced all his footsteps and found no sign of me and so he looked downstream then upstream and found no sign of me. Then he got in his pickup and drove to the upper house just as I arrived there and he unloaded a lot of Gaelic on me and told my aunt Nellie what he had gone through looking for me. She didn't help matters much as she thought it funny and he left in a real huff. I'm surprised he didn't kick us off his property. He must have been a very nice and forgiving man because we were left there and the incident was never mentioned again. He was never anything but pleasant to me even after that.

In the modern world we take our kids to swimming lessons and watch as the little ones are taught how to swim despite all the floatation devices we tie onto them to try to keep them from drowning. I learned to swim on my own. I walked down to the creek below the house to a pond that was created where Angus had dammed the creek to divert water to one of the alfalfa fields. This pond had spots that were well over my head and it was covered by willow trees so no one could see me down there trying my skills. I took off all of my clothes and I lay down in the water. I crawled forward on the bottom until there was no bottom I could reach. Then I sank and stood up coughing up water and tried it again. Several times I came close to falling into the deeper spots and had to make a real effort to get where my head was again above water. I gave up and went home and a few days later tried it again. After a week of doing that I could dog paddle across the pond in any direction and not have to stop and touch the bottom. So I really thought I was a pretty good swimmer until I saw someone really swim in the normal breaststroke manner, which was many years later.

CHAPTER 6

The Fire of 1939

IN MUCH OF THE WESTERN United States range fires are a common hazard. Idaho is no exception. Most of the native grasses have been overtaken by cheat grass. Cheat grass is a non-native grass that comes to life as the snow melts and is sprouted well ahead of the native grasses. It blocks out their needed sunlight and uses the nutrients that they should be feeding on. It grows at most elevations and dies down early in the year to become a ground cover that is highly combustible. When on fire it sends off a lot of blue smoke and since the grass is so dry it creates a very hot and fast spreading fire. Since the cheat grass is about six to ten inches high and grows even in the shade of the sagebrush and the buck-brush, it will spread a fire rapidly into those ground covers also.

I had just turned three on June 30, 1939. Then on July 11, 1939 a fire apparently started by dry lightning, began at Table Rock and raced in north and easterly directions. It moved across Ourada's Ranch and onto a wide front that covered most of Coyote Mountain and east into the timberline near Stack Rock. (There are two rocky outcroppings named Table Rock near Boise. The one where the fire started is the one toward Bogus Basin and is not the one near the old penitentiary which is known by some as Chukar Butte.) As the fire grew in the morning, smoke and then ash began to fall around our home. (the upper house.) Angus was very concerned and went out to see where all the smoke was coming from and decided that we were in big trouble.

Fire getting started at the Base of Table Rock
This picture taken by Gladys Ourada, 1939

Cinders would fall ahead of the main blaze and start spot fires that accelerated the progress of the main fire. When cinders began to appear near the house Angus took off running along his ditch system and backfired on the uphill side of the ditch. He also beat out any spot fires that would threaten to start below his ditch. He ran out of matches and yelled for more. Nellie gave me a box of matches and sent me out to follow the ditch until I could give the matches to him. I had been out on his ditches and knew where they went so I knew he would be to the east of the house on the ditch above us. I went up to that ditch and ran along the trail on the downhill side of it, being aware that just three or four feet south of me was where Angus had set the backfire that was saving our home. There was nothing but burned grass and brush on the uphill side of the ditch and on the downhill side was the trail that Angus used to walk along the ditch making repairs and keeping grass and brush from growing in it and choking off the flow of water. Damming it would it have it overflowing the banks and caused a washout with loss of the use of the ditch.

That trail on the downhill side was a small trail. Much of the way it was quite difficult for me to see very far. As a three year old I was probably three to three and a half feet tall. The sagebrush had grown well on that moist bank and there was also buck-brush, which was much taller. Most of the buck-brush was well over my head and blocking my view. Also the buck-brush had some sharp leaves that as I ran, made my skin sting. At first I walked some in the ditch, but I was afraid that if I fell, I might fall onto the coals of the burned sticks and the grass on the uphill side, so mostly I stayed on the trail. The smoke was hurting my eyes and making them water. It also made me cough and I remember crying, out of fear as I ran along, wondering if somehow I had passed Angus. But there was still the burned grass and brush on the uphill side and I was sure he was causing that, so he had to be further ahead.

I found Angus about a half mile upstream east of the house. He was using a burning branch of sagebrush to light fires ahead of himself and then would run back and forth on the ditch to make sure his backfire hadn't jumped to the lower side of the ditch. His only tool to prevent that was a wet gunnysack. I gave him the matches and he told me to go straight home as fast as I could and tell Nellie he was all right and that we would be okay. I ran home and relayed that message but we kept an eye on the mountainside and watched as help arrived to beat out the flames and prevent them from circling west to engulf us. In many spots the fire had burned across to the edge of Cartwright road.

I was exhausted and scared and went to bed in a fright. When I woke up the next morning there was a horrible stench of smoke and ash everywhere. Some small spot fires could be seen toward the Russell place to our east and there was still a stand of timber on the south side of Custer Creek burning. That was a couple of miles away and though most everything east and south of us had been burned, the Toll Gate and the upper house had been saved.

Days passed before all the little fires quit smoldering and the air cleared. Fire crews were all around but they didn't have to do any work around the upper house. Angus's backfires and ditches had played a significant role in saving our lives and property. We were told that a CCC boy had lost his life in the fire over by Chimney Rock. Later I found that to be north and east of Ourada's ranch. There had been some livestock and a lot of small wild animals killed in the fire. Mostly rabbits. I believe the coyotes and deer outran it.

CHAPTER 7

The Flood

ONE DAY IN OCTOBER 1939, after the fire, there came a long downpour.
The rain fell all day long and well into the night. When I got up the next
morning once again the world smelled of cinders and mud. There was an
eerie silence about. No cock crowing, turkeys gobbling, horses neighing or
cows mooing. Those sounds had been the signs of morning most of my life
up to then. Angus had left for the Toll Gate to see about the occupants.
Nellie told me there had been a flood and that she feared for her friends,
Mr. and Mrs. Tom Blessenger, who at that time, lived at the Toll Gate. Our
house was up on the hill about 200 feet from the creek but the Toll Gate
had been built where three creeks merged and left as one. That one is Spring
Creek. None of the Toll Gate buildings were more than twenty feet in elevation higher than the creek bed, therefore they had all been in danger.

Angus returned late in the day, dirty and tired. He told us that the
Toll Gate had suffered greatly. Mr. Blessenger was a trapper and he had
been out on a job somewhere but his wife was home. Her son informed
me recently that she had a brand new Ford which she chose to park next
to the house instead of in the garage, When she unloaded groceries,
since it was raining so badly, she had left it parked there. That saved it
as all the sheds for the machines and the garage had been swept downstream with their contents. The barn had been filled with 200 tons of
alfalfa hay, which prevented it from being destroyed. A very large log,

which was followed by tons of other debris, hit the north side of the barn and took away a good portion of the north wall. The hay inside cushioned the blow and the barn stood. On the cow barn side and part of the horse barn side floors were covered with about a foot of mud and silt.

Angus and other men from Spring Valley worked for weeks getting rid of the damage from the flood and repairing what they could. All of the machine sheds had been built very near the creeks and they were a total loss. Downstream for a quarter mile, or so, there were piles of brush and broken timbers. Mixed with that were the remains of the machines that had been carefully placed in their sheds. Much of the metal was a total loss as well as all of the buildings that had housed it.

But all was not hard work and devastation. There were plenty of good things to remember also. Before I went to school, Stack Rock School had a wiener roast for all the families and the kids attending school there. It was held after school one evening late in the fall. Nellie and Angus took me in the wagon. We arrived just as it was getting dark. I remember an enormous bonfire that was built on the hillside south of the schoolhouse. The ground had been cleared of grass and a ring of stones contained the fire to a pit that had been dug into the ground. The fire cast long, eerie shadows. Behind the fire and just a few yards up the hill were some large rocks that stood as gray sentinels watching over us.

We all sat around the fire with a willow stick approximately three feet long, with our hot dog on it. We held it into the heat above the fire until it was bubbly and dark. That was my first hot dog. Then we pulled the hot dog off the stick by putting a bun around it to protect our hands from the heat and pulling it away from the stick. We then filled the bun with pickle relish, mayonnaise, mustard, onions and tomatoes and whatever other goodies we wanted on it. I watched one of the students to see what he put on his and copied him to make mine as much like his as I could. Nellie had to help me as I had never seen these wonderful treats before. I thought that meal to be absolutely the best possible. Then to make it even better, we got to toast a few marshmallows on our willow stick for our dessert. They burned my fingers and my lips but I soon learned to let them cool a bit before putting them in my mouth. What wonderful treats they were. I believe we also had Kool-Aid to drink. It couldn't have been better.

CHAPTER 8

My Parents Come to Visit

THE FOLLOWING YEAR, RIGHT AROUND my fourth birthday, another big change came into my life. We had too many cats around and Angus was out with his .22 shooting a few of them and I was helping by pointing out where they were hiding and burying the bodies so the dog wouldn't get them. We were so busy that a car arrived without our noticing until it was almost to the house. Angus ran inside with the gun and I threw the last cat into the pit he had dug and watched the car arrive. It seemed to be full of people, so I ran into the house just as Angus was coming out to greet them. They hadn't noticed the cat thinning operation and Angus herded them into the house to get them out of view while he went back out and filled the pit he had dug, burying the dead cats.

Nellie greeted the guests and then told me all was okay. My parents had come to Idaho, along with their other children; Yvonne, Perry, Eugene and Walter. They left a daughter, Dolores, who was at a summer camp and left a note for her. The note told her she should call some neighbors, the Erhardt's, when she got home, and go stay with them until my father returned from Idaho. I was a bit confused because I knew of no parents but Angus and Nellie. Without any explanation I was just in the midst of them all and they were calling me by name and talking to me like they knew all about me.

I had no memory of any of them and it frightened me some to have that many kids around. My world was changing and I wasn't the center of it all the time. There were strangers about and they seemed right at home telling me what I could do and correcting me when they thought I erred. That had never happened before because I had pretty well done as I pleased and no one seemed to worry about it. These folks became nervous as I climbed the wall to get to bed in the attic, or ran outside naked to go to the bathroom. I couldn't even smoke my pipe while they were there. (I had a small curled pipe that I usually pretended to smoke, but sometimes filled it with tobacco and would light it and puff on it but I didn't inhale. (Now who else didn't inhale?) I did like the fact that we all got to go outside and play games of tag and hide and seek. I even tried to play catch, but the ball always hit me so I gave up. I felt that it way too dangerous for me to keep trying. There went my baseball career before it got off the ground.

I did enjoy the company of my brother Perry. He would grab a .22 rifle and we would go out hunting. He never seemed to try to make me do anything. He just invited me to join him in whatever he was about to do. He was six years older than I, so no one worried that we were out with a rifle and shooting at rabbits and ground squirrels. The rabbits we brought home for food and the ground squirrels, which were a destructive rodent that undermined the ditches and made holes that animals could step into and get injured. Angus told us to shoot as many as we could. Perry learned to be a very good shot. While he did most all the shooting, I carried the victims. He and I would skin any animals and dry the pelts on stretchers we made. We would also field dress it for cooking, if it were something edible.

Yvonne was tough on me and tried to make me mind. I didn't take to that very well and though she wasn't my favorite she was acceptable. I knew Nellie didn't care much for girls so I felt a need to be supportive of Yvonne. My aunt felt that girls were silly and not really necessary most of the time. She gave me the impression that she believed that girls should just stay out of men's way until called for then to cheerfully provide whatever service was needed.

Eugene was smart and it showed in his speech and the things he talked about. For some reason he never got into the hunting like Perry and I did.

L to r. Perry Melvin, Perry Walter, Eugene
Douglas, Walter Marlin McArthur

He seemed to more or less be in his own little world and happy there, with his own thoughts and a book or toy. He says he was a habitual "cry baby," but I don't recall him like that. I do remember that he did sunburn easily and Nellie tried to make sure he had on a hat with a wide brim whenever he was outside. Whenever he was sunburned she would rub cream from the cow all over any exposed skin and he'd be rancid in a couple of hours. Then he'd go try to wash it off in the creek. The cold water didn't help his sunburn and he would peel and burn the next time out in the sun. That was a never-ending cycle in the summer and into the fall.

Walter, also known as "Porky," was more into being manipulative of me. He could talk me into getting us stuff. He seemed to know if I asked Nellie for something she would give it to me if we had it. So sweets such as cookies and that sort of thing were asked for through me. He also would get me to try things that he wasn't sure of, such as the rope to swing across the creek, or rocks to use as stepping stones to cross the creek to keep ones feet dry. Later in the year I would be his ice tester to make sure it would hold us and not break, getting us all wet. He was just a bit over a year older than I and so the first year that he was in Idaho he and I didn't go to school. Just Perry, Yvonne and Eugene did, while Walter and I stayed home.

I didn't get around my mother much. I'm not sure she liked boys. I think she was okay with Yvonne, but was happy to avoid or ignore the boys. My father had stayed a week or two and then my mother took him to Boise and he caught the bus back to California.

My dad worked at the Tribune in Oakland. He was a functional alcoholic. He worked night shift at the Oakland Tribune running the classified ads on a linotype machine though he was almost blind. He also was addicted to the horse races and even booked bets for patrons of Walt's Club, a bar close to the Tribune building. That is where he spent his evening hours before going to work. When the races came to the Bay Area he often got a ride to the track and bet heavily on his favorites. He made a lot of money booking the horses and lost more when they were in town. This was a constant source of friction between him and my mother and severely put their finances on unstable ground. They seemed to always be on the verge of losing their home, though I never knew about that at the time I was with Nellie. She made him out to be a saint and she was sure any problems could all be traced back to the bitch he had married. My mother.

My mother kept the car and that was the first time I remember that we had a car around. My father, Perry Walter Mc Arthur, had seemed a nice quiet type that got along well with Angus and enjoyed an after dinner drink in the evening with him, I had never noticed Angus drink regularly before. After dinner my dad and he had a glass of whiskey. All of the adults smoked cigarettes except Angus. He always preferred his pipe full of Prince Albert tobacco.

My mother took us all to see Arrow Rock Dam. That was a very high dam. 348 feet in height made it the highest dam in the world when it was built in 1915. We had to go see it. We parked the car and started walking across the dam and Porky decided I should see how far the water was shooting out of the overflows. He picked me up and held me over the side of the dam so I could see. This had me dangling in his arms three hundred and fifty feet above the river. It scared me to death and I hollered for help. My mother almost had a stroke when she saw us. With all the commotion associated with that incident, Porky almost dropped me. I was never so happy to be back on my own two feet. I still don't care for heights with nothing below me.

While she was returning from one of her trips to town or the mailbox, my mother got the left front wheel off the road on a tight curve. The car stopped in the bar ditch. This had the car stuck to the point she could not move it. She had to walk a couple of miles to the Ourada's ranch and Mr. Ourada took his Caterpillar to the curve and pulled her back onto the road. To this day that curve is known up there as "Phoebe's Curve." Many of the people that know the name of the curve have no idea who "Phoebe" was.

While at the upper house, we were paid a visit by Marion and Dean Jessie James. They were Rex Jensen's daughter and son in law. Marion had just had a baby and they were proudly showing it off to my mother, Nellie and Angus. I knew all about breast-feeding having been around cats, dogs, horses and cows. I also knew about breasts on women, because my aunt had never hidden hers on a warm day. So when it came time for the baby to eat, I wanted to watch. I had never seen the full operation carried on by humans. I was shooed away as if that were some poisonous snake she was going to unleash. That seemed to really be odd to me. Had the lady just ignored me, I would have become bored in moments and been off to play. But the shrieking and hiding really got my curiosity going. I pretty much knew what was going on but I certainly couldn't understand why I couldn't watch. That has probably traumatized me for life as I find I still do have a healthy interest in ladies anatomy.

CHAPTER 9

School

Stack Rock School*4

PERRY AND YVONNE LOVED THE Stack Rock School and thrived there. Since Eugene was a late sleeper. Nellie didn't awaken him to get out and about. Therefore he was often late for school. The teacher kept tardy pupils after

---

4 Picture taken by Earl Ourada in 1950

school and the result was he often walked to school alone in the mornings and then had to walk home alone after his detention was served. Winter nights came early and he often walked home in the dark or by moonlight. He loved the school and each day out was another adventure with all the flowers and wildlife to see. Partridges, pheasants and quail would be running ahead and fly off as he got too close and there were always rabbits and maybe a coyote or rock-chuck to see. (Rock-chucks are a "Yellow-bellied marmot.")

There were several ways to get to Stack Rock School. The most scenic, but a steep climb, was to walk straight south of the upper house which meant climbing the north face of Coyote Mountain. Coyote Mountain is really just one of the foothills and as mountains are judged it is not very high. It is in the neighborhood of 600 feet from that upper house to the top at the north end then rises slowly for close to a mile gaining a height of another hundred feet at the south end. When we lived there the top of the mountain had a heavy covering of sagebrush growing on it. That was interspersed with some buck brush. No real trees up on the top of the mountain. The views were spectacular in all directions. On clear days, which most were, one could see to the west off into Oregon. A little northwest the steam from the mill in Emmitt and the mining operations at Pearl came into sight. To the north lay the ridgeline that seemed to circle the upper house from Stack Rock to Cartwright summit and wind toward the west.

When you were at the south end of Coyote Mountain, you could look off to the southwest for over fifty miles. We could often see reflections from the windows in Silver City and the Owyhee range of mountains. There was a real show at night when the valley lit up with lights from the various farms and the city lights from Boise. When there was a slight cloud cover the city lights would reflect back down in a bright red and orange color that made a beautiful halo toward the south and east. We could also see the beacon light that was a mile north of Eagle. It was there to help the airmail pilots find their destinations. On moonlit nights the contrasts were magnificent between the darkness of the trail and the reflected light on the miles of cheat grass to the west, the black of the timber line and the jutting rocks that rose up seemingly from the center of the earth. Sometimes a buck brush would seem to loom like a skeleton over the trail and get our minds to wandering over ghost stories and the Legend of Sleepy Hollow, the Headless Horseman and such. We could talk ourselves into seeing all sorts of grotesque sights along the way. We would then wonder why we came that way but really it was the beauty of nature that kept dragging us back there.

Walking to school in the winter was often a brutal thing to do. We took turns walking in the front and breaking the trail, trying to follow the trails if we weren't on the road. Walking over Coyote Mountain was very difficult. Getting up to the top was extremely hard, and if you fell in the snow you often slid for several feet back down the trail until you caught hold of sagebrush or something to stop you. This also may have made you into a human bowling ball and the kids following became your pins. Perry would become impatient with me in the lead and take over, but he sometimes fell also, then we'd all laugh and he'd be mad at us. The worst was if there was a slight crust on the snow but not strong enough to support our weight. Then each step was a chore; break the crust, force your foot forward to the length of your step and then do the same with the opposite foot. But the views made it worth climbing the mountain in summer or winter.

An easy way to school was to walk on a little road that lead from the upper house, west toward the Shearer House and just past that to Cartwright Road. I never did know growing up it was called Cartwright Road. We just said "the road" and we all knew what was meant. Then you could follow the road south to the top of Soap Hill, down to the creek and up the other side to the Mason Place. There we had the option of following a road or climbing a really steep hill to get on a flat trail that took us another half mile to the schoolhouse. If one followed the road there were still choices. We could go through the Mason Place or around it. Usually the path up the steep hill won out because it was much shorter.

A typical day in school went something like this. The teacher would tell one of the kids to go out on the porch and ring the school bell. We would all come inside and find our assigned seats. The youngest were right up front and the worst behaved also up front also, but off to the opposite side of the room from the teacher's desk. The older kids were in the back. It was one room and had about twenty desks or less. Prior to my going there it had been grades one through twelve. It was one through eight when I attended school. When it had included ninth through the twelfth grade, a tarp was hung down the middle to separate the two groups. There was just one teacher for all grades.

After everyone was inside and seated, we stood and said the Pledge of Allegiance to the flag. One of the big kids then was assigned to take a folded flag outside and run it up the flagpole, while the rest of us sang patriotic songs, "God Bless America" and such, and maybe even "Dixie." The teacher played the piano while we sang. Then she generally had a little talk of current events, how the War was progressing, and sometimes news from one of the Ourada boys. Their letters to their home were shared with us all. Then assignments were made to the big kids and we little guys had our flash card lessons or read aloud. The teacher spent a lot of time with the first graders in the morning and got us off to a good start each day.

At 10:30, we had a fifteen-minute recess to go out and play. "Anti Over" was a favorite game of ours. We were divided into two teams. One on each side of the schoolhouse and we threw a ball over the roof to the team on the other side. If they caught it, they ran around and would tag some slow kid. He or she was then on the other team. This went on until only one kid was left on one side. But we usually didn't get that far before time to go back in and resume our studies. There were then probably more flash cards, maybe numbers or sounds for younger pupils and some math problems for the older kids.

Then at twelve, we all ate our lunch together. Someone said the blessing and we all opened our lunch bags. Nellie made peanut butter and jelly sandwiches for us. We had a piece of cake or cookies and an Upjohn bottle full of milk. That would have been probably three cups. Sometimes instead of milk, we got some juice, elderberry or prunes, whatever she happened to have open or the first bottle she came to if none were open already. After we ate we went outside again to play until one o'clock.

After lunch the teacher would read to us for a half hour or more if we could beg her into finishing the chapter she was reading. That we almost always did. Next would be some more flash cards or perhaps we'd practice our printing and reading some more. Also we would sometimes go over maps of the world and learn where the countries were. Other times we would go over to the globe and learn the oceans, continents and which countries were in what continent. Also we learned the names of the seas and the oceans.

At 2:30, we would get another recess to go out and run around and play. Sometimes we played baseball. Usually a big kid would hit the ball off into the sagebrush and that would end the game as we went looking for it until the rest of the recess had passed. We also built the "Burma Road," around the hillside for our little cars and trucks. Even some of the big kids got into that with the little guys. We heard a lot about the Burma road in the news and during our current events at the beginning of the school day.

Usually after the second recess the little guys got to lay their heads on the desk for a while. After that we could go to the back of the room and look through some old books. National Geographic seemed to be a favorite of the big boys and we weren't supposed to look at them. That made them all the more to be looked at and we found that they were loaded with half nude pictures, so having lived around Nellie, that was no novelty, but they had neat old car advertisements. Four o'clock came and we got to go home. The flag guy had to take down the flag and someone had to help him fold it. Anyone that had been late or displeased the teacher would have deten-tion. If you were a half hour late, you made up a half hour after school.

My father returned the following summer. He, my mother, Eugene and Porky, all drove back to California. Once again we were without a car, Perry and Yvonne were still about and we did very well together. They were not yet out of school for the summer and the Toll Gate was vacant. Tom Blessenger and his wife had moved to another job and we were to move there and salvage what we could. There was an awful lot to do and we had to dig out the machinery to do it with. The flood had carried all the normal farming equipment down the stream and that had to be found and dugout of the debris. Angus and Tom Blessenger had gotten some of it but not all, so there was plenty left to do. Angus used his team, his shovel and his strong body and eventually we had salvaged two good mowing machines, a rake and a Fresno, two plows and a couple of harrows; a spring tooth and a spike tooth. He also salvaged a wagon. It was a light freight wagon and that became our transportation to town for groceries and anything that we couldn't carry. Sometimes it was used to visit neighbors or to attend things like a play at the school. Mostly it took us to Boise or Eagle. We went to Eagle for groceries and Boise for everything else including; clothes, entertainment, parts for the machinery, to see the dentist or to see a doctor.

Mr. Brashears and his sons, or hired men, came to the Toll Gate with a truck that had a large circular saw mounted on the bed. They would jack the rear of the truck up, remove a wheel and put a cylindrical hub onto the wheel lug bolts. They would then run a large leather belt around that hub and up to a similar hub on the axle that held the saw. They could then saw wood by running the truck engine with the truck in gear. No safeguards anywhere, just a spinning blade, maybe three feet in diameter. They would roll logs across the bed of the truck and cut them into stove lengths for firewood, or longer lengths to be split into fence posts and whatever was needed for shoring and working around the buildings. Somehow they even made a broad board that we used for a countertop on the kitchen cabinets. They may have just cut a large, wide board to length, but whatever they did it was a marvelous addition to Nellie's kitchen.

CHAPTER 10
A Trip to Angus's Homestead

I WAS ALMOST FIVE WHEN I first remember seeing Angus' homestead. Not when I lived there, if in fact I ever really did, but the first time I saw it for exactly what it was. We went by wagon, from the Toll Gate, through alfalfa fields to the Thorn-gate and over a little hill, following a fairly good road to where it crossed the creek. We had to pass through a fence by way of a gate in a barbed wire fence that had separated the Toll Gate from the Russell Place back when they had been separate ranches. We had to open that gate, go through and close it to keep stock out of the alfalfa. The hay was just coming up well and was probably 6 to 8 inches tall. That tells me this was in the spring, late enough to be warm and dry, but not hot. We had taken some food with us and just as we crossed the creek, we stopped under some nice trees that were up the bank above the road thirty to fifty feet. We had everything in some container that Angus carried up there, to the shade of those trees. There was a nice little spring there with a bit of water in a small pool and the rest running down the bank into the creek. There were a few willows around that spring and the view up toward Stack Rock was impressive. I had never been this close to it before that I could remember. I believe that we were all there, Yvonne and Perry, as well as Angus, Nellie and I. Nellie made lunch for us and opened a couple of cans of tomatoes and we had a proper picnic with sandwiches and a cup of canned tomatoes with fresh milk. I thought this must be Angus's homestead, but they told me we had a bit farther to go.

After we ate and drank from the spring we put everything back in the container, I recall it being a bushel basket, but may have been a wooden box. Whatever it was, Angus put it back in the wagon and we loaded up everything, and everybody then drove up that creek for about one quarter mile, then Angus got out and took his shovel and went to the creek and repaired a small dam that diverted the water from that creek into his irrigation ditch that ran from there, across the Russell Place and into Spring Creek. (He also had a small diversion dam on Spring Creek to put the water from both creeks into his irrigation ditch. That ditch ran above the upper house on the north side of Coyote Mountain. It was from this ditch that he had back fired the huge fire of 1939 and saved us all. So we rode the wagon a bit farther, perhaps another quarter of a mile over what was still a fairly good road, but with no hint of his homestead coming up. Bear in mind I had no idea what a homestead was so I had no picture in my mind of what it was I was going to see. All we saw was that we had now passed a few pines and there were lots of pines on the north side of the hills. That is to say on the south side of the creek we were following toward Stack Rock. It seemed to me that Stack Rock had disappeared into the pine trees that were ahead of us and I wasn't quite sure where it went.

We were in pretty country, lots of knee high green grass, many lupine, blue bells and where it was damp, buttercups. It was too early for the Syringa to bloom, but there were currants and wild roses blooming in the creek. Elderberries hadn't yet bloomed, but lots of flowers, sometimes a crocus even, yet I still saw no homestead.

When we got to where it looked as though we would cross the creek again and go straight up the hill, Angus turned left and we went up a steep little hill and on top of it was the wonderful little cabin with no one there. Then they said we are here and they got some things from the cabin while I explored the place. there had been a little pole corral that was pretty much a bunch of short poles lying on the ground. I guess the stock rubbing against it, to scratch their backs, had loosened them and they were now mostly just lying there. There were no other buildings. There were some squirrels in the trees off a few hundred yards and I recall Nellie telling me that "we" used to feed them and that they would come to the cabin to beg and Angus' dog allowed them to do this. That may be where I got the impression that I had lived there before, as by this time we were living at the Toll Gate and I was about five years old. I must have played hard and don't know what they loaded onto the wagon, though I believe it to have been at least a small pot bellied stove and all the rest of his belongings. That may have been when Mac Leod had purchased the homestead and Angus knew he was not going back to live there. I believe this took place in 1942, in the spring about the time we were moving to the Toll Gate from the upper house. We probably needed the stove to heat the bunk house.

CHAPTER 11

Moving to the Toll Gate

WHEN WE HAD MOVED TO the Toll Gate from the upper house it had been a short move. The Toll Gate was a whole new world for me to explore. The only other places I could really remember were the upper house and a visit back to Angus' homestead cabin. Both of those were small and had no out buildings such as barns, granaries, machine shed and the like. The Toll Gate had a large barn, a bunk- house of two rooms and a main house of two small houses connected by a porch. One had to go outside of one to enter the other but would always be under a roof. One of the houses was two rooms and the other just one room. Both houses were similar in size so the one room was quite comfortable and was used as a kitchen and bedroom while the two-room house was being worked on to make it into a Kitchen and a bedroom. There was a well, a springhouse and a commissary. The commissary had started life as a long bunkhouse, back when wagons came through on the toll road. That was when Toll Gate really had been a toll station, and an overnight stop on the toll road from a large sawmill on Harris Creek, to Boise and beyond. It also had a large chicken coop nearby.

The springhouse had a building with walls well insulated, as they had been filled with sawdust during construction. This building had floated off of its foundation by the flood. The foundation was also its basement and spring house. Angus and the Brashears' made up some rollers from logs and moved the above ground part of the building from the pasture where it had stopped floating, to a spot by the main house. The men set the building onto some stones to raise the wood off the dirt and prevent dry rot from eating away at it. There it served as a sort of cannery, storage and root cellar. It was filled with all the canned things from our gardens and the fruit trees. The dirt floor was covered with hay. In the fall we put our potatoes there on top of the hay then covered them over with more hay so they would remain separated and not spoil throughout the winter.

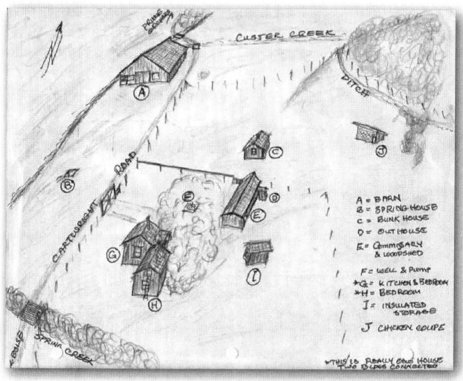

Healy Toll Gate Layout of Buildings

CHAPTER 12

The Toll Gate Barn

THE BEST PART OF THE Toll Gate was that there were so many new things to explore. To me, the barn was huge. It had a horse barn on the west side with stalls for about 10 horses with large mangers for their hay and a small box at one end of the manger for their grain or salt treats. The stalls were built sturdily with 2 X 10 lumber and the uprights were 8 X 8 posts. Everything about it was solid. There were three windows on the west wall behind the stalls with large shutters over openings, like windows without glass, to keep the wind out. When opened they served as a place to shovel the manure and straw outside, to keep the heavy plank floor clean. There were cabinets for medicines built into the walls and pegs to hang the harnesses on. At the north end of the stalls there was a 15 X 15 birthing room. It was separated from the stalls by a large door. That room was there so the mother to be could be separated from the rest of the stock. She could deliver her young without fear of the other animals causing a problem. Stallions sometimes were known to kill a young male colt, just to prevent competition in coming years. Mules were sometimes a threat to the very young colts as well, though I never heard why.

Cows also were brought there to calve when their time came. They often required outside help for their delivery and there were ropes and pulleys to "pull" the calf if necessary. I know Angus delivered a couple by that means, but I never saw it accomplished. I did see a mare squat a bit, and drop a colt onto the hay on the floor. Within a very short time the colt struggled to its feet and she licked it all clean and then she ate the placenta.

That sort of grossed me out because it made her seem like a cannibal. I have since learned there are very good reasons that many other animals do the same. Shortly thereafter, the foal was nursing and within a day or two the mother and fowl were back in the pasture by the house, but Angus kept them separated from the other animals for a couple of weeks.

I also checked out all the little cubbyholes and such in the barn and found what I thought looked like some great lemon drop candies. They had a soft waxy cover so I popped one in my mouth and bit down on it. That sent me running out to the creek to wash my mouth out. What I had bitten was extremely bitter and later I found that it was some medication for stock. So my candy search began and ended right there. I never tasted anything after that without knowing what it was and most things I had to see someone bite into it before I did. It was a good thing I hit on the worst tasting first because other parts of the barn had medicines that were poisonous if swallowed and there were also poison oats to kill rats and mice.

The center of the barn had a large haymow that I'm sure was capable of containing 200 tons of loose alfalfa hay. The hay was for all the stock that came our way and it provided a play area for me. I could climb up the wall of the barn on the studding that held the siding, or cladding boards in place. From there it was great fun to jump into the hay. I could do that from most any height within the barn that I could climb to and still not get hurt. One just had to make sure one jumped right onto the hay. One didn't want to fall short and hit the hard ground. I could play like that for what seemed to be hours. I also liked to tunnel into the loose hay, though that got to be bad because of all the chaff that ended up inside my clothes. I'd have to take them off, turn them inside out and snap them like a towel to get most of it out. Still small bits would dig into my skin and itch like crazy until I either got new clothes on or took a bath. Neither of those choices happened very often nor very regularly.

There was a sort of long narrow garage between the cow barn on the east side of the garage and the haymow. Angus parked the mowing machines there to keep them out of the weather and to do his maintenance on them. This involved oiling, greasing and replacing parts that had broken. Keeping them inside also kept the blades from rusting and the wooden tongues from getting weathered and cracked. One mower was a Mc Cormick Deering and the other was International Harvester. Both were drawn by a two-horse team and cut about a six-foot swath. It took a few days to cut a field of any size. and we had three rather large hay fields. The smallest must have been ten acres and the largest at least thirty acres.

On the south side of the barn, between the haymow and the cow-barn was a tack room that held all the saddles, saddle blankets, bridles and halters This room had some stairs in it that lead to a sort of loft that I don't really know the purpose of. There is where a box of poison oats and some blue vitriol were stored. Blue vitriol was used to treat foot rot on the sheep. I know that the infected sheep were caught and the foot rot cut off with a pocketknife and then the area was rubbed with the block of blue vitriol. I also knew Angus told me it was poisonous and to not touch it. That was enough for me to leave it alone. Blue vitriol is also known as copper sulfate.

One day while I was playing in the barn I went near the tack room and smelled a pungent dead animal smell coming from that room. I got in there and looked all around and eventually climbed the stairs and there was a dead cat and a litter of dead kittens in the box with the poison oats. I looked at the box of dead cats and was about to be sick so I decided to scoot on back down the stairs and tell Nellie or Angus about the cats. I gave the box a last look and danged if one of the kittens didn't seem to move. I grabbed it and it felt soft and warm. The kitten seemed to be barely able to move, but it was alive. I took it to Nellie and told her about the rest of them being dead and in a box of grain. I didn't know it was poison oats or what the skull and cross bones on the side of the box meant. She got Angus to go check it out and he buried the dead ones and I had been correct. Only the one kitten was still alive.

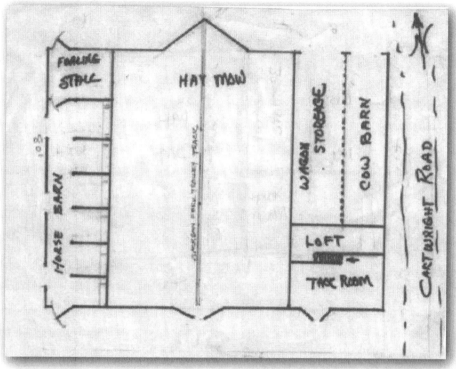

Healy Toll Gate Barn

Nellie fed it milk with an eyedropper and rubbed its behind with a small Fuller fingernail brush. I couldn't imagine why until I saw that the bristles on the brush rubbing it anus made it go to the bathroom. Nellie explained that a mother cat runs her rough tongue over that area and keeps the babies regular and clean by so doing. That also prevents predators from finding the scent of a helpless kitten for its dinner. This cat was our only full time inside house cat and he lived for many years. A couple of years later he got caught in a trap that Perry and I had set for skunks. He lost the paw that was caught in the trap, except for one claw. Then that cat hardly ever ventured out doors for more than was necessary for his toilet. He became a real beggar and would stab a piece of bread or meat with the claw on the injured paw.

We had a few buck sheep around in the spring and over the summer. One morning I took a bucket and started out to go to the Spring House and get a little water. As I walked away from the house I fell down and got to a three-point stance as I tried to get up. A powerful blow hit my bucket and me from behind. I had no idea what had happened but yelled my head off and tried to right myself again, only to be knocked sprawling again. The third time I found out it was a large buck sheep that thought it keen fun to watch me roll end over end and then present him a target again to continue our playing. Yvonne and Nellie rescued me or I may have been seriously hurt. I never got anywhere close to being bent over in from of a ram or a goat from then on. They love to play but not me. That is a real hard head they have even after dehorning.

The flood had washed out the road and the bridges across the creeks north and south of the Toll Gate. The one to the south was repaired quickly but there were two bridges north of the barn. One of those was usable after a couple of planks were replaced but the other was gone with just one girder remaining where the bridge had been. What remained was a wooden 6 X 12 crossing the creek with the six-inch side up. A motorcycle club came to ride the road and I remember some of them shooting across that plank, but one motorcycle had a sidecar and some of the members carried the sidecar as the driver carefully drove the bike across the creek on the six inch side of that girder. The less brave members forded the stream by running upstream a few yards and crossing where the banks would allow entry and exit. This was in the summer and the water was real low, so they barely got their tires wet. Going north they found the road had also been washed out on the far side of Cartwright summit, so they returned and repeated their crossing of the girder and fording the creek. That was the first time that I remember seeing motorcycles and they fascinated me. It was years before I owned one, but it was always in my mind after that.

Not long after that, a crew came and rebuilt the bridges and they were usable for many years after, at least for all the time that I lived there. The road by the Toll Gate was maintained by Boise County from Horseshoe Bend, south all the way to a point just west of the Shearer house, which sat on the county line. From there the road to Boise was maintained by Ada County. Each road had some type of grader driven over it once a year and that was all the repair that was made. Usually a large Caterpillar Tractor came from Boise County and an Adams Road Grader came from Ada County. The road that went west of the Shearer House to Eagle was not maintained to highway 55. That was the road Angus took going to Eagle and he often had to work on it a bit with his shovel where some part of it had become washed away. I never knew of any type machine to come on it to smooth it out, but our wagon could go where cars could not.

Tom Blessenger told me that the Buchannon's had a horse drawn scraper and that they had a contract to pull it up that road to the Shearer house. That was where Boise and Ada counties met and the roadwork was paid for by Ada County. Tom said that Buchannon's would come down into Boise County as far as the Toll Gate and water their team and have lunch, so they always made a pass over that short part of Cartwright Road. That horse drawn road grading all took place well before my time at the Toll Gate.

Before I was old enough to attend school, Perry and Yvonne were still in school so I had the run of the place pretty much to myself during the day. In the evenings they had books to read and homework of all sorts so I don't remember them playing with me much except on the weekends. On weekends we would feed chickens, gather wood and maybe ride an old white horse named Queen to the mailbox.

One morning we found that Queen was lying down, apparently in great distress. She had gotten into the alfalfa field and eaten an awful lot of the fresh new spring alfalfa. We went to get Angus and he looked at the sick horse and flew into action. He got an old piece of garden hose and inserted one end into the anus of the poor mare, then poured water, with a funnel, into the hose and stuck a small ball of rag in the hose to plug it off. He then used a tire pump and had Perry hold a wet rag around the hose of the tire pump, which was inside the end of the garden hose. Angus then pumped on the tire pump until the water had been forced into the intestines of the horse. Perry and Angus did that for a couple of times with Queen lying there without moving very much. After the second or third injection of water, she began kicking and trying to get to her feet. Eventually out came the garden hose followed by a lot of green water and what looked like a wheelbarrow full of dark green dung. Then Queen got to her feet and trotted around passing gas and dung for a few minutes. Angus caught her and put her in the barn and kept her there for several hours. He also made sure no other animals were able to get into the alfalfa field.

In the fall there were always many sheep around the Toll Gate. It seemed to me like hundreds of them. (Maybe because I hadn't seen bands of sheep before, that may be an exaggeration.) However, there were a lot of sheep and Angus, Colin Mac Leod and some of his men dug a ditch to bring water up on the hill west of the barn a little bit. Angus had dug ditches most every-where, so this one didn't take long to make. Then they all dug a big pit at the end of that ditch and lined it with a large tarpaulin to make the pit fairly watertight. Next they filled it with water and a few gallons of sheep dip were added to the water. I think creosote was the main constituent of the sheep dip; that was what it smelled like to me. They also had built a chute of a couple of short fences, wide at the far end and narrow at the pit, so that only one sheep at a time could pass and they had to enter the pit, which was deep enough that the sheep went in over their heads. They then swam to the far end of the pit and climbed out. In just a few hours time the men had run all the Toll Gate sheep through the sheep dip. Angus told me that the dipping procedure was to kill all the bugs and parasites in the wool and on the skin of the sheep.

That was the only time that I saw sheep run through a mass dipping. It never happened there again so I'm guessing that Mr. Mac Leod had made a permanent dipping facility at Marsing where he wintered his flocks and did the lambing operation. After the dipping operation the sheep seemed to magically disappear until the following year. I found that they had been trucked to Marsing, Idaho and there these sheep, which were all bucks, were held separate until breeding time. The breeding time was after the ewes had given birth in the spring, and the whole cycle began again. By this time the herds of sheep were numbering around a thousand and the herd of bucks we took care of during the summer were 150 to 200.

CHAPTER 13

WWII Starts

At the end of the 1930's there had been talk of war and of the Germans going into the Low Lands. At least that was what I had overheard. Nellie and Angus disagreed on most all politics but were always on the same side of the presidential race. They felt Roosevelt and his group had ruined the country and prolonged the depression and feared now that we were being drawn into a war that a better administration would have avoided. Local issues were different. On these they voted the party line, he Republican and she Democratic. It was funny to me how this always panned out and I recall only one time that it was different. That time we took the wagon and Nellie and Angus went to Horseshoe Bend to vote together. All other times Tom Bicandi would come get Angus and take him to vote and Rex Jensen would come get Nellie and take her to vote. Most everything, with the exception of the presidential election, they would essentially cancel each other's votes.

Then came December 7th, 1941. With the bombing of Pearl Harbor we were in WWII. I worried a lot about that. We had neighbors that I thought were Germans. (They were of Czechoslovakian ancestry.) We also knew of the names Hollenbeck and Hornbeck, both of those sounded suspiciously German to me. I find it strange that I worried about it to myself and never mentioned it to anyone, not even Nellie. She had told me of going to some Christening in Germany for some young boy and the proud grandparent had made a toast wherein he espoused, "This is a fine boy and when he grows older he will kill many Frenchmen." You would think that I would have discussed my worries with her, knowing about that, but I didn't.

The war didn't really affect the way we lived much. We grew a lot of our own food and we traded canned tomatoes and canned plums with the neighbors for things like pickles and some items they canned that we didn't. (Those were the same Czechs that I was suspicious of.) They were the best neighbors one could have asked for and they had seen several of their boys off to the war effort.

I remember there was rationing of butter, sugar, rubber and gasoline. Since we had no car, gasoline and tires weren't of much concern. We used kerosene in our lamps and that was only ten or fifteen gallons per year. Quinine became scarce and had been one of Nellie's first defensive medicines, but we could get a substitute called atabrine so even that was no real set back. We did observe the black out by having our lamps on only in rooms with shutters over the windows, or covering any un-shuttered windows with blankets. I believe we got the okay to quit doing that long before the war was over.

During the early part of WWII, I somehow got the impression that one of my friends, Bucky Buchannan, had been killed in the war. I believed that for about sixty-five years and found our recently that he had lived to a ripe old age. I was told that a bomb came down the smoke stack of his ship and he was killed when it blew up in the engine room where he was assigned. That must have happened to someone, but it surely wasn't the person I had been mourning the loss of all these years. The bad part is that I really did feel the loss, yet Bucky Buchannan was alive and well. Even as I retraced my footsteps in the 1970's and spent some time near the Toll Gate, passing by where he had lived, I would point out his home to my wife and kids telling them that is where a man I knew had lived. I would explain how he'd been killed in the war. Now I am wondering if there was someone I knew that really was killed in the war, and I had gotten the names wrong.

1942 at the Toll Gate was really rainy in the fall and the winter was predicted to be severe. One day a car came from the north and was headed for the Mason place. Bill Edwards and his wife Elaine were on their way there from up at the Ingram Place on Shafer Creek. They were in their 1934 Ford, it was raining, the road was wet and slippery. They ran off the road into the bar ditch, just a bit past the Toll Gate, toward the Shearer House. Their automobile became stuck in the mud to the point that no amount of rocking, pulling or pushing, would get them free. Angus got his team and pulled them back onto the road. Then they came and stayed with us for a couple of days just while the weather cleared and the road dried out a little. Then they continued on about three miles farther and settled into the Mason Place, which I understood they rented from Tom Bicandi. He owned the Mason Place along with ten thousand acres of land adjacent to it. Mr. Bicandi also owned the Ingram Place and many other properties. The Edward's became our nearest neighbors and good friends for a couple of years. Then they moved on into the Boise Valley to start farming on their own place.

Just a few days after the Edwards' left us another car came through and ran off the road in about the same place. Again Angus hooked up his team and pulled them back to safety. (I thought we should keep that rut open into the ditch to maintain a stream of company.) They also spent a day or two with us before they could get on up the hill. They were going to someplace like Nebraska or somewhere, and we never heard from them again. They did give us a can of coffee they had with them and promised some other items, but they never came through with those things. A week or two later, Porky and I worked on making it so a car would follow a rut we dug, and get into the ditch. But no car ever came by. Angus saw it one day and made us go fill it in. I imagine he knew we dug it and that was why he picked Porky and me to fill it.

Though we weren't yet in school, Porky (Walter) and I did get to be in the Christmas play, "Hansel and Gretel." Porky and I were gingerbread men. Our part was to just stand there as part of the wall of a ginger bread house. We thought that was fun and after the play there was a gift exchange, cake, cookies and some kind of fruit punch drink. We all sang a lot of Christmas songs and then we rode home in Angus's sled, pulled by our team of horses. The sleigh was full of hay and we had a nice big blanket over us, and a full moon to guide us home. Angus sang Gaelic songs and it was a wonderful ride. The only thing missing were sleigh bells, but that was okay, because though we had sung about them, I had no idea what they were.

About this time I got a lesson in manners or decent language from Angus. He had never disciplined me before that I could remember and I clearly remember this, so it must have been out of the ordinary. Angus had gotten a ride to town somehow. Maybe with the Edward's, I don't remember that detail. I do know he asked around if anyone wanted anything from town. I told him I wanted some suckers. He asked me what kind. Now being one to never pass up a lead in line, and this one I just knew was begging for a very clever answer, and I had heard someone give that answer in swearing at their stock or something. This became my chance to show off star quality as an up and coming comedian. I had an answer that would bring the house down in laughter. (Though I had no idea what it meant.) So, I had barely gotten the word "cock" out of my mouth when I and my bowl of oatmeal went sprawling off my stool, brought on by a quick smack to the face by Angus. My comedy career ended, as did my breakfast and any chance of getting any kind of suckers from town. I did learn that Angus didn't like my choice of words or sense of humor. I gave up that line of speech.

CHAPTER 14

Starting Stack Rock School

WHEN I WAS SIX, SCHOOL started in the fall as usual. Yvonne, Perry and I attended together. I learned the sounds and numbers up to quadrillions. I already knew numbers one to one hundred and the alphabet. Nellie had given me a little address book with the alphabet on it and I learned it rather quickly. The sounds were taught to us by use of flash cards that the teacher would hold up while she made all the sounds. Then she would shuffle the cards and have us make the sounds. We were also taught the basics of how to read from a "Dick and Jane" reader. I wasn't very fast at reading and still read very slowly. I did try very hard and the teacher, Miss Anna Ourada, seemed to like my progress. The first snow caused trouble though. I was not really long-legged and the snow came over my boots and melted. That made my feet cold and uncomfortable and eventually I caught a cold and found that I'd rather enjoyed staying home. At first it was just a day or two here and there. Then I gave up on school and quit entirely. Nellie continued my lessons at home and she tried to speed my reading up. She wasn't very patient with me and I was a challenging student. Probably I was just a spoiled brat, but anyway I know I cried a lot and she would let me quit my studies in order to take a nap. I still love an afternoon nap. The following fall I was seven and this time when school started I went regularly, repeating the first grade and braving the winter cold to stay with my studies.

Then in third grade, we went on a school field trip I will always remember. All field trips had to be taken by the entire student-body. School had just one teacher and about eight or ten students. On this field trip, somehow we all got to ride in cars into Boise to go to the Hotel Boise. This was a grand hotel up near the capitol that had a clientele of legislators and power brokers, much like the Owyhee Hotel did, but this one was bigger. On the top floor there was a radio station, KIDO Boise. That station was our destination and we entered a large room with a gentleman dressed in cowboy clothes, standing by a microphone with a guitar strapped over his shoulder. He was telling stories as well as singing songs on request. If no one phoned him to make a request, he just sang and talked for a few hours each morning. Then someone else came in to relieve him. This process was repeated through the day until the station went off the air late at night.

KIDO had a Tele-type machine and the person on duty would listen for it to take in a message. He could hear the Tele-type, and his audience could also, as the machine was right there inside the studio. When a message came in the machine made a racket similar to a typewriter, but much louder. The host would go over to the Teletype to read aloud what news had come his way. Then he might comment on that news, sing some more or tell another story. In our case, he asked a couple of us what school we were from and then each of us gave him our name and grade. That all was done live and went out just as we gave it to him, with our stutters, stammers and all. He welcomed us while showing us around his little studio, explaining all the various machines and their function in the broadcasting of his program. When we were ready to leave he dedicated a song to our school. After he had sung the song we applauded. Then we were herded back to the automobiles to take us back to our school.

Another field trip was also to Boise, to Julia Davis Park right by the Boise River on Capital Avenue. We had a picnic in the park and got to ride in rowboats on a pretty good-sized pond. After that we went to see the animals that made up the Boise Zoo. I don't remember any of them being elephants or that type of large animal, just the ones from around where we lived so it really didn't leave much of an impression on my mind. I had seen a good many of them in the wild and to see them in a small enclosure seemed inhumane to me. I felt they should be able to run and jump or play as they would in the wild.

A school trip also went to the Idaho Daily Statesman Newspaper. That was a really fun filled trip for me. I had previously met a man who worked for the Statesman that had been in the Printers Home in Colorado Springs with my father. They had both undergone eye surgery for cataracts there. He ran a Linotype Machine that made the lead print for the printing of the Statesman. That was what my father did for the Oakland Tribune. He made each of us a lead name stamp that we could use to print our name. That man's name was John Alden. He owned a Model A sedan, which he had driven out to the Toll Gate to visit with us a couple of times. My father had told him how to find us and he loved to drive out into the country and show off his beautiful car.

Mr. Alden was involved in a really bad accident with his Model A shortly after our school visited the newspaper. He was badly hurt, as was his car. Through the wonders of modern medicine and a good body shop, both man and machine were put back in good order. It had taken a long time to repair both. About a year after the wreck he drove the car out to show us what a fine job had been done on it. Angus and he went over every little detail and were very pleased with the workmanship. I never saw him again so I can't say how well his bodily repair held up, though he seemed to be getting on fine during that last visit. I still remember his four-door sedan with its black fenders and maroon body. That car started a fascination with Model A Fords that is with me still.

Another field trip was a joint meeting of Dry Creek School and Stack Rock School at the Dry Creek schoolhouse. The biggest impression I had of that was their outhouse. For the boys it was a three-hole affair. Never had I seen one that large before. Stack Rock School didn't even have a two-holer. I believe we were there for a Mayday type play of some sort, but we weren't a part of it. I remember we just watched them perform for us, then had a lunch and dessert before going home. I do remember they had a lot more kids than we did. They may have had fifteen or more. They had three swings and a merry-go-round. Stack Rock School had only two swings and no other playground equipment. But we had rocks to climb and wondrous sites to see. I felt sorry for those kids that had only the hayfields and sagebrush hills to look at. We could see all that and so much more. Almost every day we came across some sort of wildlife on our way to or from school.

On our way to school we often cut through the Mason Place where the Edwards' lived. One morning we noticed that something had happened to the pump over the well. It was missing and the platform it had been mounted on appeared to be broken up. We investigated and found that now the well had a dead horse in it, about twenty to thirty feet down. Yvonne ran to the house and told Mr. Edwards. He came out and was devastated. He hoped the poor thing hadn't suffered. Dumb me, I pointed out that the fall killed it. As you could plainly see its neck had been broken when it fell. That didn't console him, nor would anything right then. His wife was also terribly upset. I guess this was their one and only saddle horse and he was more of a pet than a work animal. We felt really badly for them, but had to get on to school. When we came back in the evening he had almost finished filling that whole well with dirt. Now there was no well and they had to get water from the creek from then on.

CHAPTER 15

My Brothers Return
and a Bandit's Car

ON A SUMMER DAY IN 1942; my father, Eugene and Walter (aka Porky) left California on the bus and arrived in Boise just about noontime. Each had a suitcase to carry and they walked from the bus terminal and headed for the Toll Gate, by way of Harrison Boulevard. Harrison Boulevard is a rich part of Boise with some very nice homes and the street is wide with lots of trees, so it was shady and relatively cooler there for the first part of their journey. Also there were sidewalks and lawns and it was quite pleasant, though it seemed quite a long walk to Eugene and Porky. It was a very hot day and at the edge of town there was no shade, no sidewalk, trees or even pavement, just a sandy, dusty, dirt road. The loss of the shade made the boys very aware of the heat as they plodded along Bogus Basin Road toward Cartwright Road. Part of that road was sandy and was akin to walking on a beach, that is to say, very tiring to the legs.

They trudged onward; turning left onto Cartwright Rd, and took that road about four miles to where Peirce Park Road runs into Cartwright Road. Both were dirt roads and without any signs telling the names of the roads. Two to three miles later they discovered that they must have taken the wrong choice, and were now walking back toward Boise instead of to the Toll Gate. My father decided to ask at a farm how to get to the Healy Toll Gate. In those days almost everyone north of Boise could tell you how to get there and the farmer was able to direct them back to Cartwright Road and told them to go over the next hill and continue on another couple of miles until they came to several mailboxes and another branch in the road. He told them that the branch that went to the right, uphill was Cartwright Road. As I mentioned earlier, none of the roads out there were marked with signs at that time. They were told that one of the mailboxes would say Mac Pherson on it, so they would know they were on the correct path to the Toll Gate. Eugene remembers thinking they would surely die before long. It was very hot and they had nothing to eat or drink and still had another hill to climb. They followed the farmers' directions and got past the mailboxes and onto what was then known as the "Toll Gate Road," which was that part of Cartwright Road, from Dry Creek to Shafer Creek.

From the mailboxes to the Toll Gate was about six miles. They climbed a short hill and started down the other side and at the bottom found a creek where they could dip a drink of cool water. The next hill looked as if it was higher and steeper than anything they had been up yet, which it was. They had to climb that hill and then there was just a small downhill portion and then they were climbing yet another short hill. This brought them to the Mason place and my father knew they were almost to the Toll Gate. They had about two and a half miles to go. They walked down another small incline and then started up Soap Hill. Fortunately by then the road was in the shadow of the hill for the first half of Soap Hill and it wasn't as steep as the others had been. This was a short-lived respite. The last part of Soap Hill, which was again out in the blazing sun and now no water in the creek beside the road, again no shade and they were now on the steepest part of Soap Hill. Eugene was sure they would die there, but when they got to the top of the hill and could look out across a long stretch of nearly flat road, my father told them there were no more hills to climb. He assured them that just down the hill from the house standing there in the distance they would find the Toll Gate. That house, which was the Shearer House, was more than half a mile away. It was sitting partially in Boise County and partially in Ada County. It was built to be a school and then the error of location was discovered and neither county wanted to claim it. Therefore, it stood vacant for some years and then the Shearer's moved there for a short period of time giving it the name we knew it by. After they left, it was vacant and eventually just fell down. The trio did eventually arrive at the Toll Gate and we were surprised, but happy to see them.

It was good for me to have my other two brothers back. I showed them around the Toll Gate, we jumped in the hay and played all day in the creek and on its bank. We built roads for our cars and made things from shingles that were still around from the flood. We also dug a pit in the sand and covered it with a piece of corrugated tin we somehow found and thought we had really done something. Nellie and Angus both put a stop to our digging in the sand. They were afraid we'd eventually dig enough that it would cave in and bury us, so that endeavor was abandoned and we were relegated back to digging our roads and such in the bank of the creek. We would spend days there entertaining ourselves.

One day Eugene, Walter and I were playing beside the road, roughly half way between the Shearer House and the Toll Gate. We heard a car coming and thought we'd have company. We stood in the road waiting for the car to stop, so we could visit with the occupants. It didn't even try to slow down and we had to run or it would have hit us. It just roared right on by. That scared the dickens out of us and we wondered what in the world could possess someone to drive like that. The car had been gone a little while and then we saw it coming back. This time we got well out of the road and way up the bank so as to not be a target. It shot past us, and all we could tell was there were two strangers that didn't look our way or wave. They obviously were not friends of ours.

The next day, or so, as we were going to the school we saw a large object in the distance that looked like it was blocking the road. That was up past the Shearer house near, the top of Soap Hill and about a half mile away from us when we could first see it. We began to speculate as to what it could be. Walter thought perhaps someone had opened a hotdog stand there. When we got closer we could see it was a car lying on its side across the road. Then we thought of the car that had raced by us and we became a bit scared and hurried on to the Mason place and told Mr. Edwards that the car was there and about how it almost had run over us. Somehow the authorities were notified, the car removed and things got almost back to normal, although we took a little longer walk up over Coyote Mountain to avoid going past that spot for quite a while.

We found out later that the occupants had robbed and killed a lady in Peaceful Cove, which is very close to Boise. They had stolen her car for their escape. After they crashed the stolen car, they ran off to Highway 55 and hitched a ride to get away from Boise. They were caught in Denver, as I recall. We never did find out all the details of what became of them after that.

CHAPTER 16

We Get a Swimming Hole

ONE YEAR A CREW OF Forest Service workmen came in the spring or early summer and camped north of the barn. They had a bulldozer and were to build some roads from the Toll Gate to the ridge by Stack Rock and on to connect eventually with the road to Bogus Basin. This was exciting to me. I had never seen machinery like that up close. Now here it was, only a few yards from our barn with men working it. I would have watched more, but as soon as they started the engine I was told to get out of the way, probably by Walter or Eugene. I was afraid of the machine and went back to the house. Noise had a way of frightening me, and pushing curiosity to the back of my mind. Escaping noise became paramount in my thinking and actions.

At the end of each day, the bulldozer was left at the end of the road-work and the crew would ride back to camp in a pickup. They transported fuel and oil in the pickup and didn't have to drive the tractor back to camp each night. That saved a lot of time and probably saved wear and tear on the machine. So the crew would return to camp, fix their dinner, then come over and visit for a while before retiring for the night. The next morning they would fix their breakfast, pack a lunch and return to work with the bulldozer.

One morning after they had gone from their camp, Walter and I decided to snoop around. We found they had made some extra breakfast and thrown it out for our dog, or for whatever critter came by. I had never seen a pancake before. Walter assured me it was food, so I tried one and liked it. We went back and told Nellie that the crew had made a delicious pancake and she told us she could do that also. The following day, or so, she did make pancakes and we put honey on them and they were better than the ones the crew had thrown out. Later I found out that the pancakes were also good with Log Cabin Syrup.

After a couple of weeks the Forestry crew was done building their roads. They consented to use the bulldozer to create a small dam in the creek for us so that we could have a proper swimming hole. This was a double blessing; we kids got a swimming hole and Angus got a good diversion dam to help direct water into his ditches that irrigated the pasture around the Toll Gate buildings and our garden. We had a couple of acres of garden and close to three-acre pasture, that were all kept very nice and green. The animals kept the pasture looking like a lawn.

About this same time, a Game Warden, Mr. Bauch, came around. He was very friendly and brought us all soft drinks and took our pictures. He was even interested in getting pictures of us swimming. He brought us some swimming suits that he got from the Natatorium in Boise, but his main interest seemed to be getting a lot of pictures of us swimming totally nude, as we usually did. He was very particularly interested in many pictures of Yvonne, both in a swimsuit and out of one. Probably much more interested in the out of the suit pictures. It seemed he could spend hours patiently photographing all of us. He took pictures of us other places also, but his main interest was at the swimming hole. On his next visit he would give us copies of the pictures. Though it seemed he had taken a hundred pictures, he only brought us about three or four of the boys and just a couple of Yvonne.

Mr. Bauch had also shown a great interest in Indian artifact that we had found. He said he would donate them to the collection that was on display at the State Capital in Boise. (I later spent a lot of time in the Capital going through all the displays and I never saw any of the arrowheads or pestles that he had taken from us to go on display there.) We did find a lot of arrowheads and some pestles while planting our garden by the house. As Angus would plow the soil, we would follow and pick up anything that was out of the ordinary, especially black obsidian arrowheads and anything that resembled a stone-age tool. Mr. Bauch always seemed thrilled with those trinkets and would reward us with soft drinks and candy on his next visit.

Suddenly Mr. Bauch quit coming around. No more pictures, coke, beer and watching us swimming. I wonder now, if Angus may have seen some of the pictures of Yvonne and had a quiet word with him. I'm sure Nellie would have thought it all innocent fun, but looking back on it I'm sure there were devious plans in the works somewhere in Mr. Bauch's mind. Yvonne was about thirteen or fourteen years old, at that time. She was very pretty and a well-developing young girl.

CHAPTER 17
My First Paying Job

WHEN I WAS EIGHT IN early summer 1944, Mr. Echanove came to the Toll Gate and hired us boys, and Angus, to go to his farm on Dry Creek to help put up his hay. We all made up a bedroll and took our clothes in a sack, piled into his pickup and he drove us to his farm. It was very large, probably totaling one hundred and sixty acres or more, all irrigated flat land. The fields were covered with alfalfa, which had just been mown and raked into rows. The alfalfa fields seemed to go forever. The house was a beautiful two-story stone structure with ample barns and sheds for his stock and machinery.

This was back in the day when local farmers and ranchers that I knew of did most everything with horses. I believe Mr. Echanove had one tractor and a Model A Ford that had been converted into a sort of tractor, with a buck rake in front of it. The tractor had been used to mow the hay. Horses had been used to rake the mown hay into rows. The Model A Ford with the buck rake could bring hay to the haystack from out in the field. However there were also several teams of horses that pulled a flat type of sled that we called a slip. Men would pitch the hay from the rows onto the slip and the horses would pull it to the haystack when the slip was full.

I had been hired to drive a derrick team. The derrick was positioned next to the haystack. The function of the derrick was to lift the hay from the slips up into the air to maneuver it over the haystack. The device that took the hay into the air was called a Jackson Fork. The Jackson Fork was attached to a boom on the top of the derrick by a cable and pulleys in such a manner that as the ground end of the cable was pulled, the Jackson Fork would rise with a portion of the hay from one of the slips. My job was to drive a team of horses pulling a cart made from an old horse drawn mower body, to which the derrick cable was attached. I drove the team of horses straight away from the derrick until given a signal to stop. When, at the right height, the boom on top of the derrick would be swung over the stack. There was a man on top of the haystack, called the stacker. He would direct the entire hay stacking operation, including stopping me. When the hay on the Jackson Fork was where he wanted it he would signal a man on the ground. The man on the ground would pull a trip rope that would allow the Jackson Fork to drop its load of hay. The dropping of the hay was my signal to unhook my team from the cable on the ground and return to my starting point. The men at the slip would swing the boom back to position it over the slip load of hay. When they had the Jackson Fork over the slip they pulled the trip rope to bring the Jackson fork back to the load of hay, where the cycle began again. As the Jackson fork returned to the slip location, the cable my team had pulled was retracted and brought back to my starting point, near the base of the derrick. I hustled back to that spot and reattached the cable to the cart and awaited the signal to haul the hay aloft again.

Recently Pedro (Pete) Echanove asked me if I had remembered his brother. That question surprised me, as I did know he had a sister, but hadn't met a brother. We talked some more and he told me that his brother had driven the derrick team and that the team had run away for some reason and his brother had been killed as a result of the runaway. I was hired because his mother didn't want their only remaining son to drive the derrick team. That had all taken place a couple of years before I was born.

Angus, my brother Perry and rest of the men worked pitching hay onto horse drawn slips. When they had a load the filled slip was brought to the haystack, where it was unloaded with the derrick and Jackson fork as described above, then back to the field for another load. There were probably three slips with three crews working them, so the stacking operation was fairly continuous. We worked until just before 12 o'clock, at which time we went to the house for our noon meal. That meal was a big one, steaks and chops and stews with all the trimmings. Almost everything was homemade and all made from fresh ingredients.

The Echanove's had a telephone and during breakfast it would ring and there would be a pause as all the farm wives in Dry Creek picked up the party line, then they would discuss what the lunch menu would be and how they would prepare it. Most all of this was done in the Basque language and I didn't understand it. Mr. Echanove's son, Pedro spoke English and he had explained to me what all that chattering was about. They made wonderful meals and lots of everything. The men worked hard and were well fed to keep up their strength. The women prided themselves in the quality of the meals they put on the tables. On any given day, all the Basques in Dry Creek served the same lunch that day to their crews. The phone call was to make any last minute adjustments to the menu and discuss preparation. The night meal was left over's from lunch and was usually served cold. Both lunch and dinner meals were followed by some sort of dessert, cake or pie. Coffee, tea and milk were available during all meals.

The Echanove's also had a radio and they let me listen to it. I don't recall ever having seen one before that. It stood in their entry in its own cabinet and had a large dial as big as a saucer, with rows of numbers on a circle around the face of the dial. There were several controls that had to be adjusted whenever one changed from one station to another. I listened to country western music. All the station's broadcasts were in English only, and no one worried about vulgarity, as in those days it wouldn't be on the airwaves if it wasn't fit language for all ears. KIDO Boise was my favorite station.

We worked ten-hour days, with an hour off for lunch in between. The workday was seven until twelve, dinner, and then one until six, then supper and bed. Breakfast at six and the day started over. I believe we worked for two weeks. The workweek was Monday through noon on Saturday. I believe that we just had one Saturday afternoon off and then Sunday was rest day also. Saturday afternoon, Pedro, (Pete to us) took us bowling in Boise. That was the first time I had been in a bowling alley and I enjoyed it very much. I believe Sunday we all just rested and ate more good meals. I doubt that we were driven back to the Toll Gate until we were done working the fields. My pay was fifty cents per hour and everyone else got a dollar per hour. That was good pay, for the time, and kept us real happy. Nellie made me put my money in the bank in Boise and told Angus that was my money, not house money.

I had one bad moment in that job. The first morning when the ladies served breakfast, one of them handed me a plate with half a dozen eggs on it. I took them all and proceeded to eat them. I was told by someone, that I should have taken two and passed the plate on. That embarrassed me badly and I never did anything vaguely wrong at the table again. I waited until everyone else was served before I started eating and hoped everyone forgot my initial mistake. That was the first mealtime I had been served family style in my life. Nellie had always dished up what I was supposed to eat and that was it. No questioning or refusal allowed as there were seldom any other choices to be offered.

When all the hay had been stacked, we rolled up our bedrolls, filled our clothes sack and piled into Mr. Echanove's pickup. He drove us back to the Toll Gate and paid us our wages. Then he went back to his hay ranch and we resumed our normal life as if we had never left. Nellie and Angus then seemed anxious to get to town and spend the money we had earned. Nellie did make me put all mine into a savings account at a bank in Boise and I don't think the rest of them saved a dime. Perry bought a J. C. Higgan's shotgun, a 20 gauge, which helped us in our bird hunting.

CHAPTER 18

Good and Bad Food Choices

No matter the time of year or what our circumstances were at the time, we always had a Dutch oven full of beans on the stove and loaves of fresh bread to eat. Nellie had to make bread almost every day and she did that very well. She also would bake biscuits and cinnamon rolls that were a favorite of all of us. She made cookies and cakes on special occasions. Quite often really, as we all seemed to have a sweet tooth and since we seldom had candy, these things substituted. There was an apple tree at the Shearer House and we would bring her apples from that tree. She made the best apple pies I have ever had from what we brought home. She also made pies of most anything else we picked such as plums and berries. There were something called a "choke cherry" up near the Burnt Timber. We would walk up there and pick a bag full, which she then made pies from.

We were told to be careful picking the chokecherries and to watch out for bears. One time Perry and I had been picking them and had gotten our bag about full when Perry told me to "Get going home, now!" I didn't see what the fuss was but he seemed alarmed and had backed off from where he had been picking and was walking back down the road backwards until I joined him, then he and I ran toward home for a while. I didn't go too fast so he finally stopped running and waited for me to catch up. He asked if I had seen the bear, which I had not. He said it wasn't very big, but it had made a grunting noise as it reached for the same fruit he was reaching for.

For some reason we were there without our normal firearms, so we just ran away with our bags of choke cherries.

One winter day Eugene and I got the bright idea to kill a magpie and cook it. We had been watching one that was eating something dead close to the house. We began by throwing snowballs at it until we hit it. The effect of the snowballs was that it couldn't fly well. We chased it from pillar to post until the poor thing finally succumbed to our onslaught. We picked all the feathers off it, took out the entrails, then rubbed it in the snow to clean up any blood or anything that didn't look like fresh meat. We lit a fire of dead sticks and grass and positioned our meal on a stick. We toasted it like marshmallows for a few minutes over our fire. When it got looking rather black we each took a bite. Right then we knew why no one was eating magpies or crows. Besides being really raw, it tasted really bad. So our food gathering plan went down with the first bite. We left it there for the dogs and put out our fire and went home to a real meal. It was probably beans and some other meat from something actually edible.

The best berries we knew of were blackberries from the Mason Place. I picked them and Nellie made a wonderful pie from them. They were hard to get at with lots of stickers. Nettles were also growing there. I found an old door and threw it over the blackberry patch and crawled out on it so that I could really pick with ease.

This worked so well that I didn't pay a lot of attention to the plants I was getting into and one day as I was headed over to the Ourada's house, after having picked a sack of berries the day before, I had noticed that my face itched a bit, but didn't think much of it. When I got to the Mason Place I went back to my berry patch, just to eat a few more and I saw that I had put the door over a bunch of poison sumac as well as the berry vines. By the time I got to the Ourada's my left eye was swollen closed and the other was just a slit. Mrs. Ourada had some white powder that she mixed with water to make a paste and put it on all over my swollen face. This stuff really worked, and she gave me a small sack with some in it to take back home. That worked so well that though I had been able to see only a little from one eye, by the time I got home I was using both eyes and the next day there was very little sign of the outbreak. Later in life, I asked her what that powder was and she could not recall, though she did remember I had shown up at their house almost blind. That was a shame that she couldn't remember. As a teenager and young adult I contacted poison oak rather often and really had it affect me badly a couple of times. I certainly could have used her good home remedy as it worked much better than calamine lotion.

The first time I was at the Ourada's by myself, I had gone over there to play on a Saturday morning. I don't remember if I had been invited or if I just gotten the urge to go, but go I did. The girls and I did some playing inside and outside, and eventually it was lunchtime. Mrs. Ourada asked me if I would like to join them for dinner. Nellie had told me that you cannot gracefully, or properly, just accept an invitation to a meal, etc., until after the third time the offer is made. You are required to turn it down twice and when they ask the third time it is perfectly proper for you to accept the offer. I'm sorry to tell you that none of the Ourada's appeared to have been made aware of that rule, so I sat in the living room starving, while they spent the better part of an hour having their dinner. The noon meal, dinner, was the biggest meal of the day, on most farms and ranches. I learned then that politeness does have its price. After that I accepted meals the first time people asked.

In the summer, we were treated to another four visitors. Nellie's sisters, Maud and Carrie came to visit and brought Carrie's grandson, David Philip Armstrong and Ione's son, Jackson Coffin. Both of these aunts were good cooks and made all kinds of goodies for us. The boys sort of were a, "them against us," thing of another nature. They seemed to think we were a bit backward and openly showed that they were much more "worldly" than we were. We did play some together, but they seemed to do better by themselves. We eventually made it a practice to exchange chicken droppings with them. Since they didn't want to touch them, and they didn't know enough not to pick up the fresh chicken droppings, besides being out numbered and on our turf, they got the worst of it. The aunts all had to reprimand us, and make us quit picking on the poor city kids. We did mostly leave them alone after that and they didn't search us out.

At the end of summer, Aunt Carrie returned to Idaho, picked up David Armstrong and took him to his mother's home in Beverly Hills, CA. Jackson Coffin stayed two more years and he and I became good pals. Jack went to Stack Rock School for his seventh and eighth grade schooling.

CHAPTER 19

Perry and His Ear Infections

MY BROTHER PERRY SUFFERED FROM terrible ear infections and they got so bad something had to be done. Nellie's brother Eugene lived in Rupert, Idaho and his son-in-law was a doctor by the name of Otto Moellmer. Nellie and Perry talked to him by phone when we were in Boise. He told Nellie to come over and he's do what he could for Perry. Nellie, Yvonne, Perry, Jack and I all boarded a Greyhound bus for the four-hour trip over to Rupert. I had a wonderful trip as I had no knowledge of much besides Boise, Eagle, Melba and Nampa. So to see the sights along the way and especially Thousand Springs was beyond belief. Here were just lots of springs with water gushing out of the side of a cliff and making a waterfall into the Snake River Gorge. Then we got to Rupert in the late afternoon. It was a lovely town, not much bigger than Eagle, but not spread out so far as Boise.

Dr. Otto Moellmer's house had an office in a building behind it. He built electric trains as a hobby. Whenever he wanted a snack, he could send a note by train to the house and it would return in a few minutes with his order filled. That just fascinated me. They also had a toilet in the house. Even in Melba, I couldn't remember anything but an outhouse, even at the Jensen's, which I considered the ultimate in houses. Maybe the Jensen's had an indoor toilet, but I don't recall seeing it on our visits there.

Dr. Moellmer examined Perry and treated his ear infection with penicillin. Perry had to wash his ear with hydrogen peroxide and cotton swabs every day and for about two weeks he had to inject himself, into the muscle of his leg, with white goo, that looked about the consistency of tooth paste. This white goo was penicillin, and those shots must have really hurt, though he didn't complain and the ear trouble seemed to get better. He was troubled with bouts of ear infections for the rest of his life.

While in Rupert we went with some kids to a county fair. We went on several of the rides and one was called a Loop the Plane, or something like that. It did all kinds of twirling and motions that didn't do my tendency for motion sickness any good. I was sick and embarrassed and they had to take me home. The next morning I felt a bit better and had to go to the bathroom. I sat on the commode and in walked some young girl and embarrassed me to death. I didn't know that you were supposed to lock the bathroom door.

Yvonne had to go back to Oakland for high school and Perry was also gone for a while but came back to attend Boise High School. He lived in Boise during the week in a small house the Ourada's had there. On the weekends he was back with us at the Toll Gate. Jack and I walked to school through all the various paths that we could find going that general direction. We would often go over the top of Coyote Mountain and on a clear winter day we could see the trains as they went east and west down the rails from Boise to Caldwell. We could often hear the whistles if the wind was still. Also we could hear the large trucks going up the highway toward Horseshoe Bend, counting their shifts as they changed gears on the steep grade. This led to a lot of daydreaming and idle chatter about what we thought was going on in the world, the war effort and some rather deep thoughts. Even then, we couldn't solve all of the world's problems.

CHAPTER 20
Jack Coffin

JACK WAS A BRIGHT PERSON and he scored well in school. He also was inquisitive. He and I found a lot of fun stuff to do. We found a large tin full of black powder and a few blasting caps. We made a fine little bomb with a blasting cap, some fuse and a Copenhagen snuffbox full of the black powder. That worked real well on bringing down a dead cottonwood tree. With Perry along, we found it would bring dead fish up in a beaver pond on Shafer Creek. Beat the heck out of a day with a fishhook and a worm. You could get a pocket full of fish by just scooping them up.

We also found that the neighbor, at the Mason place, Mr. Bicandi's man, Clyde, had left the Mason place for the winter. In the shop were a forge, bellows and charcoal. We heated some steel and beat on it with a hammer, quenched it in water and broke it when it got brittle. That was interesting, but I had seen that at the blacksmith shop in Eagle, and so had Jack, so we branched out into heating some linseed oil. We had heard of boiled linseed oil somehow and decided to boil our own. We did and both of us paid for that by getting violently sick to our stomachs from the fumes and since we were doing this on our way home from school we had empty stomachs. There was nothing to vomit. This was a very bad situation indeed. I'm still not enamored by the smell of linseed oil, boiled or not. It took us a couple of days to get over the effects of those fumes and we gave up on the forge.

Jack and I went to the mailbox and eventually walked down to Echanove's and up Mac Farland Road, through the Turner place and made our way home by that circuitous route. At the Turner place we gathered a large sack of black walnuts beneath a few of the trees there. Along the way we got a rock and pounded open the hard shells and ate a lot of those walnuts. I'd have been as well off boiling linseed oil again. I still have trouble with the flavor of black walnuts. And to add insult to injury, for some reason I also had diarrhea, so both ends were in trouble. This time Jack didn't get sick so maybe I ate one that was spoiled and he didn't. But I never had the urge to eat any more of them.

Jack and I noticed that Nellie was acting more strangely than normal. Not that she didn't have her quirks before like talking to herself and getting in violent arguments with herself, so much so that at times we could hear her from a mile or more away. But now she was doing things that were even out of character for her. One morning she got in a physical fight with Jack. She grabbed a garden rake and came at him with fire in her eyes and swinging that rake so that he feared for his life. We were on our way to school and had our Upjohn Bottle full of milk in our lunch sack, really it was a flour sack, and Jack hit her over the head with the lunch sack so hard it broke the bottle and we ran off to school.

That evening, as we were in no hurry to get home, we walked up on top of Coyote Mountain and spent hours surveying the sights in the valley and plotting what we must do. We thought of calling the authorities and having her put in some hospital or home, but we didn't know whom to call, nor did we have a telephone to call with. So at about nine in the evening we went home and she was fixing our dinner as if nothing had happened, except for a obvious large bump on her forehead and a black eye that a prizefighter would have been proud of. Nothing was ever said about it and she must not have told Angus how she got hurt.

That winter she had a terrible time with her teeth and gums. Eventually she had all her teeth extracted. I wonder if that had been a factor in her strange behavior. After the teeth were removed, she seemed to act more like herself and seemed to enjoy life a lot more, though she had to cut food into pretty fine pieces as she didn't get replacement teeth for a while and then those she got didn't seem to help a lot. I have heard that they weren't made for her but had come to her from someone who owned a funeral home. I do not know the truth of that though it wouldn't surprise me if it were true.

While Nellie was in town getting her teeth pulled, Jack, Angus and I were at the Toll Gate. I seem to recall that Roxie Jensen had come and taken her for the procedure and that we had been left behind to fend for ourselves. That wasn't a problem, Angus could cook beans and she had left us with a few loaves of bread. We had canned goods and lots of fresh things that had been stored away in the springhouse.

Angus had fed us lunch and had settled in for his nap. We had been in the room doing some model building and as we got up to leave we noted that Angus was snoring quite loudly and would probably wake himself up fairly soon. Jack showed me a .22 shell and motioned for me to get Angus' pipe, which I did. We took the slug out of the .22 shell, dumped the tobacco out of the pipe and dumped the powder out of the .22 shell into the pipe, replaced the tobacco and tamped it all down a bit. I put the pipe back where I had picked it up from and we went to a table and played a bit of rummy while we waited for Angus to wake up.

Presently he woke up and after a few moments reached for his pipe and sort of examined it a bit, then reached for his Prince Albert can. As he put a tad more tobacco in the bowl, I eased over near the door and watched as he pulled out a match and lit the pipe. Jack began to join me near the door as Angus took a few deep puffs to get the pipe going well.

Suddenly there was an eruption of flame in front of Angus. Tobacco and sparks flew out from the pipe. Angus beard was sizzling and we were running for our lives. I had the distinct feeling that we might not survive this attempt at humor. Angus said something in Gaelic and I picked up the pace. Surely he would kill us when he caught us. I had never been able to run fast and Jack had disappeared in a flash. I headed toward the road and when I saw the gate was closed I had to decide my next move. I decided to jump it, though I had a fear I would die in the attempt. I was so scared that

I cleared it with room to spare and landed outside the fence still running. That was my first and last successful high jump.

Later that night Jack and I snuck back to the house and went to bed. The next morning Angus was up and fixing our breakfast as if nothing had taken place, though his beard had some awful ratty looking edges to it. We quit with the practical jokes, happy to have survived.

CHAPTER 21

Jack Leaves, I am
Terribly Lonely

JACK GRADUATED FROM THE EIGHTH grade at Stack Rock School and was tied for the highest score in the state of Idaho testing of eighth graders with Aurelia Ourada, who was also in his class at Stack Rock School. They broke Earl Ourada's record test score from when he graduated from eighth grade. (I was no threat to ruin the standing of any of those folks.) Jack then left us and returned to high school wherever his father lived. We lost touch for the next twenty years or so. I do know he graduated from Annapolis Naval Academy and flew jets for the Navy before he went to work as a chemist in Southern California, from which he retired to Texas. He has visited a couple of times since then.

With Jack gone and Perry attending Boise High School all week, I spent a lot of my time alone. At first I walked to Ourada Ranch Road and Cartwright Road with Perry, where the Ourada's would pick him up on their way to school, but later in the year that was only on Mondays. They would all spend the rest of the week in Boise. Perry and Earl were both in the ROTC and looked like regular soldiers in their handsome uniforms. They seemed to do well with their rifles in the ROTC and I am sure that they honed their skills. Both were expert marksmen already with just the training, for Perry, from Angus and what he read in Field and Stream, and such magazines.

In the depth of winter I would often be off to school before the sun was up and then going home as it set. If I went to the mailbox, it would be quite dark by the time I got home. I always loved the view of the Toll Gate as I got within sight. The contrast with the snow and the darkness of the unpainted wooden buildings, the bright yellow shafts of light coming from the windows were the light cast by the kerosene Aladdin Lamps. The three Box Elder trees had lost their leaves and were like giant skeletons hovering over the main house. If the moon were out, then there were more shadows being cast by all the buildings.

I was afraid of the dark and welcomed the moonlight, but hated the shadows. I imagined all sorts of bad things lurking there to pounce upon me and do me harm. While I walked I often looked behind me to make sure that no one or anything was sneaking up behind me. A couple of times I would see some large animal following my tracks in the snow, though they always stayed well back. The following day if the wind or a fresh snow hadn't covered the tracks, I would find whether it was a dog or coyote, or some large cat. The large cat tracks following me were only found a couple of times, but they would worry me for weeks afterward. In retrospect they weren't cougar, but possibly a bobcat. Several times a coyote or a dog had followed me for quite a distance.

During these cold and lonely walks to and from school I was very melancholy. I often got worried for my own welfare. I was afraid that no one really cared about me or how I was doing. I also wondered if it was really possible that I was the only human, and that I might be asleep and somehow dreaming all of this. I had no one to discuss my feelings with while out of the house and I was too embarrassed to admit that I worried, or that I had fears. I prayed a lot, to any God that might be listening, crossing myself like the Catholics did, just in case. I sang to myself and talked aloud to keep up my courage and was always very happy to arrive back at the Toll Gate and the warmth and safety I felt there. Going past the Mason Place wasn't a thing to enjoy like it had been when I had company walking by and we'd go in and look around to see what we might have missed.

Now that I was walking alone, and during that time of year when no one lived there, I gave it a wide berth and hurried past as quietly and quickly as I could. Even the ruin of the Shearer House seemed to be a place someone or something might be hiding.

All of that passed when I got inside the house and smelled the bread and the bean pot on the stove. I would get my tin plate and load up my meal, get behind the stove with a glass of milk and have my dinner. There was almost always some sweet rolls or cake for dessert. Then I would read my books, do my math or whatever small bit of homework I may have. When that was done I may engage in a game of chess or two with Nellie and then go to bed. Usually if it were snowing or the wind was blowing hard, there was some noise from the trees creaking and maybe the dogs checking things out and I'd be afraid again. I might have to light my candle and read for a while to forget it all and go to sleep. If Perry was about, these things were no problem and I slept like a kid should.

CHAPTER 22

Van Den and Our Animal Disasters

WHEN WE FIRST WENT TO Boise in our wagon, there was a livery stable near the railroad in downtown, just a few short blocks from the Idanha Hotel. We could go to the hotel and within a few minutes Angus would be back, having dropped the team and wagon off for the duration of our stay, at the Livery. But, that ended rather quickly in my memories of going to Boise. Then he would drop us off at the hotel and go back to the edge of town and leave the team and wagon with a fellow that had a small ranch and junk business. This was a man named Arnie Van Den. I was told his name had been Van den Berg when he first came to Boise, but that he had changed his name after a few run ins with the authorities over some hauling of dead animals and his junk business. It appears he didn't always dispose of the dead animals properly and would sneak them to some out of the way spot behind someone's property and eventually he got caught and in effect, run out of town. That, and some spousal abuse made his presence in town undesirable.

I didn't know any of that and he always seemed to treat us well and was not charging much to watch after our stock and the wagon. His wife, or whatever she was, made lye soap in large frying pans. We would buy a pan or two and that would last us for a year or more. It was made from lard and lye and, I believe, some ashes. Whatever it was, it was tougher than any washing machine ever was on clothes and hands.

Van Den also sold us some pigeons and we had a large flock of them for a couple of years. They seemed to multiply rapidly and evade predators fairly well. Then one day they rose up like a cloud and every one of them, as if on a signal, turned south and flew away. They had been with us for several hatchings and only a few of the original birds remained, but off they went and they all appeared back at Van Dens. He never offered to replace them and I doubt any of us cared. They were messy birds and left droppings all over the barn and even in the hay.

Van Den next sold us some rabbits. These were chinchilla rabbits, we were told, and much in demand. They also multiplied rapidly and they had a body about the size of a cottontail rabbit. These were very good eating and we also could sell the furs to Mueller's, so they were a welcome addition. The problem was containing them, and we didn't do that well. In a few years they had all just disappeared, though the sagebrush was now fairly full of cottontails that looked a bit different than they had in years past. Some had changes in fur coloring and the size of the rabbits was larger than they had been.

At another time we got some ducks. I believe that they also came from Van Den. They nested and since they seemed to not have enough eggs, Nellie added some turkey eggs to the clutch. Of course that worked out just fine until they hatched and, as a duck will, mama took them for a swim. That worked out well for the ducklings but was a disaster for the turkeys. Those that didn't drown had to be caught and raised in a small chicken coop and eventually they got adopted into the turkey momma's brood. But the majority of them had drowned.

We had hogs. Hogs are a great animal and will eat anything. We were without a boar and the sows left on day in search of one. Whether they found him or not, I don't know. What I do know is that they found a sheep herders camp on their way to where ever they were headed, and smelling food they destroyed most everything that was on the ground looking for that food. They even ate all his bacon. Then they continued on their way. He came back to a disastrous scene for him, everything in tatters and most of his food gone. Those days the camp was a tent on the ground and so he lost virtually everything he didn't have with him.

That evening, as he was trying to make a meal out of what was left, the hogs came back by and nosed over to see if they had missed anything. They found out what they had missed was his .44 magnum and its ammunition. A couple that showed up at the Toll Gate that night were wounded, and the rest were either dead, or dying, between his camp and our house.

CHAPTER 23
Visiting the Sheepherders

THE SHEEPHERDER BECAME A GOOD friend to Perry, Jack and me. We gave him some bedding and enough food to get him by until Mac Leod came out to resupply him. This time his home was a camp wagon and we were very careful to make sure our pigs did no more wondering. We also acquired a boar of our own.

He taught us all kinds of ribald songs and dirty jokes and we thought he was wonderful. He was the only sheepherder I knew that didn't have a camp tender and he carried a pistol instead of a 30-30 rifle. That year was the first and last time that we saw him. A few days later the flock of sheep and he were up by Stack Rock and if he came back in the fall, we missed him.

Usually the sheepherders had been Martin Woods, he was the herder, and John Garamendi, was the camp tender. They were good to us kids and had spent a bit of one winter with us at the Toll Gate, sleeping in the bunkhouse with Perry, Yvonne and me. They even had me come visit their sheep camp when they came through in the next few years. I sometimes went to their camp and spent the night sleeping in their tent with them. Nothing peculiar ever happened, but I wonder now about the propriety of letting a seven or eight year old go out and spend a weekend in a sheep camp with some older men. It turned out okay, but I wouldn't have let my kids do that.

Martin Woods had a brother, Michael, that came over from Ireland, and was his herder and Martin was the camp tender. They would sing and tell stories and Mike had an accordion that he played quite well. Mike spent the time to teach Perry to play a harmonica. Later, at the Toll Gate, Perry and Nellie would play a duet. Both were pretty good at it. I never heard Perry sing, so I guess he stuck with the harmonica and let Nellie and Angus do the singing, I could do neither, play an instrument, nor sing worth a hoot, so I usually just listened and begged for more.

One Friday, I hitchhiked out to Marsing and spent the weekend at the sheepherders housing there. I even had my own bed there and was treated like visiting royalty. I didn't get to go into the lambing sheds though, so I never did see that operation. But I had three meals a day and a good pile of books and magazines to go through while the men worked at the lambing. Then one of them called one of the wranglers from Spring Valley and he came and took me back to the spot at Spring Valley where we always started our walk back to the Toll Gate, whenever we hitchhiked anywhere. (That was where Spring Creek came into Spring Valley Ranch, about a half mile, plus, south of the ranch house. This was as close as cars could get to the Toll Gate in winter, and left us with an hour walk to arrive home.)

While at Marsing, the Woods brothers had told me the date that they and their flock would be coming to Spring Valley on their annual drive of the herd to the summer range near Garden Valley, Idaho. That was forty miles or more northeast of the Toll Gate as the crow flies. They would first be trucked to a spot on Eagle Road about a third of the way between the beacon light in Eagle and the mines at Pearl. They told me to come out that road toward Pearl to the second real creek and follow it east to their camp. They would be there all set up, and told me which Friday they would be there. My schoolteacher took me to the beacon light after school on the appointed Friday and I walked north on that dirt road for several miles, until I came to the second real creek, then I turned east. I walked for several more miles and it was getting dark. Then it dawned upon me that I hadn't seen any sign of sheep droppings nor could I hear any sheep in the distance. I wondered what to do.

I retraced my steps and went to the next creek north, thinking I was counting some dry wash as a creek, and that this one must be it. I walked up that creek and it was really dark, but a few miles ahead I could see a campfire out on the hillside ahead of me. I stumbled along, and though I saw no tracks of signs of sheep and heard none, I knew someone had to be at that campfire, so I kept on toward it and along about midnight I got there. It turned out to be a Boy Scout Troop out for an overnight camp out in the wilderness. I asked how far to Spring Valley Ranch and none seemed to know even where it was. The troop wasn't from Boise and I believe they were from Emmitt.

By now there was a halo of light in the east and I knew the moon would be up shortly, so I again began to travel east, knowing that I wouldn't find any sheep camp tonight, but with luck, Spring Valley Ranch's main headquarters lay just ahead. Then it would be another hour to the Toll Gate and I would be home. But I was hungry, thirsty and on a very dry hillside and the Scouts hadn't offered any type of food or drink and I was too proud to beg, so I was hoping that I'd at least find water real soon. I walked for about two more hours and was very tired and contemplated just sleeping on the ground, but there wasn't even any brush to break the wind and I still was in dire need of water, so I plodded on. Thankfully now I had a nearly full moon to light my way and it did appear I was getting near to the top of the ridge just west of the Spring Valley Ranch. When I topped that ridge and could see down the other side, the east side, there lay Spring Valley Ranch still a bit farther north than I thought it would be, but at least it was in sight.

The ranch house was still a couple of miles off, but I knew I could get water sooner from a spring that I had seen on earlier trips to the ranch house. Finally, and this must have been getting close to three in the morning, I got to the ranch house and sang out a few "Hello the house." Eventually a light came on and a kid I knew, Orion Givens, came down from his room and took me inside and made me a sandwich and we went up and went to bed. That was the first time I had been inside the house, except for the kitchen.

Orion had let me sleep in and about nine o'clock I heard younger kids and a girl's voice. That was new to me. I didn't know of any girls at Spring Valley. The only woman I knew of at Spring Valley was the manager's wife, Orion's mother, and she was in her fifties. I had to get dressed and investigate. I found that they all were up and about and had saved me a large plate of breakfast and were all curious how I happened to be out alone at that hour of the night. I relayed my story and ate a fine meal and was about to take my leave, when a pretty young girl, just a year of so older than myself, asked me to stay a while and play with them all. So what's a boy to do? She had captured me, and nothing would do but to stay and watch her every move. I was totally smitten with something, maybe puppy love?

We all played some board games, did a bit of walking around checking out the stock, and I found out the young kids and the pretty girl were all cousins of the boy that I had already known, Orion. His father was the manager of the Spring Valley Ranch. At noon we had a good lunch and then all went into the living room and the pretty girl sang a song, while playing the piano, then went into telling a long mystery story that had us all quietly sitting on the edge of our seats and quiet as could be. Except for myself, I held off for as long as I could, but eventually gas escaped me with a roar and everyone, including the pretty girl fell into hysterics laughing and I was so embarrassed that I ran out of the house and was half way to the Toll Gate before I quit running. I never saw any of them again and never went back to Spring Valley Ranch until years after they were all grown and gone, and I was married and living in California.

CHAPTER 24

Bounty Hunting and Trapping

PERRY AND I HUNTED, TRAPPED and shot all sorts of things. The Fish and Game paid a bounty for some things. Magpies and crows were worth three cents each, a coyote was worth two or three dollars as was a bobcat. Cougar was worth fifteen, I believe, though we never got one of those. We also sold pelts of rabbits and small skunks that we called civet cats. There were also weasels and in the winter they were white and they were called ermine. The white pelts brought more money and we tried to catch them all winter, with varying degrees of success. Sometimes we'd catch two or three and another time one or none, but the combination of all the bounties and the pelts gave us a bit of spending money. With that we bought more ammunition, a few hunting knives and traps

We sent away somewhere for some scents that came in a rack of small bottles. They were theoretically the scents of the animals during the mating season and they must have been. We would set a trap near a stream and place a small piece of newspaper over it, drop a few drops from one of the bottles and then sprinkle dirt, snow or leaves over the trap. The next day or two we would come back and there would be a skunk or weasel in our trap. I was the holder, and Perry was the skinner. Skunks were the worst and I had a tough time getting through skinning one without losing a meal, though I never did. It was always close though. Then I'd have the dang pelt in my pocket until we got home, which might be several hours later, and with luck, several pelts later. They stunk to the high heavens and it was almost impossible to wash the odor off our hands without soap and warm water. We dried the pelts on a rack of wire or on a shingle cut to the size of the pelt. After it was dry we would ship it to a Mueller's in Denver and they would send us a check.

Magpies and crows were our main form of bounty money as they flocked in every night to roost just a half mile away to the east in a thicket of thorn trees that we called the Thorn Gate. On a good night we may shoot about fifty of them. Perry was the better shot and did the majority of the shooting while I fetched the victims and made sure they were dead. He would try to line two up at once and on moonlit nights that was fairly easy to do, so we tried to do most of our shooting on moonlit, winter nights where the moonlight often made it almost like daylight. We'd take the body's home and pick the soft breast feathers for pillows, remove the heads and string them on a single strand of wire and hang them out to dry. We also raided the nests of crows and magpies. As cruel as that seems to me now, I thought of it as a goldmine at the time, and it didn't cost us any ammunition.

When we had a bag full we'd take them down the creek to Highway 55 and hitchhike into Boise to sell them at the Railway Express Office. Several times some nice person, in a nice warm car, picked us up and we'd happily ride for a while toward town, and they would begin to squirm and look about, finally asking what is that smell coming from. We would tell them that it's just the magpie heads warming up. With that we would have to hold them out the window for the rest of the ride and you could bet they wouldn't be picking up kids with sacks from then on.

At the Railway Express Office, we'd proudly present our sack to the little girl at the counter who would look horrified when she heard what was in the smelly sack, and run in the back for her supervisor. He'd come and ask us what we had and Perry always upped the tally by a couple or three. I just knew we'd get caught and sent to jail. But without a second look, the guy would grab the bag and disappear for a minute and the reappear and pay us off. The little girl wouldn't ever be seen until the next trip in. If it happened to be the same girl she'd dash off as we approached the door and we'd be dealing with some serious looking gentleman again.

One of our biggest problems, and this applied to all of us that lived at the Toll Gate, was keeping our feet dry in the winter. We didn't have modern boots and we used to develop holes in our shoes and boots. These we filled, as best we could, by wrapping our feet and socks with newspapers and changing the paper as often as it got wet and cold. But on long walks we didn't often have enough paper and the snow would get into the shoe or boot and melt, thus making the socks wet and before long we'd have feet that were really cold. We bought some legging from an Army Surplus store and that really seemed to help keep snow from coming over the tops of our boots. But, our wet feet were a problem that only new boots could cure, and we just didn't have them often.

Another problem in winter was that washing clothes was not a pleasant task, which therefore seldom got done. One of our worst beatings came at Nellie's hands, after we had been warned not to play on the ice in the creek, as it wouldn't hold us. As mentioned earlier, Walter had an ice tester and sent me ahead on a little pond just below the Spring House. I walked across fine and Eugene, Walter and I then took turns skating across it several times. Eventually we lost all caution and all three were in the middle when suddenly the ice beneath us gave way and all three of us fell into the muddy bottom of the shallow pond.

We jumped out quickly and since we were soaked and filthy with mud we ran to the bunkhouse and changed our clothes. There was a ditch close to the road that was also frozen over so we returned to our skating on that ice. We hadn't mentioned to Nellie that over in the bunkhouse were the clothes we had fallen through the pond ice with. Need I tell you that it wasn't long until we repeated the fall through the ice again into the muddy bottom of the ditch! This time Nellie had seen us, as we again scampered to the bunkhouse for yet another change of clothes. This time she came over and beat the stuffin' out of us with our wet tennis shoes. She now had to wash three outfits of Levis and shirts plus all our underwear.

We didn't own enough clothes to have complete changes and we were forced to wear women's under pants for a couple of days. That was worse than the beating and the clothes we had to put on were things that she drug out of her ragbag. We feared someone at school would find out and we'd die from embarrassment, but that never happened. Our clothes were more rinsed out than washed, then hung on the fence to freeze dry during the next couple of days, when they were brought inside for a final drying over chairs. We didn't fall through the ice anymore.

CHAPTER 25

The Hupmobile
Becomes a Wagon

AT THE UPPER HOUSE, THERE was an old Hupmobile, approximately 1925 model, a four-door sedan. We kids had played in it after it was determined that the car was beyond repair. I never knew who owned it, or where it came from, but I had never known it to run. Because of the war, metal became in demand and Arnie Van Den was just the man to jump onto this derelict auto and get some money for the metal. Angus and he made some kind of deal. Arnie took the car away to his place and after awhile we got the chassis back from him. It had been converted into a very sturdy wagon with the mechanical brakes working and a decent seat to sit on. It wasn't anything gaudy, just a very heavy wagon, with rubber tires and a full automotive spring suspension. We thought it would be a wonderful wagon for our trips to town. There would be no wheels to soak, and the brakes worked just like car brakes, except these brakes were applied by a handlever that the driver pulled. This was just like other wagons, but much better brakes, as these were on all four wheels, not just rubbing blocks working on the steel tires of the back wheels.

One day we got up early and took our new vehicle to Eagle to buy groceries. Angus, Perry and I rode down to Hwy 55, by way of what is now Brookside Drive. The horses had been fresh when we started and they managed to pull the new heavy load up to the top of the hill by the Shearer house with just one short rest. From there to a sandy stretch had been all downhill and on a very solid road of dried dirt. The rubber tires rolled easily and Angus had to apply the brakes quite a bit to prevent the wagon from pushing the horses into a trot. The springs made it seem to float over the imperfections in the road. The last mile or so, just before Hwy 55, was always tough on the horses. The wagon wheels would sink into the sand and there was a mile or two that was very deep sand. The new wagon did fine to that point, but the horses had a bit of a pull to get it through the sand, but when we hit the highway it was again a bit downhill and this was a spot that the horses seemed to like to get up and go. Sometimes they would gallop for several minutes and then trot all the way to the Overland Station at the junction of Beacon Light Road and Hwy 55. This time they just trotted a bit until they got to where the road was flat and there they slowly walked along.

We got to Eagle after noon and gave our list to the ladies in the store and they put together our order as we walked a block east of the Mercantile and had some lunch at the Eagle Grill. For me lunch was usually a chiliburger and French fries. We had water to drink and on the way back to the Mercantile; Angus would buy us a shake or malt at Orville Jackson's. By then it was time to help load the wagon and be on our way home. All told we would be in Eagle about three hours. That was just enough time to get the horses a little rest, a drink, and a bit of hay from the wagon.

The ride home went well until where we turned off Hwy 55 onto the sandy part of the road. Again the tires sank into the sand and the horses leaned into their traces to make the pull to the solid dirt that lay ahead. This time Angus had to rest them several extra times. It seemed that the pull was much heavier with this wagon than with our old wooden freight wagon. By the time we got to the solid dirt where the wheels were totally free to roll, the team was too tired to pick up the pace. Every little incline took its toll and we had to rest the team again. Perry and I got out and walked, to lighten the load. Angus had to stay on the seat to drive and set the brake when the team stopped. By the time we got to the top of the hill by the Shearer House, the team was a mass of frothy sweat and their breathing was labored so they sounded like steam engines. Angus was kind to them and hadn't pushed them, but they wanted to get home. They had put in a hard day, pulling that metal monster and its contents to the top of the hill. We had made a stop at a stock pond and Angus had unhooked them and led them to the pond for a drink, which they had readily taken.

Once we made it to the top of the hill by the Shearer House, we knew it was okay, the wagon would get its load home to the Toll Gate and we'd have accomplished our mission. Going down the hill was easy on the horses, but Angus had to have Perry help him pull the brake a time or two as the mechanical brakes had held the wagon back much better when it was empty, but now that it had another half a ton of flour, sugar and groceries, it was pushing the team down the steepest part of our whole trip. We pulled into the yard under a full moon and Nellie was glad we hadn't had anything go badly wrong. Usually these trips to Eagle got us home about sunset. This trip had taken us well on toward 10:00 at night. The horses still sounded like their lungs would burst and Angus told us to come to the barn and we'd rub them down and go over them with a curry comb while they had some grain and salt for a reward for their hard work. That wagon was put up on blocks and never was hooked to a team again. It probably would have been fine with a four-horse team, but we never worked horses that way with a wagon.

We returned to using a smaller general-purpose wagon for our main means of transportation to and from towns. Also when we went to the orchard to pick fruit the smaller wagon was used. The last I saw of it, about 1970, the body was sunken into the bank of the creek near the springhouse. The wheels and tongue had been removed and all the metal was deteriorating in the hard water that it was exposed to. In the summer of 2011, I was there and went in search of it and could find nothing left. The creek is overgrown with willow trees and both banks have eroded to gentle slopes.

CHAPTER 26

Tommy Bicandi and Paul Jaio

TOM BICANDI HAD A SON also named Tom. I don't think he was a Jr. so we just called him Tommy and everyone knew we meant the younger one. Tommy had a friend named, Paul Jaio. We called him Jay Oh, but I heard his name was properly pronounced phonetically, as "Hi Oh." Tommy and Paul bought a 1927 Fordson tractor and a plow. They plowed and planted some grain at the Mason Place. They hired Mr. Ourada, with his combine, to harvest their fields. Tommy told me they did quite well, getting forty bushels to the acre. They had planted several hundred acres and the rains had been kind to them. Also the grasshoppers and crickets didn't appear in hordes like they often did. That was a very good yield for that ground and dry farming.

While Tommy and Paul were plowing to plant their grain crop, I would often ride on the draw bar of the tractor while holding onto the seat. Somehow that entertained me, to watch the earth turn over as the plow blade was drawn through the soil. I could do that for a half hour or more after school and still get home before dark. One evening I was doing my usual ride and Tommy was driving the tractor, when the tractor began to make strange noises and backfire. After one backfire that sounded like a rifle being fired the motor died and wouldn't restart. Tommy took the carburetor off and, as there was no shut-off valve in the fuel line, gasoline began to run down onto the ground and the tank would soon be emptied. Tommy jammed his finger over the line to prevent the fuel from flowing and told me to go get Paul. I saw what he was doing and said I could do that, so he let me plug the leak and he took the carburetor apart and blew dirt out of it. He then put the carburetor back on the engine and restarted the tractor.

All was again well and I rode a bit more, then I got off and walked home. Along the way I began to get a burning sensation on my back and under my arm. I also smelled just like that gasoline leak did. I took off my coat, which was an Army Surplus Eisenhower jacket, made of wool. It was pretty well saturated with gasoline all across the back and down the sleeve of the arm I had been using to plug the leak. I hadn't been as successful in plugging it as I had thought. So I carried the coat home, after washing myself off as well as I could without soap, in a little creek at the bottom of Soap Hill.

When I got home, Nellie washed my back and arm with some of her lye soap and put some cream on my skin. But my back was still quite red and looked like it had been sunburned. Cream was Nellie's answer to sunburn, so why not this? This was a chemical burn from the gasoline, but it was still just a first-degree burn much like sunburn, so cream did do some soothing and cooling of the burned area. Then she hung the coat out on the fence for a couple of hours, later bringing it back into the house and hung it over a chair to finish airing out and drying.

The following day, when I arrived home from school, Nellie told me that the coat had hung there in the sun drying while she was in the kitchen, which was just through an open door. Then she heard a loud 'whoosh" sound, and smelled burned cloth. She dashed in the room where the coat had been drying and found the coat had been consumed by fire. Also the curtain behind it was ablaze. She grabbed the dishpan from on top of the kitchen stove, which was usually full of water and threw it onto the curtain. Then she got more water out of the reservoir on the end of the stove and put out the rest of the fire. We almost lost the house that time. Had she been out in the yard, in the barn, or woodshed it would have burned to the ground and everything we owned would have been destroyed.

CHAPTER 27

Rodeo at the Mason Place

AFTER BILL AND ELAINE EDWARDS had left the Mason Place, Tom Bicandi brought his hired man Clyde, there from his place on Shafer Creek, the old Ingram place. Clyde spent the winters there because the Ingram place wasn't very accessible during the winter months. Mr. Bicandi and Clyde built a corral and moved in equipment to transform the existing barn into a cow barn and dairy operation. They set up a gasoline engine to power the milking machines. Clyde, I never did know his last name, was a jack-of-all-trades type of person. He did any kind of ranch work and cooked very well. Tom Bicandi and his son, Tommy, would spend the days at the Mason Place and go home to Boise at night, just as they had done at the place on Shafer Creek. They always brought the mail up from the mailbox with them. That gave us kids a ready excuse to go over there and listen to the tall tales that old Clyde loved to tell, though they must have been mostly off color jokes, as I don't recall any of his stories. (I don't remember the jokes either.)

We did hear tales of cowboy rodeos and such. With the new corral there, Tom, Tommy, Clyde and another young French Basque, Paul Jaio, decided it was time to get us involved in the real thing. They had a few head of stock that needed cutting, branding and earmarking. One time, while he was living with us, our cousin Jack Coffin and I were invited to come over and try our hand at rodeo riding. When all the work was done, there was a feast of mountain oysters, steaks, beans, Basque bread and cheeses. Then it was time for the siesta, which was a long nap.

Later in the afternoon, after our nap, Tommy and Paul brought some young colts and steers into the corral area. One by one Jack, Tommy, Paul and I all tried our hand at riding them. I ate an awful lot of dirt that day and the elder Tom and Clyde were well entertained. Paul and Tommy put on a good show of riding ability, but Jack and I went flying early into almost every ride. It was all good fun and I wouldn't trade that experience for much. Neither would I make a career in the rodeo. All the aches and pains did seem worth it when you could stay on for thirty seconds, which is close to a lifetime' on a bucking bronco or calf. That did not occur often for me. When the fun was over, we limped off home to the Toll Gate and within a few days most all the stock had been moved back to Shafer Creek for the summer and we wouldn't see them at the Mason Place again until fall, just before the first snow fell. Rodeos were never repeated at the Mason Place while I lived nearby.

Most all summer, Mr. Bicandi would drive from his home in Boise up to Shafer Creek and then drive home at night. I went with him a couple of times to Shafer Creek to see what was happening at the Ingram place. His day seemed to consist of going up to his ranch, eating lunch, taking a long nap and driving home. He did pull a few weeds or tend a small garden for a half hour or so, but I don't think he or Clyde did anything but make sure that the gates were securely closed, the stock was safe, and check that the fences were in good shape. Clyde did have to gather firewood and cook a large lunch. It seemed a nice quiet life to me, the serenity of being out in the woods, the convenience of having groceries and dry goods delivered almost every day, and no hay to mow or real crops to take care of, a small number of cows about and a mule or two, plus a dog for company when everyone else left for the day. There were fish in the creek and I'm sure that Clyde wasn't above taking advantage of the deer that wandered into the pastures. It was many miles from any travelled road and no one would likely hear a sound if he shot one.

CHAPTER 28
Another Embarrassing Moment

I WAS IN TOWN ALONE in late spring and it was very cold and rainy, with snow on the ground. This would have been late 1946 or 1947, making me 10 or 11 years old. In the late afternoon I went to a movie; saw two feature films, comics and some newsreels. During the intermission I went down to the bathroom, but it was crowded so I decided to wait until the movies were over. I bought a large coke and popcorn and sat through the longest movie I had seen. I definitely had to urinate, but was determined to see the end of the movie first. When it was over I raced from the upstairs down to the bathrooms, which were crowded as all the ground floor had gotten in there before me. Hardly a need to tell you the next, but I was soaked all down my left leg and front and totally ashamed. It was dark out on the street and I had a shopping bag in front of me, so I wondered out to State Street and tried to get a ride, but it was dark, I had on jeans and a dark coat and nobody stopped.

After perhaps 20 minutes of hitchhiking on State Street I found myself to be just about a half block from Jimmy Mac Leod's house, so I went there, put the bag in front of me and begged a room for the night. Mr. Mac Leod was a cousin to Angus. He and his wife had befriended me in the past with room and a meal or two. Mrs. Mac Leod took me in and wanted me to eat or take my coat off or do something normal, but I wouldn't have it. I went to the room she pointed out and the bath she told me I could use, and tried every way I knew to get my pants to not give me away. I had washed the color out with snow before I even started hitchhiking, but in the light, that had done very little good. So I took my bath and washed my underpants and wrung them out inside my bath towel and put them back on. They would dry while I slept and I put the wet pants over a furnace vent that never sent out any hot air all night.

In the morning I looked a bit strange, juggling my bag in front of me, as the pants had only partially dried. They fed me breakfast and I guess they didn't have a car or for some reason it was decided amongst us to asks Tom Bicandi if he'd take me as close to home as possible. He drove me to the mailbox in a very new 1947 Chevrolet pickup truck. He obviously could go no farther that way. There was over a foot of snow on the road from the mailbox up the hill toward the Toll Gate. Mr. Bicandi offered to take me a few miles west, then north, a long way around, and let me out at Spring Valley Ranch, as this would have made my walk about three miles instead of six. We had been taught to turn down offers twice, only then could we accept the third offer. Like Ourada's and my missed meal, he didn't know that rule, so I had to pick up the mail and walk home in about two feet of new snow, with half dried and shortly, thoroughly frozen pants. I managed to get home and by then most of me we was wet and frozen anyway, so I just went and got my older clothes and dressed in them. My ordeal was over. I was sure that everyone in Boise, and probably all of Idaho, was laughing at me and I never saw Jimmy Mac Leod again. When I was much older my kids, Nelda and I did go see the Bicandi's. He had never noticed my plight.

CHAPTER 29

Fires and Firefighting

IN OUR AREA, FIRES WERE always a concern. I remember the day in 1939 when our whole world seemed enveloped in smoke and soot and how bravely everyone had tackled getting that fire put out. But I also knew a Civilian Conservation Corps boy had lost his life in that fire. Often as we would walk home from school, in the summer and fall, we saw large columns of smoke in the distance. Mostly over to the west of us and we would read about range and forest fires in the Statesman newspaper. A good many were near Jordan Valley, Oregon and even further, but the threat seemed to always be there. I don't ever remember fires to the north of us, but I know they did happen. Their smoke must have blown easterly. Sometimes the fires to the west and southwest caused so much smoke to be generated that the sky took on an eerie yellowish cast. When that happened, Perry and I would walk up to the top of the hill west of us and make sure that the fire wasn't close to us.

One morning we got up and after breakfast we were thinking about going rabbit hunting. As we went outside, we noticed a bit of smoke to the west, and as was our practice, walked up to the Shearer house and took the road to Eagle a half-mile, so as to locate the source of the smoke. Once we topped the ridge, we got a good look and determined that this fire had the potential to become a real threat to us. The fire was east of Eagle, but on the north side of Dry Creek and east of Hwy 55 near what is now the golf course beside Hwy 55 and Brookside. The fire was putting up a huge column of smoke that was beginning to cause the yellow cast to the daylight. The day seemed to be getting much darker than it was when we left the Toll Gate. We decided to walk down to the fire line to see if we could assist in some way. This one had to be stopped or once again our known world would be threatened, and that had me scared, so we walked very quickly.

It took us close to an hour to get to the head of the fire. Perry and I found that the Grange Department's trucks were now coming our way to get ahead of the fire. They drove to a spot on Broken Horn Road that was just about straight east of the rock crusher*[5] at the southern end of Spring Valley's home ranch. (The location would now be about a half mile north from where Broken Horn and Brookside roads meet). There we met a tracklayer that had pulled a disc to create a firebreak from Highway 55, to the dirt road we were on. This was a mile or so, east of Highway 55. The next move was to pull the disc back toward Hwy 55 to expand the firebreak the disc was creating. I was chosen to pull a rope that had been soaked in a bucket of diesel fuel and set alight, behind the tractor to create a backfire. We used the freshly plowed firebreak, as the means of stopping the advancing fire. A large group of men, with wet gunnysacks, followed behind the tractor and my burning rope, and made sure no fire jumped to the dry grass on the opposite side of the firebreak.

Disking of dry grass doesn't make a perfectly dry dirt surface, there are many tufts of grass sticking up and the fire had created a wind that was blowing up the hill toward our home and Spring Valley, so these men put in a good hard hour or more while we set the backfire. I can attest to swinging a wet gunnysack for any length of time, as being a hard job. I had done that a few times when we did controlled burns of weed patches at the Toll Gate. Add in the acrid smoke from the grass and sagebrush, a normal hot summer day, which can be over one hundred degrees, and the added heat of the backfire causes one to wear down rapidly. It is difficult to drink enough water to keep your mouth from becoming very dry and

---

5 This may have been a quarry or mining operation. Everyone we knew just called it the Rock Crusher.

your throat will get sore shortly. We accomplished the firebreak and back-fire and when the two fires met it was almost magically all over. Not quite though, for many more hours, men had to go around the burned area with Indian tanks, which are a portable fire extinguisher, to make sure none of the hotspots flared up again and started sending cinders into the air. The Grange Department trucks also wet down any suspicious areas near the dirt road and along Highway 55.

Perry and I were done for the day and were about to go home, when the fire boss came over and got our names and Social Security numbers. I didn't have one, so he told me that one would be created for me and mailed to me. I don't think that took place, as I don't recall having a Social Security Number until I was out of the Marines when I signed up for one to work at Sunshine Biscuit Company.

Another time we were out in the front yard of the Toll Gate cutting some firewood and happened to look up to the ridge to the left of Stack Rock. We thought we saw some smoke there for a while, then weren't really sure it was smoke, so we went about cutting more firewood. An hour or so later we were again thinking we saw a puff of smoke and then nothing. Now we were intent on looking for sure so we went in the house and got out an old telescope Angus owned. Perry and I both took a real long look. Sure enough there was some smoke around the base of a stand of pines. We could tell it was too big for a campfire so we saddled up our horses and rode up the fire-trail to the site of the smoke. That was a long and steep climb, so even being on good horses it took us more than an hour to reach that spot near the top of the ridge. We had each brought a shovel and a wet gunny sack, but by the time we got there the sack was useless, being completely dry. So, in reality we had two shovels with which to fight a forest fire.

Perry told me to hold the horses and he would venture into the fire and see how big it was and I should not leave until he came back. Off he went into the smoke and I stood out in the fresh air and all I could do was listen to the crackling of the fire, and the steam being forced out of the damp logs on the ground. This sound was much like the fire in a fireplace with some wet wood, along with a good supply of dried wood. Every once in a while there is a loud cracking sound and a spark would fly into the air. This was exactly what I was hearing, along with a steady digging and panting sound of my brother digging a trench around this fire.

It was about an hour later that an airplane flew over and someone threw a small parachute, with a weight on it, out the window. I watched it descend right into the area beside the fire. I yelled to Perry and he told me to stay there, he would be out in just a little bit more. It seemed a couple of hours and I don't know how long it really was, but he did finally come out, black- faced with swollen red eyes and his nose black and running profusely. We had a water bag and he about drained it in one continuous swallow. He asked me if I had seen the smokejumper, and I had not. Perry told me the little parachute fell a few yards from where he was working and the plane circled to make a second pass. This time a guy made a leap out with a parachute and an air current took him another mile or two northeast; almost to the bottom of Shafer Creek. I didn't see any of that, as I was not high enough on the ridge to see any of the far side toward Shafer Creek.

I had been where I could see the Toll Gate and heard a siren blow from that direction. I couldn't tell what type of rig it was but it had red lights and a siren, so I knew help was coming. We watched it pass the Toll Gate and head for Cartwright summit, so I knew it would be a long time in getting to us, that was probably six or eight miles of very rough road. Had they come from the Toll Gate straight up the fire-trail, as we had, it would have been much closer, but I guess they didn't know about, or were afraid it was too steep, for their little tank wagon to climb the fire trail. The fire rig was a Dodge Power-wagon with a tank of 250 gallons of water and 200 feet of one-inch hose. It also had a small pump to supply the water pressure to the fire hose from the water tank. These were very effective little fire rigs for just this type of fire, but were also very limited in how much they could do without a ready source of water close by.

Perry went back to his digging and I kept the horses still for another three quarters of an hour, then the tank wagon turned out onto the fire-trail I was on and the men came and asked me why I had started this fire. I was a bit upset by that and explained that we had seen it from our house, and I pointed out the Toll Gate, which they had just driven past. They were skeptical and wondered if we had been there since early in the day, why hadn't their lookout tower on Shafer Butte seen it. I couldn't answer that and they went in to look for Perry and a few minutes later came out in disbelief. Perry had dug a trench around the whole fire, which was almost an acre and a half, through about six inches of duff. They knew he couldn't have done that in any short time.

Then the fire-boss told us to go on home, they had it under control. Perry stood our ground for both of us. He said he had worked real hard for the last six hours and wanted to be paid, so we gave them our names and they reluctantly wrote them down. Several weeks later we each got another check for our firefighting, this time from the Forest Service. That was the end of my paid fire-fighting career in Idaho, though I later in life became a firefighter in Oakland, CA.

One early afternoon we were coming home from grouse hunting up by the prune orchard and we decided to burn a large area of morning glory that had infected our hayfield north of the barn. We took our game home and went back to the hayfield with shovels and gunnysacks that we had saturated in the nearby creek. Angus had mowed the field and the hay was in the barn. All that was left was a three-inch high stubble. The remains of the morning glory was dry so we figured burning it would kill the seed and the fire would be very easy to control. We scraped around a bit with our shovels and lit the center of a circle on fire. We took the wet sacks and beat out the fire around the edges of the scraped area and then trouble set in. A little whirlwind passed right through our fire and spread it over about thirty or forty feet of stubble. That fire then took hold and began to burn in two directions away from us. We each took a side and started beating the fire out, but it was gaining headway and soon would be in the willows in the creek and who knows where it would be stopped.

Angus came running and we all shoveled and pounded with wet gunny sacks until we stopped the fire from burning west, but to the east we were in real trouble. The fire crossed the creek, and just as we were in real despair a small plane, piloted by Marvin Hornbeck, flew over. He circled real low and saw we were in trouble so he pulled up and made a dash to the Floating Feather Airport. That was probably ten air miles away There he called for help. Again the little tank wagons were sent, this time by the Grange Department. Two of them arrived at the Toll Gate within about a half hour of the plane leaving us. They ran to the head of the fire with their hose streams and quite rapidly put it out, stopping the spreading of the fire. The rest of the night they pumped water on any hotspots they found. We didn't dare to submit any hours for that fire as we had caused it, though we never told Angus just how it got started. He never asked, but I think he knew we had something to do with it.

CHAPTER 30

My Brother Perry

MY BEST FRIEND DURING MY early life was my oldest brother Perry. He was the one that I looked to with any question I had. He always gave me an answer without telling me that it was a stupid question or that any halfwit would already know the answer. He took me with him as he was learning to shoot a gun. We liked discovering what game we had around the Toll Gate that was edible and what animals were just good for their bounty or their pelts. After his schoolwork was done, he read all he could find in the hunting magazines and the newspapers, to learn as much as he could about the habits of the deer, bear, rabbit, beaver and porcupine. He read also about the upland game birds and their habits.

One spring, Perry found a nest of snowy white owls. He took one of them to the teacher at Stack Rock School and she took it home and raised it to adulthood. It lived in her basement and did rather well until she got a couple of bushels of cherries and put them in the basement to be stored there until she could find the time to can them. When she checked on the owl, she found it had eaten lots of the cherries and had died. Cherry pits have cyanide in them and I guess the poor owl hadn't read the label. It had been a beautiful bird. She would buy mice to feed it and never thought about it eating the cherries.

My reading was about pirates and their ships, Gulliver's Travels and books about antique firearms. None of my reading was going to put food on our table or money in our pocket. I also read a lot of western magazines that told the tales of the outlaws of the old west. Comparing our reading, in my mind, I wished that I had the interest in learning about the animals and birds that Perry did, but then when we would be out on a trail somewhere and I'd ask him about some tracks or feathers, he could tell me wonderful things about them for an hour or more. I determined that I'd just stick with the pirates and cowboy stories. If I needed any information on game, I'd ask him. He was all the encyclopedia of wildlife that I would ever need.

I tried to learn to shoot like Perry did. I was fairly good with a shotgun, but a blind person would have been also. The grouse flew slowly and were very loud in the process, sort of like a living model airplane. That gave me an edge over them, but things that had to be responded to with lightning reflexes were pretty safe around me. Not being very observant, many times a bird or animal would take flight, or run across my path and it would startle me worse than I had scared it. Often a good meal simply avoided me by sitting still until after I had passed and I'd find its footprints in the snow while returning home empty handed.

When Perry and I went out together that was usually a success story for the hunters, and a bad day for the hunted, be it birds or four-legged game. Perry could read the signs that the game left behind and know from what he was seeing what type of game it was and how long ago it had been there. He could relate to where it had likely come from and where it was likely going to, so he had a way of just looking into a small valley and seeing where the game was most apt to be found. Sometimes he would have me make a big circle and get a half-mile or so ahead of where we were and then I would trudge back toward Perry scaring the game toward him. This was a very successful type of hunting practice for us.

A few times we would reverse the assignment and Perry would go off after telling me to stay put for twenty minutes, then walk the creek or road just as we had been doing. When I did that, I would be on high alert, as I knew he had a sense there was something edible going to cross my path. I would have my rifle or shotgun ready for action as well as my eyes and ears open to the sounds around me. This was how I shot my first and only deer though Perry had wounded it first.

We were about two miles from the Toll Gate, on Custer Creek. Perry told me to walk to a spot he pointed out a few hundred yards further along the road. He told me to sit still there until a deer came my way or until he came back. I had a .22 pump with about 15 rounds of long rifle ammunition in the magazine. I walked to the appointed stake out and Perry disappeared into the snowdrifts and dead timber to the east of me. I knew he would be a while climbing the hill across Custer Creek from me to the south, then he would go east for a half mile and come back toward me through some dead timber that had been killed by the fire of 1939. I had visions of a huge buck walking down the hill and ending up in my sights, just 50 yards away, across the creek, where I couldn't possibly miss it.

Well it didn't quite work out that way. I sat where Perry had told me to stay. My eyes were sweeping the entire hillside of dead timber. The only movement was every so often the wind would dislodge a pile of snow on a dead branch and it would silently fall to the ground. Then I hear the boom of Perry's 30-30 and figured my hunting was over for the day. Then Perry yelled to tell me, "He's coming right at you."

I really snapped to attention then. I could hear a deer coming down the hill just as I had suspected would happen. Suddenly, there he was, chest deep in the snow, trying to bound over the drifts, but without the normal grace of a deer. He seemed to be more plodding straight through the drifts. He was now close and I could plainly see him so I stood and fired. Boy did I fire. I'd wager a pump .22 had never thrown so much lead in the general direction of an animal before. Then my rifle jammed. A cartridge had been smashed against the chamber it should have slid into and I had to clear that. I did and another burst of my lethal fire brought the poor beast to his end.

I was elated that I had brought him down with only a couple of shots. Then looking about I saw spent cartridges everywhere I looked. I yelled to Perry, "I got him!"

Perry yelled back to not do any more shooting, saying he'd be right there. So I decided to reload and found that I had used all the ammo that was in the rifle. The barrel was quite warm. Now I knew about "Buck Fever" and was totally embarrassed that it had caught me and I had blazed away like a mad man. How on earth would I face Perry?

I went to the dead deer and arrived there just as Perry did. We both checked to make sure it was indeed dead. Then he gave me all kinds of Hell for losing my mind like a greenhorn. He said it sounded like two bursts of machine gun fire. He had buried himself behind a log until I had shouted to him. He knew bullets were flying all around that hill, not just at the deer. I knew he was right.

We field dressed the deer and saw that his 30-30 shot would have been fatal. I had hit it twice right where I aimed, right by the heart. Those were probably my first and second shots, before I fell apart and made a burp gun out of my rifle. We cut the deer in two parts and we each carried a half and headed back to the Toll Gate. I was a bit subdued with embarrassment because of the Buck Fever, but Perry didn't ever mention it again and Angus and Nellie just heard that I had killed the buck he had wounded. Now we had food for several weeks.

The following winter, we were hunting above the same spot, but we were both together, on the ridge south of Custer Creek, approaching that same batch of burned, dead timber where I had dispatched his wounded deer. As we got close to a spot where we would enter the timber Perry put his finger to his lips in a "Hush" sign, and we both dropped to the ground to listen. We could hear deer in front of us, seemingly quite close, so we began a slow and very quiet crawl toward the timber. Just as we got into it, we saw a small herd of does and a rather large buck, just thirty yards ahead of us browsing the chaparral along the edge of the timber. Some of them were pawing through the snow and eating the grass. They were beginning to pick up a bit of our scent and were acting a little nervous.

Perry gave me a "Hold it" sort of sign. I just lay there and he rolled on top of the 30-30 to cock it without the noise being telegraphed ahead, giving us away. Then ever so slowly he rolled back and brought the rifle to his cheek, took aim and fired. The big buck shrieked some-thing terrible and leaped up straight into the air before collapsing dead where he fell. At that moment, I knew for certain that I could never kill another deer.

The scream of that buck and the rifle shot put the rest of the animals into a rather panicky circular motion. Perry levered another round into the chamber and shot one of the does. It fell silently and lay still in the snow as the herd evaporated into the dead timber and chaparral.

The second shot had taken me totally by surprise. We had never shot two deer at the same time. This shot shocked me. I was afraid that maybe he had some sort of "Buck Fever" also, but he didn't. He had fired two shots, killed two deer, and our meat problem for this winter was now over. At least we thought that at the moment. We took the livers from the field dressed deer and went back to the Toll Gate. The next morning we brought our horses and retrieved our deer meat. Nothing had bothered them dur-ing the night.

There was just one real problem with this hunting trip. It had been on a weekend. That meant there were people out skiing on the Bogus Mountain ski slopes, which were only a couple of air miles east of where we were killing our winter meat supply. Someone surely heard the two shots, know-ing that it was poachers, shooting deer. The Fish and Game Department was notified and within a couple of weeks some officials came to the Toll Gate and wanted to discuss the carcass hanging in the tree by our front door. They didn't buy the tale my uncle Angus tried to spin about having butchered a goat. They could see a deer hide nailed to the commissary wall, drying in the sun. Thankfully they didn't look at the other side of the building. They would have seen the other hide drying there also.

They made some threat of going for a search warrant. Angus said that he had to admit that he had shot a deer because we were starving. The near truth prevented them from finding the other deer, which had been salted down in a barrel. So they told him that they would have to take him to Boise for trial. He agreed to go along with them. They took the deer down and took it to court with them. They left Nellie behind so she removed the other hide from the far side of the commissary and hid it under her bed.

Angus told the law officers that we lived in Ada County, which meant they had to take him to Idaho City, not Boise. The result of that was for this arrest they would have to drive over 100 miles. The officers and Angus would also have to spend several hours in a strange court, taking up the better part of a day.

In Idaho City they presented their case to a Justice of the Peace. His Honor fined Angus $25 and $3 court costs, none of which he had, so they took him home. The deer was to go to the poor and Angus told the Justice of the Peace that was where it had just come from. We were the poorest of the poor. Your honor wasn't impressed enough to give it back to him so the meat was given to the VA Hospital in Boise.

Angus was instructed to mail the $28 within some period of time or he'd have to serve some jail time. He told Your Honor that he'd do his best and I believe that his fine was sent when we sold some horses in the spring. In 2008, Nelda and I searched the records in Idaho City. There is no mention of the entire proceedings. Perhaps his fine was put into "petty cash," for the office coffee fund.

CHAPTER 31
More Horse Stories

WE MANAGED TO ALWAYS HAVE at least two saddle horses at the Toll Gate. Perry and I sometimes rode them to the mailbox or anywhere else on the ranch and nearby. They were named Pigeon and Racer. Pigeon was a mare that was quite pigeon toed, but even so was very sure footed. Racer was, as the name gives away, some type of racehorse stock. He very fast, with a long and lanky build. He was prone to falling and though he didn't get hurt, one of his falls just about did Perry in. We had been out near Angus's cabin and were coming home just past dark. As we got about a half mile from home; we let the horses have their head, and they galloped along at a very fast pace. Perry and Racer were ahead of me a bit, and as it was dark, neither of us, or the horses, saw a mound of dirt in the middle of the road. (Angus had hauled some logs down the road and when he made a small turn, the logs piled loose dirt into a mound that went all across the road.) The mound across the road was only six to eight inches high, but racer hit it full tilt and did a summersault, landing so that the saddle-horn hit Perry in the center of his chest. This happened right in front of Pigeon and me and we crashed over the top of both horse and rider, and though Pigeon stumbled she did not fall. I leaped off and ran back to Perry and thought he had been killed. I decided I had to do something, even if it was wrong, so I dragged him over the bank, and down to the creek. I dipped some water and threw it in his face. That seemed to get him going again.

We stayed there for half an hour or longer and eventually he could talk and tried to stand. He could do a little walking with my help, so we took it very slowly and finished our trip to the barn. I took the saddles off the horses and turned them loose, than we continued on to the house. Nellie kept him awake for a long time and made him as comfortable as she could, then when she determined that he was better she let him sleep. He bore the imprint of the saddle horn to his grave and I have no idea how he survived the full weight of a falling horse on his chest. I just know all his ribs had to have cracked. It was a month or so before they quit hurting. He had a bad cough for a long time. None of this prompted us to even consider seeing a doctor though.

Perry and I were riding Racer and Pigeon to the mailbox one spring day. The weather was quite warm and the roads dry and hard, making for a pleasant ride without any dust being thrown up by the horse's hooves. There were a lot of quail and partridges running through the grass and brambles beside the little creek at the bottom of Soap Hill. We were unarmed as this was the time of year that the game was reproducing and that was when they were perfectly safe from us. We never wanted to interrupt the reproduction process. The game birds would provide us food for the coming fall and winter.

There was no such safety net for the crows and magpies though. Year round we tried to gather as many of these marauders of the game birds nests as we could. This day, as we passed the Mason Place, just a short bit before the Ourada Ranch road, we came across a loud chattering of magpies in a little plum tree. There were two nests in the tree and both were full of magpies that had not fledged yet. This meant easy pickings for us. Perry had me hold the horses and he went over the fence beside the road, across the little creek and climbed the plum tree to raid the nests. While he did that I was standing in the road with the reins in my hand waiting for him.

As I stood there, I heard the sound of a car coming. This presented a bit of a problem, but nothing too serious. I just had to control the horses' fear of the approaching vehicle and hold the reins tight, keeping both horses as close to the edge of the road as could be. There was a fence right at the road on the downhill side so the only way we could move was to the uphill side. The problem with that plan was that there was about a six-foot embankment on the uphill side of the road.

I began to realize that I was in trouble and tried to lead the horses quickly back toward the Mason place to a wider spot in the road, but the car overtook us before we got to the wider spot and it passed us without slowing much at all. This scared the horses into jumping up onto the bank to get away from the car. The horses knocked me into the bank and though I held the reins tightly and they dragged me up the bank with them as they leaped. A horse' hoof caught me right in the lower jaw and about knocked me out. I held on and after the car had passed the horses settled down. I had bitten through my lower lip and my whole face was a bloody mess. Pain suddenly made itself known and I began to cry my eyes out. I was afraid I had also lost all my teeth, though that hadn't happened.

Perry came running over to check on me. He tried to shut me up and took the horses reins from me and led the horses back to the wide spot in the road He tied them to the fence and had me follow him over the fence to the creek where he washed himself and me off and examined my wounds. I had bitten clear through the lower lip in the front but it was a pretty clean bite without a lot of tearing and strips of flesh hanging anywhere, so he washed it plenty and then had me hold my bandana over it tightly for a while. I had the devil of a time quitting crying because it hurt so badly. Both upper and lower teeth were loose but they were all still there.

After Perry got me patched up with the bandana and I had quit bawling and bleeding like a stuck pig, he got the horses and we continued to the mailbox. We got the mail and didn't go any farther. We had planned to go to Pete Echanove's and visit, but by then I didn't look good enough to visit anyone, nor did I feel up to it. We decided to go back home. I still have the scars on my lower lip and don't see how I didn't lose some teeth, but they turned out fine and so did the lip. We did get about sixty cents worth of magpie heads from the two nests, so the day wasn't a total loss.

Sometimes life presents us with unforeseen learning experiences. I had been to quite a few western movies where the cowboys and the bandits, Indians or whatever, engaged in running gun battles while riding their horses. The good guys could often blast the bad guys right out of their saddles and save the day. Shooting off the back of the horse was a given.

One day, while returning from the Spring Valley Ranch house, I was carrying my .22 Marbles Game Getter. This was a small rifle with a folding stock, which we had broken and removed. So it had become a pistol with a .22 top barrel and a .44 / 410 bottom barrel. I usually carried it as a .22, with no ammunition loaded in the lower barrel. While riding up Spring Creek to the Toll Gate, I had not even thought of firing at anything. I was just sitting there in my saddle enjoying a quiet ride home after having been fed a good lunch at Spring Valley.

This all changed when a large rabbit bounded up the trail ahead of the horse, then seemed to wait for us to catch up to it before it would bound off again to some other spot and wait for us again. I pulled the reins slightly and Pigeon stopped. I took aim and fired.

I learned that one is able to get off a horse quicker than one can get on. I also learned, that one shall then have to walk home. Your ride will have left you for the day. It also became obvious that I did better shooting from a sitting position on the ground than I did from on horseback. I had only sore spots to show for my effort, a couple of miles to walk home and the embarrassment of telling Angus and Nellie why I wasn't with Pigeon when she got home. The rabbit was safely in the bushes, none the worse for my show off shooting, with no audience.

CHAPTER 32

Perry Leaves Idaho

A COUPLE OF WEEKS BEFORE Christmas 1948, Perry and I went to Boise and did some shopping for ourselves: ammunition, shows and good food. Perry also bought me a box of half a dozen toy trucks of all models; lumber, mixers, general freight and whatever else there was. I have forgotten what all was in the box, but they all were very realistic and I knew I really wanted them. We stayed the night in Boise at a cheap hotel, the Hotel Overland. I recall it cost us thirty-five cents for a bed for the night. The bathroom was down the hallway. We ate breakfast in a café the following morning, then hitched-hiked our way to Spring Valley Ranch. There we found our rifles where we had hidden them near the highway. Then we walked the three miles up the stock trail on Spring Creek to the Toll Gate.

When we got home in the late afternoon, Angus was really upset that we had spent all our money and really only had ammunition to show for it. Perry and Angus got into a very heated shouting match about the trucks being little kids toys. Perry responded by saying that if Angus got off his butt and found some work then money wouldn't always be a problem. There was a stunned silence, Nellie was crying and Perry stalked out the door. I was very upset and nervous that this had gone way beyond any reprimand we had ever received for anything. They had both said things about each other that would have been hard to retract. But I hoped that Perry would go sulk a bit in the barn or the bunkhouse and that Angus would take a nap and all would be well.

That wasn't to be. Perry had gone back to the highway and hitched rides to California. Angus had taken his nap and apparently forgotten about my involvement in all of the argument, as he treated me well and never mentioned the trucks again. I made a point of taking them over to the bunkhouse and never playing with them around anywhere that Angus would see me. Eventually I felt they had caused the family rift so I put them in a dresser drawer and never opened that drawer again. I never knew what became of them.

Later in the winter and spring of 1949, Nellie would give me a dollar or two almost every weekend. She told me to go to the Overland Station and get myself whatever I could for lunch. I realized we were out of meat, except for an occasional bird or rabbit that I shot. I was a little hesitant to go shoot a deer by myself. I really didn't want to ever kill a deer again. Also I didn't want us to get caught poaching and fined again. I was pretty sure the Fish and Game would be watching for us to start hunting again. So I'd walk down to Highway 55, at Spring Valley, and hitchhike to the corner of Highway 55 and Beacon Light road. That was just called "the Junction," though its official name was The Overland Station. It was a gas station with a lunch counter and had some groceries. I often bought a large bag of cookies or some cakes to eat on the way home, but I did buy a hamburger, so I got some red meat.

After I was sure Perry was gone, I got to thinking about what would happen next. I had to finish my school year and I had no real prospects for a job. The Echanove's and most every farmer in the valley could put up his own hay with the family doing the work and didn't need the big crews they had needed back in earlier years. The hay was all being baled and it took fewer men to clear a field than when it had all been loose hay and pitchforks. Mac Leod had hired Perry, but had never offered me work. Ourada's had a gang of kids and didn't need outside help. Rex Jensen paid very poorly and would have been my last choice for employment. I had worked for him once before and when it came time to settle up, he had paid me thirty-five cents per hour and I had furnished my own meals. Angus and

Nellie were receiving some kind of an old age pension from the County of Boise, but the blow up with Perry had driven home how desperately poor we really were and how bad our future was looking.

I did discuss this quite a bit with Nellie and she told me that when seventh grade was over I could go to California. There I would have better chances for an education and work, though she had never wanted me to work. She had always dreamed of me getting into politics and let others pay my way through life. There was something about being a politician that made me think they were all parasites. I could not understand, nor would I have ever been comfortable with that type of lifestyle. She had told me all my life what a wonderful person Senator King was and how he had always been there to help those in need. But she also told of a lavish lifestyle that was paid for, not by the good Senator, but by the folks that put him in office. I couldn't balance the contradictions this presented and believed I couldn't bring myself to live well off the backs of folks that worked for a living. She also told me not to mention to Angus that I was planning on leaving. That would not be something to share, just our little secret.

So now there it was laid out for me, a plan for my future. "Go west young man and seek your fortune." I spent a lot of time daydreaming about how I was going to pull this off. I had a bike and thought that I could ride that over to Portland and then down the coast to Oakland. I feared going the shorter route through Winnemucca and Reno, into California, because of all of the desert and the mountains I would have had to climb. With my bike being a one speed and heavy, I felt the flatter trip west across to Portland made more sense. Then there was also the bus. I had no idea what that would cost, but I did have a couple of hundred dollars savings in a bank in Boise that I could use. Though we hadn't discussed that I was pretty sure Nellie would sign a note for me to withdraw my savings for the purpose of traveling to California.

School was over in mid-May and I was 13 years old in 1949. I had decided upon taking the bus to California. I was afraid of the trip to Portland and down the coast of Oregon and California, as I didn't know how far it was. I hadn't a clue that gas stations would sell you a map, and I was worried I might get lost. From most of the places I could remember having been before I could see; Stack Rock, Shafer Butte or War Eagle in the Owyhee Range. They were visible from any high point. I worried that once I was far away, those landmarks would no longer be visible; I worried that without the familiar landmarks to guide me, I might wander off in the wrong direction. Also I wasn't real sure how long bicycle tires would last on pavement. My tires were getting pretty well worn and there was also the issue of luggage. So my mind was made up. I'd go to Boise and catch the Greyhound for Oakland. Once there, I would then take a taxi to 2233 Auseon Avenue. I could think of no reason to tell anyone I was coming, so the plan was finalized, in my mind. I doubt I ever thought about telling anyone, Nellie and I knew and that was enough. Any more people in the know and my plan may get thwarted.

Then Mr. Bicandi threw a monkey wrench right into the gears and spoiled all my careful plans. He hired Angus and me to build a fence along his property line from Stack Rock, down to the Ourada ranch, near Camel Rock. I could have cried, but instead went with Angus and Mr. Bicandi, bedroll and all, up to Stack Rock. We set up our camp and I was trying to determine a way out of this when Angus, unknowingly, came to my rescue. He told me he had forgotten to bring coffee. I told him I'd go home and get some. He said that could wait until Mr. Bicandi came back, but I insisted, and as evening set in I left the camp on the mountain and began a slow walk to the Toll Gate. As soon as I was real sure I was out of sight, I picked up the pace to a fast trot and ran all the way to the Toll Gate. It was about three miles and all downhill, so I could do that in less than an hour.

I had hoped for a note from Nellie giving me permission to withdraw my money from the bank. My plan was to jog down Spring Creek to Highway 55, and hitchhike into Boise and begin my journey. Nellie insisted that I remain the night, have a good dinner and rest up. So I spent the evening getting warnings about life in the city, watching my money, watching out for girls that were just lurking everywhere waiting to catch a young and innocent boy, get into a fast marriage and live off him from then on. She also reiterated that she had hoped that I should never have to work for a living, that I could get into politics and be like the King family, travel the world and do good things for others, while the taxpayers supported me in a grand style. Finally, with all the warning ringing in my ears I went off to bed but scarcely slept a wink.

My Escape is Made

THE MORNING CAME AND I was sure that if I didn't get underway immediately something would happen to cancel my plans. Nellie gave me a letter for the bank and a couple of dollars in change to get by until I should have my own money. Then I put a couple of things in a suitcase and headed to the highway. In another hour I was on Highway 55, hitchhiking a ride to Boise, headed for my future life. The first car to come by stopped and I was taken into Boise, arriving there about 10:00 AM when the bank was opening.

I headed straight to the bank and withdrew all my money except twenty-five or fifty dollars that the banker thought I should leave there to keep my account open. I explained that I was going to move to California, but he still talked me out of closing the account, so I left the minimum to maintain it and took the rest in cash. I then dashed over to the Greyhound station to catch the next bus for California. Surprise for me! The next bus left at five thirty in the afternoon. It wasn't a Greyhound Bus. It was the Boise-Winnemucca Stage Company, which ran a smaller bus out of the Boise Greyhound Terminal. I bought a ticket and sat in the depot for a while. Then I became frightened that by now I had been found out, and Mr. Bicandi would come to the bus station and haul me back up to Stack Rock to build his fence. So I left my suitcase in a locker at the bus depot, and went to hide in a movie theatre. At about four o'clock, I again went to the Greyhound Depot and got my suitcase and awaited the bus.

The bus was late by a couple of minutes and I was afraid that Mr. Bicandi had held it off so he could get me before I fled. Then it came in, I boarded and went to the rear and hid in a corner of the back seat until the bus began to move. We stopped at several stops and each time I was terrified that I'd get caught and be dragged off to finish that dang fence. Not until we stopped for a rest stop in Jordan Valley, Oregon, did I feel safe that I had made my escape. Then it dawned on me that I was tired, cold and hungry and I hadn't brought much of a coat. The bus was packed and I was sandwiched between two large Mexican men on the rear bench seat. I tried to go to sleep. One of the men wrapped his large serape over me and I slept to Winnemucca, waking once when the bus stopped at Mc Dermitt, Nevada. At Winnemucca I got off the Boise-Winnemucca Stage, and got onto a real Greyhound bus. This was a bigger bus and had a heater, comfortable seats that reclined and were covered in cloth, not the cold artificial leather of the bus I had just left. This one was scheduled to go all the way through to Oakland, California.

I slept most of the way to Reno, which was our breakfast stop. Harold's Club, Reno was a casino and also the bus stop. I went in and saw a slot machine. I put a couple of my nickels in it and won fifty cents. 9Thus began my career as a professional gambler.) With my earnings, I went to breakfast and had bacon and eggs for less than half a dollar. Then we boarded the bus and I had a window seat about three rows back from the driver, on the right hand side. We went along the highway at a pretty good pace and when we got into the climb out of Verde to the top of Donner Summit, the road became quite windy and I began to have a queasy stomach. I had to have the driver stop when we got almost to the top and I stepped off and threw up my breakfast, dinner and everything but my toenails, though I was sure with one more heave they would be up also. Then I got back on, some lady got a wet towel and wiped my face off and the bus again was under way.

I then slept to Colfax, where I got off the bus and had a drink of water. We went on and the next stop was Auburn, all I remember of that was a big trestle for a train and a beautiful old courthouse. I believe Sacramento was the lunch stop, though I didn't feel up to eating. Then we were off to Vacaville, where I smelled a strong odor of onions as we went through town. I also remember how dry everything looked there. The grass was a golden brown and some places it had been burned. The grass in Idaho had just gotten a good start growing and everything seemed green and fresh. California seemed quite dry and dirty. Realizing that made me feel some remorse for running off so fast from Idaho. I wasn't so sure that this was a good move now that I was nearing my goal of Oakland.

After several more stops, the bus arrived in Oakland. I retrieved my suitcase and walked out to the cabstand on San Pablo Avenue. I asked the gentleman next to a Yellow Cab to take me to 2233 Auseon Avenue and he whipped out his map. He gave me a long look from head to toe. First authentic hayseed he'd seen in awhile since the influx of the Okies before and during the Second World War. While I settled into the back seat, he searched his map for Auseon Avenue. This was one of those avenues that has a name and was found in the numbered avenues between 86th Avenue and 87th Avenue, in east Oakland. About a hundred blocks from the Greyhound Bus Depot, It was in a part of Oakland that had seldom seen a taxi. It was mostly working class people then.

I guess the taxi driver hadn't seen a real country bumpkin in a long while. I had on a pair of faded out Levi's with holes in both knees, which had been patched with some odd scraps of unmatched cloth Nellie had found. These scraps of cloth she had darned on under the holes, rather than sewing it on. The patches were on the inside of the legs and the loose edges of the holes had been darned down with a yarn of whatever color Nellie had found near the top of her sewing basket. I had a plaid flannel shirt with holes in the elbows that hadn't been patched. My light coat was striped gray and black. Around my neck I wore a large red bandana. I had a pair of Keds on my feet with Argyll knit socks that showed, as my Levi's were a couple of inches too short because they were my good school clothes, bought the summer before and I had grown a couple of inches. I was also wearing a pair of badly smudged, wire rimmed, eyeglasses with round lenses. My hair hadn't been cut or combed since around Christmas time, and I hadn't bathed nor washed in more than a week. Other than the above I was right in style with the rest of the California teens.

We left the bus depot and the cab traveled through downtown Oakland to Lake Merritt and east to East 14th Street. The Taxi took me along East 14th Street for what seemed a very long time. After a few miles we made a left turn onto Auseon, which certainly didn't look like Harrison Blvd in Boise. The cab delivered me to my parent's door. I paid him and probably tipped him a quarter, then grabbed my suitcase. I started to go inside, but Yvonne, Eugene and Walt attacked me, on the porch. Then my mother came out and they all pushed me inside rather quickly, lest any of the neighbors should see what I looked like. Everyone was in shock and probably my mother was dismayed at this sudden turn of events. But they took me in and showed me the house and where I would sleep. I was to use a bunk bed that was normally Perry's. He was in Ukiah, California, in the Redwood country, working at a lumber mill. I could have his bed for a couple of weeks until his job there was done.

My mother took a close look at the clothes I had on with a bit of scorn in her eyes. Then I mentioned that I had some money and she told Walt to take me to Gabardine's, a local clothier on East 14th Street near 96th Avenue. He was to help me purchase some decent clothing, including a change of clothes, so I'd have a spare outfit. Walt and I walked to the store and he picked out a couple of pairs of khaki pants and two shirtsleeve shirts for me. Then we got a pair of shoes, socks and underwear. Walt also bought himself a new outfit, which was done with my money also. That seemed okay with me, knowing full well one brother wouldn't take advantage of another. Then we went home with our purchases and later we went to the show at the Eastmont Theatre. That cost ten cents entry, but the snacks ate up about a dollar, or more for each of us, all of which I paid for.

About two weeks after arriving in California, as we all sat at the dinner table, my father asked my mother, "Doesn't that kid have anywhere to go?" My mother told him something to the effect that I was his youngest boy and that I was now home to stay. He said something like, "Well I'll be damned." And that was it, welcome to life in the big city.

CHAPTER 34

Pete Pivoda

SCHOOL WAS STILL IN SESSION in California when I arrived. I knew of only one person, outside of family in Oakland. There was a friend of Perry's, Pete Pivoda, who had written letters to Perry while he was in Idaho. Pete was an accomplished artist and sketched a lot of ink cartoons of incidents that Perry had described to him after they had happened in Idaho. I don't know if he ever saw pictures of Nellie or Angus, but he made a very convincing likeness, in cartoon form, of all of us. He pictured the horses, Nancy and Stobie, running away with the wagon and groceries flying as the horses, wagon and Angus careened over a cliff, Angus yelling, "Whoa, you SOB's. Whoa!" That was one of his cartoons that hadn't actually happened to us. He did do cartoons about our hunting, fishing, haying and other adventures that were based on truth. Nellie and Angus looked forward to his letters and cartoons as much as Perry and I did. So that was the one person that I made sure I met and we became good pals, hunting and trapping up above Knowland Park. He had a .22 pistol that we took everywhere, with it stuck in our belt.

For some reason I was afraid of the phone. I would ask my mother to dial Pete and when he got on the line, only then was I okay with it. In the few times I had used a phone in Idaho, I had always verbally given the number I wanted to the operator, and she had connected me. I feared I would break it or make a wrong call and who knows what would have happened. Certainly I wasn't up to speed on much of the electronic things.

Coffee pots and toasters were a challenge. I didn't drink coffee, but I was asked to prepare it a couple of times until the others figured out that it was easier to make it themselves than to explain to me how to do it. Even the electric toaster was a challenge at first. It was so old that the slices of bread were placed over the element wires on each side of the toaster and little doors were closed over the bread. When one side was toasted the doors had to be opened and the bread turned over and the other side toasted. It took me a few tries to not blacken one side or the other.

Pete and I explored around the hills outside of town and went to Upper San Leandro Reservoir to swim. That was a several mile walk, through lots of underbrush. I got a real bad case of poison oak, since I had no idea what the plants looked like and we had walked for miles through lots of it. I wished for Mrs. Ourada's cure, but had to settle for calamine lotion.

On one of our trips to the hills, Pete and I were near the south end of Skyline Boulevard near a place in the road where it passed between two long rows of eucalyptus trees. We heard a car coming and it sounded quite different than any car I had ever heard before. It was a Tucker, one of 51 that were made and I never saw one on a road again. Its three headlights fascinated me. It had one in the center of the grill that I learned later turned as the driver steered the car, to illuminate where the car would be going. The whole car was quite different than anything I had seen before.

On that same trip, we were off the road and heard a model airplane engine. Finally a little plane passed over us, and a few seconds later it was quiet. We figured it had run out of gas and that the owners would come get it, so we watched a while and never saw anyone, so we looked for it ourselves. We looked for it for quite a while and couldn't find it. I found out years later that it most likely was flown off by my future brother-in-law and his father, and they didn't find it either. It had made its maiden flight and went into aviation wonderland, never to be seen again.

CHAPTER 35

My Mother, Sister Dolores and Making Friends

MY MOTHER HAD A FRIEND, Ethel Millman, whom she did some house-work for. They also did other things together and one of those things was to go to the Golden Gate Fields racetrack in Berkeley. They took me there and I saw my first horse race. They bet on some nag and we cheered wildly as it came in second and they both won a small amount. Then they were really into the next race and bet on another horse that came in first, but was the favorite and that paid practically nothing other than getting their money back. They seemed to both bad-mouth my dad for betting on the horses and here we were where they were doing the same thing and enjoying their day quite nicely. That seemed to me to be a little bit hypocritical.

My mother took me to San Francisco to go shopping. We took a train out to West Oakland, to the ferry terminal. There we got on a ferry and rode it to the Ferry Building in San Francisco at the foot of Market Street. We then walked up Market Street and I felt like we were in canyons where only occasional light from the sun fell on us. My mother bought some clothing for someone, not for me, and we retraced our journey, though on the return we rode a bus on the lower deck of the Bay Bridge. I was amazed to be on something so massive and found it interesting that the Bay Bridge was really two bridges, one a suspension bridge and the other a cantilever similar to the railroad and highway bridges I had seen before, but on a much larger scale. That was a memorable ride to me. Cars went both directions on the upper deck and trucks and busses were on the lower deck, also going both directions, which were separated by train tracks for the small electric commuter trains that ran between the cities of the Bay Area.

I had a sister Dolores, whom I had never met. She was born before my father and mother met and she had never been to Idaho, so I didn't know her. I had heard wonderful stories about her husband, Richard Ennis. He was a career Navy man. They lived in Alameda and one afternoon she and her husband, Ennis came to visit. They brought a folding Army cot for me, so I would have a bed when Perry got home from his job in Ukiah. That Army cot was my bed for a couple of years and eventually I moved it out to the garage so I could have my own room. There was no working automobile in our family at the time and therefore none in the garage, though it was fairly full of junk.

The first summer in California was full of new adventures for me. My brother Walt and I did a lot of things together until all my money was gone. Then he went to earn some money at Sequoyah Golf and Country Club most mornings. He would either play cards in the caddie shack or get a "double," which was to carry the bags for two golfers. That paid him pretty well, as he was not only a gifted golfer; he also had the ability to discuss most anything with just about anyone, regardless of age or station in life. Most members were very well to do and tipped him quite generously.

When I went to caddie a few times, if I got any work, it was usually to shag balls for those members that were too cheap to actually play a round of golf. When I did get a "loop," which was to carry a bag of golf clubs for someone playing a round of golf, it was usually some cheapskate who wanted a "B" caddy, so they paid the three dollars for me to carry their bag for eighteen holes and maybe a quarter tip, not the three to five dollar tips Walt usually received nor the ten to twelve dollar caddy fee. There was a reason for that, as I had no idea what club was needed for the upcoming shot, didn't know where the next hole was and had no idea how far it was to the green. Also and these wealthy golfers intimidated me. I never initiated any conversation and answered, "yes, no and I don't know," to any question they might ask. I also didn't know that it helped to share the tip with the Caddy Master, the old "pay to play." He was the contact between the golfers and the caddies and those in the know slipped him a few dollars often. Caddying wasn't my cup of tea!

I did find that I could make a few dollars on a weekend mowing lawns and got a few of the neighbors to try me out. They usually liked the job I did and many had me come back fairly regularly. But that was good for thirty to fifty cents and maybe a quarter tip, for an hour or two of work. The edging was done with hand clippers on most lawns. Many of the driveways in Oakland were just two strips of concrete and they ran to the rear of the houses, so if the driveway was seventy five feet that meant three hundred feet of edging, just on the driveway. With luck, some lady may offer me a drink of ice water or lemonade in the middle of the job. The men just growled out orders to make sure I did all the edges and warned me not to step on any flowers. This was not a very lucrative job either.

Some friends of my sister Dolores, Betty and Frenchy Poletti, had a young daughter Simone, whom they would pay me to baby sit, while the adults all went out to dinner or a movie. My brother-in-law, Rich and Frenchy were very funny and entertaining types. Frenchy would talk to me, and start to tell me some cock and bull story, and as he told it, one eye would drift shut. When one is paying attention to an older person's sincere story, these things become noticeable. I would stare and then he'd forget his story and bark at me to stop staring at his disability. Then he would go on a tirade about, "How do you think that makes me feel." I would be very apologetic and I'd try to say I hadn't noticed until he pointed it out. It all made me feel really bad thinking I had treated my sister's friend so poorly and I'd almost be in tears. Then I would notice him start to do the same thing to some other unsuspecting soul and I realized I had been the victim of another hoax. But they did pay well for the babysitting and they used me several times.

I was put onto a rather fast learning curve, coming from the Toll Gate, where Nellie had done about everything that would at the time, be considered women's work. Washing clothes, ironing and cooking were all things I really knew nothing about. My mother assured me it was high time I learned. I was to vacuum the rug in the living room as one of my chores. One of my brothers told me I had to keep it moving or it would burn a hole in the carpet. Helpful hints to the naïve again. I also learned to iron my clothes and that was helpful when I got into the Marines. It took several times for me to learn to wash my clothes. The water was pumped out and then refilled to rinse. Also city folks didn't wash blue jeans and whites together, I learned.

The Mc Arthur house seemed to be the neighborhoods hang out. We had no car, so the garage was used sort of like a clubhouse for the boys and a few of the more adventurous girls, who seemed to appear quite often. Some of the older boys would sit out on the porch and teach my sister Eileen to swear, or pull other useless tricks on her and me. I was naïve, and fell for every tale they told me. I was sent to the store to ask if they had left handed monkey wrenches and all sorts of non-existent things. They also had a way of getting me into fistfights. I was usually the loser and found that I was better served to avoid the company of most of the older guys that came over to our house.

There were a couple of guys about my age, only a year of two ahead of me in school. We got along well and would often go to the park a few blocks away to play football. I wasn't good at any sports and couldn't run fast, so I was always a lineman and seldom touched the ball, however I loved the game and the opportunity to have some company that didn't take advantage of my inexperience around people. Almost all the boys had bicycles and we rode them everywhere we went during the day. Since I didn't have one, I did the peddling and the owner rode the handlebars. That was fine with me as I was very strong in the legs and could peddle two of us up most any hill that a single rider could go up. We went as far as Niles Canyon on bikes, which must have been close to twenty-five miles round trip.

CHAPTER 36

School and Other Pass-times

ABOUT THE END OF SUMMER I bought a bike and that made us all on even footing. I could now keep up with the best of them, and I could go without having to peddle someone else on the handlebars. That lasted until the first day of school when I rode the bike over to Elmhurst Jr. High School, on 98th Avenue. I parked it with all the rest of the bikes and after school it was gone. Somebody had done the unthinkable and stolen it. That had been something I had never considered. In Idaho, I had left my bike leaning against a tree or parking meter whenever I rode it to Boise, even while I went to the show, or visited the Capital Building, or whatever I did. Maybe I had just been lucky, but I never thought someone would actually steal a bike, but here was mine stolen right at the schoolhouse. I was shocked beyond words and my friends all were a bit disturbed that they hadn't warned me not to take it to school. It was many years later, before I had another bike.

School was another change. I was going into the eighth grade, and knew no one in that grade or any other person in that school. I had just come from a school with six kids in all grades, and now I was in one with about 300 in my grade. Walt was starting tenth grade and so I was on my own at Elmhurst. I hadn't been there before, but I had a general idea where it was. I could go down the railroad tracks to 98th Avenue, turn right and would find it two or three blocks ahead on my left. As mentioned previously, I rode my bike to school and watched where the other kids parked, and that was where I went. Then I went inside the main school building and not having a clue where to go, I went to the office. Bells rang and kids ran, and more bells and faster running.

I was so scared I considered going home. Somehow that thought scared me worse, so I sat in a chair in the office until finally someone asked me why I was sent there, and asked me where was my paperwork. I then had to go talk to a secretary who asked someone else and then the person in charge came over and asked me if I had my transcripts from my last school. I didn't, and had no idea what they were. Then I was asked what grade I was going into, how old I was and why I was only in eighth grade, and on and on. After a good hour or so, I was sent to the gym. I had to ask directions, as I had no idea what a "gym" was. I found out it meant gymnasium. The staff, by using the incorrect word, confused me even more than I had been. After all, this was a school. I went where they pointed me and took a seat in the back, behind another dozen or so kids. Some man was up front reading names and assigning homerooms, whatever that was, and eventually someone from the office came in and gave him a paper with my name on it and he told me to go to a "portable," and he gave it a number. He also gave me a paper that had a list of times and room numbers on it.

I really had no idea what a "portable" was, so I wandered back to the office and someone there told some girl to take me to my homeroom just as there was another ringing of bells and everyone walked out of that room and more kids came pouring into it. I had never seen so many people as at this school. I went in and was told to take a seat and the teacher said she would assign seats when everyone got in. I did that and she called her roll and assigned everyone a seat, except for me. I had had to get up to let some kid sit in my seat and when she got all done she asked me why I wasn't in my seat. I explained that she hadn't called my name and she looked on her list and I wasn't there, then I gave her the list I had been given and she told me I would be in a different room for second period, I would be in her room for my home room. By then I was getting the idea that this would be different than Stack Rock School. She told me to go to my next room and sent someone to guide me there.

I found out that a "portable" was a one-room building, about the size of the whole Stack Rock School building. They were made to be temporary in a way that they could readily be moved from one school site to another to meet student-seating demands. They were wooden buildings, low in height, with minimal amenities, perhaps a coal stove and a few overhead lights. They had swinging windows that were hinged at the top and when open would often be hit by someone walking by outside, as they jutted out at just the right height to knock one silly, if they weren't paying attention, as the bottoms were head-high to the average student, when open.

The next teacher about had a fit because I was late and threatened to send me to the office. I explained I had been there for a long time and that I had been sent to the gym and a portable, now I had been guided here. That time, my being late was forgiven, and a seat was assigned and I was given a book and told to read the first chapter. This was one class where I actually learned something new. The book contained some California history, something I hadn't studied before.   Because it interested me I did quite well in that class.

The next time when the bell rang some guy told me he was going to my next class, so I followed him. After that was lunch and they served a hot meal in the cafeteria that was just fine. That cost thirty-five cents. I ate and looked for my next classroom. It was another portable and the class was math. I did well there also, as it was a repeat of what I had studied in fourth or fifth grade in Idaho. We had two more classes, and then we were out for the day and it was only three o'clock.

One of the worst classes for me was gym. I was not one of the munch-kins. When the teams were chosen, at first I was a very early pick. Then as the players found out I had no idea how to play any of the games, they filled their teams and no one had chosen me. So while they played, I did a lot of bench warming. The gym teachers only paid attention to the kids that played the best and maybe a second string team. Those received a lot of in-dividual instruction and they were observed during every game they signed up for. A couple of us were duds and the coaches just made sure we took a shower. We received an "A" if we took a shower every day. I hated gym class but loved the chance to get a warm shower and avoid the fight for a bath at home. (Yvonne and Eugene spent an inordinate amount of time primping and preening in the morning and evening, or so it seemed to me.)

There were a couple of classes that I really did enjoy. Mr. Couch taught an art class that I did okay in. No one had shown me anything about how to draw and he impressed on me that shading added depth and reality to my scribbles. In those days one could draw pictures of guns without being expelled, and I loved to draw the old flintlock and matchlock rifles, which I had taken quite an interest in. I also tried my hand at ships of the old sailing days and found that interesting. There was a lot of detail to all of these and I knew the names and functions of the various things that I drew. A good drawing could explain things better than I could put them into words. My favorite picture of my own drawings was an elaborately adorned early Navy Colt Revolver. I had studied it at the Snow Museum in Oakland, standing for hours before the gun display case and memorizing what I saw. Unfortunately I was able to take that class for just one semester and never had another art class.

Another class I liked in Elmhurst was choir. I couldn't sing well, but I had a good time trying. At the end of the semester, which was Christmas Season, the choir went to the Oakland auditorium and sang our little hearts out. I had to buy a white shirt for that, first one I had ever owned. The sad part of the class was that many of us were not in there because of singing ability, or even because we wanted to be, but the person that as-signed the class to us felt we'd be less trouble there than in an advanced type study class. In plain English, some of us were just dumped there for lack of a better place to put us, and a disinterest in finding out what would have been most beneficial for us. The result was boredom for some, and a lot of misbehaving in a class lead by a person who could not maintain order, so she would go out into the hall and cry often, and the class would learn nothing. I tried to not become the one that made her dash out into the hall and for that, I believe, she gave me a "B".

I had a shop class that taught us how to work with wood a bit and one that taught us a bit about making things from metal, like a set of tools for a fireplace and such. I learned how to soften metal and work it with a hammer and tongs and how to quench it to harden it. It was all good stuff that I have used over the years.

Another shop class was lead by a teacher who was the assistant principal at Elmhurst, Mr. Campbell. It was a sheet metal shop where we learned that he seldom was in the classroom, but was tickled pink to come back and catch one of us doing something he has determined shouldn't be done in his class. He got great pleasure out of having the offender grab his own ankles and then he would apply a paddle to the butt of the student. He had varying degrees of punishment, base hit, double, triple or homerun. A homerun would cause him to break the handle off the paddle. This form of discipline seemed to not do a thing to keep his classes in order. I think all that did was satisfy some sadistic thing in his makeup. I believe that was why he left the classroom so often, so he could catch a victim, which he invariably did. I made a dustpan in his class and I'm sure he had no idea, nor cared what I made or even what my name was. He gave me a "C."

We had lockers then, no backpacks, and we were supposed to take our books home as needed to complete our assigned homework. Most often, I left my books at school and did my homework during the roll call in the homeroom. It would be hurried, and my grades were marginalized, but I did usually manage to get on the honor roll.

After school, time was mostly spent with my friends, Ricky and Ronny. They would come by and we would sit in the garage and tell stories, smoke cigarettes and hide from our parents. None of mine would venture out there, I'm sure they didn't care what we did, as long as they didn't hear about it. After dinner, if we had any money, we often went to Mac Arthur Blvd at about 82 Avenue. There was a little café there, called Combs, with a shuffleboard and pin ball machines. A play on the pinball machine cost five cents and one could win a bunch of free games, if you were good. If not, a wire drilled through the side of the machine would allow access to trip one of the high score spots a few times and thus cough up a free game or two. This was frowned upon by the owner; a Mr. Combs. Only the most daring took part in that adventure, but we all knew it was possible.

The shuffleboard cost a dime and the owner was often a player, so that was out of our league. There were no free games to be won, either, so we seldom played shuffleboard. Some of our older friends and brothers did though. Walt was good at it, as was Perry, but I stuck to the pinball machines most of the time and when my money was gone, I'd go home. Older girls spent time there also, so Walt and Perry, and others of the "older folk" spent a lot of their time and effort there. I don't recall Eugene going to Combs; it may have been due to his senior classes taking a lot of his time and effort. He had plans to go to UC Berkeley after High School.

My mother discovered that she had cervical cancer within a few months of my arrival in California. For me, that made it very difficult to have conversations with her. I knew she was sick, I never had known anyone to have cancer and survive it, so I tried to be as inconspicuous as possible. I knew she felt really terrible and she took a lot of that out on my baby sister Eileen, who was three years old at that time. She screamed at her and I would run out to the garage so I didn't have to listen to her. Thankfully this didn't happen often, but it made me very nervous and confused. We must not have had any type of health insurance and so she went to the Alameda County Hospital in San Leandro, Fairmont Hospital, for some treatments. My older sister, Dolores took care of Eileen through part of this ordeal and though she wasn't very good with kids either, it was a slight improvement.

Along toward fall of 1951, my mother spent more and more time at Fairmont Hospital. Eventually she was admitted there for the duration of her illness. I had never been informed that her cancer was terminal. I took the bus out to visit her a few times but didn't really know anything about her, nor did she know much about me, so neither of us had much in common to talk about. That made me feel bad, because I knew normally children should be terribly sad that one's mother was sick. I just felt a sense of relief that she was away and no one was yelling at me, or Eileen anymore.

That was a mixed blessing, as I really felt better that she was away and it seemed to me that we were all safer from her wrath, yet I felt guilty for feeling that way. I also never told a soul how I felt, nor did anyone appear to care, if or how, I may have felt. I did feel very much alone. Eventually Eileen went to live with Dolores for a while.

CHAPTER 37

My Mother Dies

THOUGH I HAD NEVER BEEN a very confident and outgoing person, this move to California had made me even more of an introvert. I was overwhelmed by the size of everything, the school, the City of Oakland, the Bay Area. I felt that they were all so big that I'd never be able to get around in any of them and I really only had about three friends that I could hang out with and they were all older. Then some kid in one of my classes at Elmhurst, I can't recall his name, got to having lunch with me once or twice and even asked me by his house one evening, after dinner. I went over there and we were alone, watching television, which was also very new to me. He offered me a drink and I took it and discovered it was whiskey and 7 up. Not a bad combo, so I had a couple more before I went home. Then I was very ill and got the dry heaves. That pretty much ended my career as a professional drunk. When I got home and to bed, I just fell into a deep sleep. The next morning Eugene woke me up and asked me where I had been and informed me our mother had died, and they had tried to let me know, but no one had any idea where I was.

The news that my mother had died came as a strange blow to me. I knew I should be feeling badly and be crying, or somehow showing it, but I didn't really feel all that bad. I knew that she had been in terrible pain and was not herself for the last several months and it seemed to me that now she wasn't hurting anymore. I was hurting inwardly, but not because of the loss of my mother, but because I didn't really feel like I had lost anyone close to me. I felt more like a neighbor down the street, that I may not have cared much for, had passed away. What hurt me, was that I felt that way about my own mother. Of course that was something else to keep bottled up inside. So no one ever heard me talk about that.

I had never been to a funeral and had no good clothes to wear to one, just an old white shirt. Now I was going to a family member's funeral and must dress accordingly. Eugene had a friend in a church he went to who gave me a double-breasted suit and I bought my second white shirt. Someone loaned me a tie. I don't remember much about the service, nor do I know where it was. I know a big black car took us there and brought us to the graveyard on Piedmont Avenue. After the burial, the same black car took us home and that was that. No reception or anything like that, no friends over to the house. Everyone just went off each his own way, and I sat home alone trying to figure out how I was supposed to feel. I guess I felt worse for my plight than for the loss of a parent. Now I was pretty much on my own. My father worked nights, Perry worked full time, Yvonne was living away on her own, usually with Walter staying with her, and Eugene had his circle of friends from church. Eileen was also gone.

The pastor at Eugene's church, Elmhurst Baptist Church, 90th and Holly Sts., had a daughter about Eileen's age, which was four years old. He and his wife had a couple of other children, or at least on the way. They took Eileen and raised her as their own daughter, until she was in her late teens. Probably she had the best opportunities of anyone in our family, for a well-balanced life and education. I didn't see her later on, as they had moved to Southern California shortly after my mother died. There he became pastor of a much larger congregation. They eventually lived in Bell, California, which is a small town between Los Angeles and Long Beach. It was a nice bedroom community and a safe place to raise a family.

I went back to school after a couple of days and misbehaved in class. The teacher came by and picked me up by the ears, set me on the back of my desk and slapped me a couple of times, across the face. I don't believe I had ever been so embarrassed in my life and I dearly wanted to cry, but with a full classroom watching me, it wasn't going to happen. The teacher made me come back to her room after school was out for the day. When I did, she read me the riot act about my deportment and said she wouldn't stand for any more of it. Funny thing now is that I can't recall what I had done for sure, but I may have been chewing tobacco and spit out the window of the portable. At the end of her tirade she asked me what I had to say for myself. So I told her that I was sorry, my mother had just died, and I wasn't thinking clearly. Somehow that got her to crying and hugging me and then she was the sorry one, and I got to go home. I hadn't tried to manipulate her, it just happened. I behaved well in her class after that and she never said an unkind thing to me again. I ended up liking her, and did my best to earn good grades.

Another summer came, 1952, and I went to the Sequoyah Country Club to caddy. I also worked a few days at the zoo when they had a big event, helping to empty trash and making sure kids on the train had a ticket. I don't remember if that paid anything or if Mr. Snow, the owner, just let us in to the park free. I also made a few dollars every week by mowing some lawns. I still had my same three friends and we went to the show, played football at Arroyo Viejo Park. We went to Bob's Hotdogs on Mac Arthur Blvd, near 78th Avenue or Combs near 82nd Avenue, to play the pinball machines. Sometimes we walked to San Leandro or San Lorenzo to a show, but normally we didn't venture very far to the east after dark. There was a policeman that would stop us and make us stay on the north side of East 14th Street if he felt we were out of our territory, and he decided what that territory was. There weren't the number of gang problems then as there are now, but he was being proactive by keeping different groups of teenage boys away from each other. Only one of our friends seemed to resent the policeman's friendly directions and later in life he ended up being murdered in Oakland by an unknown assailant wielding an ice pick. Another one of Oakland's unsolved murders. (As a Lt. in the Oakland Fire Department, I responded to the incident and had no idea who he was. I learned a few years later from his mother and had the good sense not to tell her I had been called to the scene.)

CHAPTER 38

Church, Salvation and Women

I WENT TO EUGENE'S CHURCH one Sunday. I thought the preacher, Pastor Paul Horn, was talking to me the whole service. I had often wondered about God and spiritual things. I had even read a lot of the New Testament, prayed a lot for things to get better in my life, including more money and some friends. His sermon just seemed to remind me of everything I had read and I determined then to accept Jesus as my Savior. Vernon Woods, a member of the church came and prayed with me and we talked for a long time in some quiet spot. I went home and told Eugene what I had done and then we started having some prayer sessions at our home. Eugene had quit going to Cal after our mother died and had started to go to the Baptist College in San Francisco. So we set about converting the few friends I had and making our lives over a bit. That worked, with varying degrees of success. I believe most of them went along to placate us.

We lived a couple of miles from Oak Knoll Naval Hospital and some of the sailors from the Hospital would go to some of our religious functions at church. Some of them stayed at our house and they got talking about people they met on ships and such. One mentioned a Pete Pivoda and said that Pete had a friend from Stack Rock School, Cleo Stover. Eventually I met Pete and Cleo again and even went out to the Aircraft Carrier Antietam, where they were stationed. This was at Alameda Naval Air Station. I was there for a movie and spent the night aboard the ship as a guest. The ship was in Alameda for repairs. They came around for a couple of weekends, then back to sea and off to the war in Korea again.

My good buddy, Joseph Ronald Alexander, "Ronny" to all of us there in East Oakland, found some girl that he wanted to take out. She had a friend and I think the deal was that she would go with him if the girl friend could tag along. So being sixteen or so, and having a friend close to that same age, he went along with it and set us up to be a "blind date." I was excited, but scared, I had never actually been out with a girl, didn't know what to say to one, and sure felt this one would be way too pretty to be seen with me. We all agreed to the double date. Ronny and I were to take them to the zoo, I believe. We met them somewhere along the way and I was immediately stumbling for some excuse to go home. The poor girl was as skinny as a toothpick and looked more scared than I felt. We toughed it out and went to the zoo, or where ever we went, and I couldn't wait to get away from them. She probably felt the same about me. I was sure that would be my first and last "blind date," and it was.

Eugene had a girlfriend. Her father was the gentleman that had given me the suit for my mother's funeral. He invited us all over to his house for Thanksgiving dinner, Eugene, my father and me. We went and I found out that the hosts had four daughters, one married, one a year or so younger than Eugene, one in my grade, but in a different Junior High, and one much younger. They had a very nice dinner for us and had great desserts. I was beginning to like the whole family, what with all the great food and especially tasty desserts.

Eugene suggested that we go to a show and I could take the girl that was in my grade. Terror set in and I had mixed feelings about the whole day. I loved the thought of taking her to the show, dad even doled out a couple of dollars to assist in that, but I was not sure what I was expected to do next. So off we went, walking to the Granada Theatre at about 89th and East 14th Street. That was about 20 blocks from their house. I have no recollection of what was playing, I knew that the guy was supposed to hold her hand and walk on the outside. I wasn't really sure of the "hold her hand" part, but that seemed okay with her. Eugene was holding his friends hand and they knew all this stuff. Throughout the show, when we weren't eating popcorn or drinking Cokes, I put my arm over her shoulder, just like the rest of the couples in the theatre. I even checked and that was what Eugene was doing. I didn't want to be a problem so I made sure that no real weight fell on her shoulder. At the end of the movie, my arm was almost paralyzed and I was in agony with a cramp in my arm and back.

After the movie there was more terror, now my arm just hurt, not paralyzed anymore, but I had not spoken ten words the whole evening and I was afraid that I was either hated or that I would have to kiss her good night or both. Also I had never kissed a girl. When we got home to her house, we didn't linger on the porch, but went right into the house. Everyone had gone to bed and left a dim light on for us, so I said a quick "Good night," and sprinted out the door and walked home alone. I was cursing myself for not having at least tried to kiss her good night, but how would that have gone over if I did it wrong? But obviously I had done the whole thing wrong and knew it.

There was an older girl across the street from our house on Auseon Avenue, and down toward Bancroft a house or two. She and I were friends enough to say "Hi," back and forth. One fine day she invited me into her house under some pretense of needing some help, while explaining there was no one there to help her, and wouldn't be for a long, long time. I did whatever it was she needed help with and she asked me to have a seat and chat. Well I could do that, so I sat on a chair and she got us a Coke, or something and she chatted. She told me she knew everyone in my family and liked all the boys, particularly Perry. Then she asked about my girl friends and I told her I didn't have any. Our conversation got deeper into why not and eventually I had to admit I had never kissed a girl. Immediately I was given a lesson that took my breath away and sent me dashing to the safety of my own home. But I was still hoping against hope, for another lesson. She seemed awfully warm and cuddly.

A couple of days went by and she called me over again. This time we were to play checkers. That we did and she asked me if I thought I knew how to kiss a girl. I told her I was sure I could, so she gave me a test and I passed. This time I was a bit braver and didn't dash home. So she got out the checkers again and we played a few more games, all the while she explained to me that her folks wouldn't be home for hours, so if I had any other questions, just ask, that was what she was here for. So we played checkers and she said it was too warm. She went to her room and changed her top and came back with one that was much more comfortable, very wide at the neck and didn't hide much of anything. There was an awful lot to be seen, all covered in pretty freckles and sweat, heaving with every breath she took. I was hard pressed to not get caught staring. She didn't seem to mind and moved often to lean far forward and give me a better view.

We played more checkers and we each won a game and then she took the checkerboard, checkers and all, and poured them down the center of her blouse and then told me, "It's your move next." I was so astonished at that display that I sat there speechless for a minute and then it came to me that she probably didn't really want to play checkers anymore, so once more, I bolted for the door and ran for the safety of my own home. Close call, but as President Clinton would have said, "No cigar." She didn't invite me back right away, but did come over to visit a few times, when I was home alone. I would go out on the porch with her, where I felt safe. She eventually tired of that and totally gave up on me.

CHAPTER 39

Perry Got Married and I Find Girlfriends

PERRY GOT MARRIED ABOUT THE time I started Castlemont High School. His wife, the former Miriam Faye Malone, was a beautiful eighteen-year-old Navy brat. He had met her while taking dancing lessons at Arthur Murray's dance studio in downtown Oakland. Soon they were married, though I don't know where that happened. I believe that they first lived in a trailer parked in our driveway. Later they moved into an apartment at the end of our block, real close to Castlemont High School. She and I played a lot of cards and I missed a lot of school because of playing Canasta. I thought that she and Perry were the greatest couple in the world, but after a year or so, she went back to her parents who had been transferred to San Diego. Her father was an officer in the US Navy. Perry was devastated and had a real hard time coping with that breakup. He moved home and was very despondent.

As I started Castlemont in September of 1952, another event brought on some changes. I was still very shy and had the same three friends that I could hang around with. Then Eugene came home from a church camp trip and told me that on this retreat, or whatever it was, he had met some blonde girl that knew me. I didn't recognize the name, but the next day at school she found me. She told me she had met my brother. That touched off a real change in me. I liked her and she seemed to like me, so I asked her to go to a football game with me, Castlemont at Hayward. I even arranged a ride, with another older couple, so we would have a way there and back. The older girl lived close to our house on Auseon. Her boyfriend worked as a carpenter with Perry and owned a car. My newfound friend accepted and we became almost a couple immediately. Only problem was that I had again become afraid to kiss a girl. She went along with the hand holding and a few days later, I asked her to a swim party that the Elmhurst Baptist Church was giving, which she agreed to attend with me.

The swim party was at a public pool in Hayward, called the Hayward Plunge. Transportation was arranged through the church. A few of the older guys had cars and would share a ride with us youngsters that didn't. So we went to the swimming pool and went our separate ways to put on our swimsuits. When we came out I saw that she looked very healthy in a cute two-piece swimsuit, and I tried to look my best in my suit. I thought we were good to go. We had been swimming for a while, when the Youth Minister followed me to the bathroom and told me that I had to talk to her about her attire. Two- piece swimsuits were inappropriate swimwear for good girls, in his view. I told him I'd tell her, but there was no way I was ever going to discuss her choice of suits. I was embarrassed and it spoiled my evening. I noticed that same guy seemed to not take his eyes off her very often. I didn't know how to handle that. I thought about talking to Eugene but I knew he and that guy were good friends, so I didn't talk to anyone. (It turned out the guy was having sexual identity problems and soon ran off with his boyfriend.)

A while later we went to a swim party at Muir Beach. I worried that I'd get censored or something for not making her wear something different. To my relief, he didn't go and no one else seemed to have any trouble with her outfit. On the way home, one of the cars didn't run right and the guy we were riding with pushed the errant machine all the way back to San Leandro. I was impressed that we never bumped the cars together with any kind of a bang and our driver explained that he had been a fighter pilot during the war and could really feel the contact between himself and both cars, so that was his secret of success.

During this time, my aunt Nellie showed up at my father's house. I guess she wanted to get away from living alone at the Toll Gate as Angus had been stricken with a stroke and was in a care facility in Boise. She didn't want to stay alone out so far from town. I didn't remember hearing about the stroke and was trying to concentrate enough on school to pass into the eleventh grade. Nellie found out about the girlfriend and one day went up to visit the folks and see what type people I was dealing with. I was embarrassed almost to tears when my friend told me that she and her folks had met my aunt. I know Nellie had probably dressed up in her best to go see them, which would have been a dress with some material added to the bottom, sewn on with a darning needle and contrasting colors of yarn, a large floppy hat, a veil, and tennis shoes with bulky white sox. She may have worn a green eyeshade under the hat. My friend didn't elaborate and I tried to change the subject quickly to something less embarrassing.

The problems shifted from the bathing suit and aunt Nellie to my fear of a kiss goodnight. The young lady told me that the lack of kissing her was just wrong. She wanted me to rectify that or we were through. That came to me in a note in a class we had together. It was signed with "Te amo" which didn't mean anything to me either. I wrote her back that she'd have to teach me how she liked being kissed. She did later that day and we got along great for a while, no more trouble with kissing now that I had been properly instructed.

Then it became time to figure out "Te amo," as I still hadn't a clue what that was all about. She explained that it meant, "I love you," in Latin. This astonished me, made me very happy and scared the wits out of me, all in one emotional moment. No one had ever told me they loved me before. I had no idea of how I was supposed to respond. In the movies that always came to the surface just as the movie ended and the couple rode off in a blissful state. I had been warned by Nellie of this type of thing, but yet to feel that perhaps someone did really love me was a whole new ball of wax for me. I had never been told that, nor had anyone been outwardly concerned about me, other than giving me warnings, such as Nellie had.

This love thing had jumped out and become a very involved, terrifying condition.

Then I got tired of a lot, of what seemed like petty situations. Her parents were divorced, her real mother was in LA, the lady I thought was her mother was in reality the cause of the breakup of her parents, or at least that is what I got from someone's sniping. One day she loved her then the next she couldn't stand her. So somehow we drifted apart. Another reason for that drift was her stepmother seemed to be pushing for us to get engaged and I wasn't ready for anything of that magnitude. That same grandmother seemed to infer, to my understanding anyway, that she would give us a home to live in when the right time came. This was all moving way too fast for me. It also seemed that we were sharing a lot of stuff that I probably shouldn't ever know about, at this point in a new relationship.

Later that year I went with Eugene and his friends to Mt. Hermon Christian Camp in the Santa Cruz Mountains. We stayed in a cabin and went to meetings in a large hall. While at one of those, I met a quite pretty blonde girl about my age. She gave me a "come hither" look, so I came thither. I was immediately smitten with her Nordic good looks, blond hair and ice blue eyes and ample physical assets. We palled around through the rest of the meeting, which I believe was just a long weekend. We were sorry it was over and promised to write to each other. She lived in Citrus Heights, east of Sacramento, which was as good as in New York, as far as I was concerned, having no car or money. We did write a lot and I got her phone number, but that was a long distant call which cost more than I could afford, therefore there was no way I could call her.

Perry had come home, told us his marriage was over and after a couple of months he and Yvonne rented a place in Hayward. He finally snapped, drove home to pick me up and asked me to drive him to San Francisco. I thought that odd, but agreed and so off we went. He explained that he would jump off the Golden Gate Bridge and I could have his car. With that I pulled over to the curb and asked him if he would like to help me first. It was a Friday and we could drive to Citrus Heights and I would introduce him to a lady I had met, who happened to have a sister that I liked. He finally agreed and so we headed for Sacramento by the river road, because it was a Friday and traffic would be heavy on Highways 80 or 50. He seemed to look forward to not jumping off a bridge and I thought I was a real help with this alternate plan.

He drove like a mad man, having taken over the driving from me. It appeared we now had no time to waste to get to Citrus Heights. We drove wildly until we got to Freeport, just south of Sacramento, then the timing gear on his car broke and we coasted to the end of our driving for that day. We called a tow truck, which took us to a mechanics shop, which was closed for the weekend. The owner lived close by and we somehow got him to come down and look at the car, give us an idea of what was wrong and a ball park figure to repair it. Then we called the girl in Citrus Heights and I told her of our car problem and exactly where we were. She assured us that she and her sister would come and get us.

They arrived after about a half hour and I introduced Perry to the sisters. We then went to a Mel's Drive-In for a quick dinner of hamburgers, fries and a shake each. While there, we got to know each other, and it seemed everyone got on quite well. The girls decided to give us a ride back to Hayward, where by then Yvonne and Perry were renting a little house. We all agreed that would be the thing to do and I learned later that the last thing their parents had told the girls was, "Don't you dare take those boys back home." But take us there they did, and then after we all had a rest, they went back home. We promised to be back in a week, which we were. And we were back and forth a lot in the next few months.

The following weekend, as planned, we went to Freeport and picked up the car. Someone must have given us a ride there, but I cannot recall who it was. But get the car we did and continued on to Citrus Heights and met our newfound friends and their family. There were a passel of kids, two or three boys and a younger sister. Their father was an engineer on the trains. He would drive the train over to Sparks Nevada, from Roseville, and then drive one back to Roseville, on a return trip. Then he was done with work for a few days.

Perry and the big sister, got on a lot better than I did with my friend, even though the big sister was engaged to be married to a minister, when he would finish his studies at Northwestern University in Chicago, or so she told us. She seemed much more than casually interested in Perry, for someone planning to be married soon.

The girls' parents spent a lot of time in San Francisco and other spots near there, leaving the rest of the family under the watchful eye of the oldest sister. That meant that when Perry and I came up there, we would take the kids to a show, swimming or whatever we did all weekend. We slept in our car and would travel as far as Donner Lake in two cars, Perry in his 46 Chevrolet coupe and me driving a load of kids in the family 38 Ford Fordor Sedan. (That is not a misspelling of "four door" as Mr. Ford called them "Fordor.") How Perry could afford all this, I don't know. I had little or no money the majority of the time. The older sister must have helped with more than just her friendship. Perry and she always were in the coupe and if more than four of us went anywhere, I had the rest of the brood for a quiet, romantic evening, or whatever.

CHAPTER 40

Ronny and I go to Idaho

As SCHOOL WOUND DOWN AND with a new summer coming on I let the friendship in Citrus Heights persist, but was thinking more of what to do to earn some money over the summer months than how to perpetuate this erratic relationship. The answer came to me on how to spend the summer when we heard Angus was back at the Toll Gate and Nellie was going back home. I asked my friend Ronny if he wanted to go with me and we'd spend the summer at the ranch. He decided he could do that, so we put some clothes in our suitcases and went with Nellie when school was out. We took a Greyhound bus and left late in the evening for about a twenty-hour ride, with a transfer in Winnemucca, Nevada.

At about noon or so the next morning we were crossing Nevada and heading for the Oregon line, having transferred at Winnemucca to the Boise Winnemucca Stage. Crossing that desert in the old bus with no air conditioning meant that in order to maintain some cool air and air movement, the driver would open a few vents near the front corners of the bus. One vent was in the entrance door. Ronny and I were sitting just behind it, opposite the driver and half asleep. We were awakened be a loud thump in the door and looked to see what it was. There trapped inside the door was a meadowlark, evidently no worse for wear but it had gone in through the screen over the vent and now was walking back and forth inside the door looking for some way out. There really was none as the screen had flopped back over the entry point and there was a grill on the inside of the door.

The driver had to stop the bus and use a screwdriver to remove the grill and let the bird out, which happily flew away. He put the grill back on and away we went.

Since it was later when we got to Boise, we put up for the night at the Idanha Hotel. Ronny and I walked out to the street and stood there trying to decide which show to go to or if we wanted to go eat. Along came a gentleman in a pickup and slowed down and yelled at us, "Do you boys want to work?" We ran to his truck and told him yes we did, "what do you have?"

He told us he had 100 acres of hay baled, in his field, and needed it stacked inside his barn. He told us to be ready at six the following morning and he would get us and take us to his field. The pay was to be one dollar an hour with board and room. He told us to go get some gloves. So off we went to buy some leather gloves and skipped the show.

The next morning we were on the same corner waiting and he took us out toward Meridian to his farm and we started to gather baled hay onto a wagon and haul it to the barn. Again, I made the mistake of saying I knew how to stack baled hay, so I handled half of the bales in the field and Ronny handled the other half. The boss drove the tractor pulling the wagon we were loading. When the wagon was loaded we took it to the barn where I handled every bale again. The gentleman we worked for was very nice to us and we worked hard for him. His wife turned out delicious meals that were hearty enough to keep two growing teens well fed.

Each day Ronny and I swore that this would be the day we'd go to the canal after work and swim some and really get clean. When evening came and dinner was over we would go back to the bunk- house and collapse on our beds until the next morning. Both of us got sore hands at first but by the end of the week we were in great shape and felt no after effects of all the hard work. I believe we just worked seven or eight days straight through until all the hay was stacked in his haymow and then he paid us off in cash. We walked over to Highway 55 and hitched a ride up to Spring Valley and walked up to the Toll Gate.

At the Toll Gate we did a tour around to show Ronny where everything was, where we would be sleeping in the iron bed outside, with the canvas up over us if it rained. I showed him the guns and how they worked and we went looking for rabbits, but I don't recall that we found any. Nellie made her bread and we had the beans on the stove, day in and day out. Just like when I had been living there. Angus was pretty much okay and I don't remember any ill effects of the stroke he had suffered. He seemed fine with his plowing and planting the garden, though it was late in the season. He was able to do all that and take care of the stock that remained, which were just some horses and a cow or two.

Ronny and I often went down to Spring Valley, though I don't believe we ever went to the ranch house. We would walk across the lower field to Highway 55, hitchhike a ride to Boise to swim in the Natatorium or to Horseshoe Bend and swim in Payette River. The Natatorium had a high diving board that we both dove off once. After that we'd just jump off. I forget if it was fifty or thirty feet. Whichever it was, it was very high and had been higher in the past. Someone had been injured badly and maybe even killed there, so the powers that be, had the diving tower lowered to a safer height. But it still scared me and one dive off it was plenty for both of us.

We found that the Payette River was quite cold. The water in the large millpond, just below Horseshoe Bend sawmill was much warmer, so we went there and swam. Nobody ever said a thing to us about it being a working sawmill, where logs were dumped into the pond and taken out for processing, at any time of day. We would get tired of swimming and walk downtown and buy a Coke and something to eat then hitchhike a ride and return to the Toll Gate.

We even hitchhiked to Mc Call, on the Payette Lakes to do some scouting out of the country. I had never been there, but had heard it was beautiful. So we ended up going there to the beach with all the rich people, or so it seemed to us. No one would give us the time of day. Eventually we got concerned that it may be cold at night up there and we didn't want to pay for a hotel, so we hitchhiked back to Spring Valley and walked home.

One day Julius Jaker came up to the Toll Gate from his hay ranch on Dry Creek and hired me to come down to his place and cut and rake hay. This paid the same dollar per hour with board and room, for wages we had made at our previous job. I begged him to take us both, but he was a bit thrifty and figured two of us might goof off together and he could watch one, so I went with him and Ronny stayed at the Toll Gate. I think he also had just one tractor with mower attachment.

Julius was a hard taskmaster and wanted me to start work in the field at 7 AM, not leave the house at 7. Also, I was to sharpen sickle bars on my own time and do maintenance on the tractor and mower twice a day, before 7 AM and before 1 PM. That is, again, on my own free time. He had asked me if I could drive a tractor, which I couldn't, but I had told him I could because I was sure I could, since I could drive a car. I got on the tractor and couldn't start it, so I told him I was used to John Deere's and this was a Farmall. So that flew, and he gave me a quick lesson in how to make it work. I drove it out to his field and became a very good operator in no time. I loved mowing alfalfa except for the couple of times I could see that birds were running through the tall hay I was about to mow. I would stop and hope they ran away, but when I stopped, they would stop, and then when I got going again they'd stretch up to see if I was near and the sickle bar would lop off their heads. I hated that part, as these were baby pheasants of which there never seemed to be enough of, around our place, or at Dry Creek.

I cut hay for a week and raked it for another week and then went back to the Toll Gate to discover Ronny had gone back to California. His job at the Oakland Zoo had come open and someone had contacted his mother. She had written him a letter. He went home and went to work. That didn't pay as well as the haying job, but at least he did have work.

At the end of the summer school break, I again hopped onto the bus and returned to Oakland. I had made a little money for school clothes and did all the shopping by myself this time. That seemed to work out a lot better than when Walter had taken me shopping. But I was lousy with money, didn't really save a dime and within a month I was again broke and mowing lawns or going up to the golf course in hopes of getting a job there.

While Ronny and I had been in Idaho, I had kept writing to the girls back home in Oakland, and Citrus Heights. They said they missed me and I missed them, but wasn't ready for a lot of the stuff they seemed to be gearing up for. At least the one in Oakland seemed ready for matrimony, or thought she was. I think most of the relationship in Citrus Heights was one of convenience for my friend. She often had some excuse why she couldn't be home until late on a Friday night when we were coming up. Then she would appear, much worse for wear, and too tired to go to the show, or whatever we had planned. I began to tire of this arrangement and Perry and I began to have other things to do on some of our weekends. Eventually this driving to Citrus Heights to baby sit kids became too much for me and I renewed my local friendship, mother, grandmother and all. Her dad was a union boss and there was a vague promise of work in the lathing trade if I could stick with it, or she didn't dump me. There was some talk of an apprenticeship on the girl's part.

CHAPTER 41

Joining the Marines

SCHOOL BECAME A DRAG, AS I wasn't doing very well, bored to death and getting mostly terrible grades. I was afraid that I wouldn't graduate with my class because of bad attendance, poor grades and lack of inspiration. My brother Walter had joined the Marine Corps, as had the brother of my friend Ronny Alexander.*6 Ronny and I decided to also join, but I was just seventeen so we had to wait until I was eighteen to sign up. I don't think either of us told anyone of our plan to enlist and we didn't tell anyone good-bye. I know for sure that I didn't, not even the on-again, off-again girl friends in Oakland and Citrus Heights. I didn't tell any of my family.

Ronny and I went to the Marine enlistment center in Hayward to investigate, a day before I was eighteen. The enlistment folks treated us really special, giving us lodging in San Francisco, meals and passes to a show. The next morning we were taken to the SFO airport and told they would fly us to San Diego, where we would be sworn in and become Marines. We sat in the airport at SFO for the entire day, awaiting an opening on a flight to San Diego. Later in the evening they called our names and we boarded a DC-3 and took off for Burbank. I looked out the window and noticed a little oil trail developing behind one of the engines. By the time we landed in Burbank I was sure we had lost ten gallons of oil down that wing, but nobody else seemed concerned. We were in Burbank long enough to refuel, clean the oil off the wing and took off again for San Diego. We must have

---

6 This was the same friend that spent the summer in Idaho with me.

arrived there past midnight. Everyone had been really pleasant to us so far. The airport personnel even politely directed us out some side doorway to an awaiting Marine Corps bus, out of view of anyone but the bus driver, a Marine Private and a Marine Sgt. who would direct us from then until we arrived at MCRD. (Marine Corps Recruit Depot, San Diego.)

That was the end of "nice" for several months. We stood outside the bus and the Marine Sgt., called our names after telling us to respond "Here Sir." The first response was a weak one and that got the culprit yelled at and all of us informed, "I can't hear you!" yelled at us by the Sgt. in the loudest voice I had heard in my life. The next guy yelled his "Here Sir" and was told to board the bus. Unfortunately for him, he was wearing his hair in a queue, which the Sgt. "mistook" for a handle, which he grabbed onto to help the recruit aboard the bus. They missed the open doorway and the recruit slammed head first into the side of the bus with the full weight of the Sgt. pushing him, resulting in a resounding thud, then the recruit sank to the pavement, half conscious and so on it went until he revived himself enough to drag himself onto the bus. We finally all survived the roll call and the boarding procedure. Some recruits got more help than others, and none of it needed, nor warranted. Thankfully we didn't talk back. It just seemed that would be the wrong thing to do at the moment.

We were driven to the Marine Corps Recruit Depot in San Diego. Recruit Class 180, July 1, 1954. There we were directed to enter some building and find a bunk. We dashed inside and found a bunk to our liking, just a bunk, no mattress, a spring, but nothing else. Just bare bunks, one up, one down and row after row of them. Some sat on them, others tried to lie down and catch a nap. That lasted just long enough for us to think we were okay doing this, when in bounded some miniature Cpl. with an attitude of a seven foot tall bully, and informed us that he hadn't given us permission to sit, lie down or to do anything. In his presence, from now on we would stand at attention beside the head of our bunk until he gave us permission to do more than breathe. From this point we were to breathe quietly and the Marine Corps would inform us of everything else we were to do. We were to do nothing on our own, only with the express permission of the Marine Corps, which meant for us recruits, from anyone in uniform.

There was an hour-long tirade about what all he wanted from us and what the ever benevolent Marine Corps was providing for us, which was everything known to man to insure our survival and nothing else. There was nothing we needed that wouldn't be provided and if we had anything that wasn't provided to us by the Marine Corps, woe unto us. We were to wear what we had on until chow in the morning, after which we would be given clothes to wear and a bucket with all our necessities in it. Chow tuned out to be S... on a shingle, which I immediately threw up, and the clothes were dungarees, lest we look too pretty.

We were informed that we would be placed on a schedule, when the Marine Corps determined that we were ready, which turned out to be a month later, when the USMC finally found a Drill Instructor for us. Until that time, we ran, marched, did pushups and duck-walked throughout the days and half the night, directed by some wanna-be drill instructors. We spent the days picking up cigarette butts and cleaning our barracks, which were Quonset huts with concrete floors. We would scrub the floors with buckets of sand, water, and soap, and then do it again the next day. We marched for hours and ran farther than we thought was humanly possible. We did more pushups than any of us ever thought possible and learned to wash clothes with a bar of soap and a bristle brush, outside on a wooden wash table with cold water from a garden hose.

Eventually we were put onto a schedule and had a real bear of a Drill Instructor and a fairly nice Assistant Drill Instructor. The schedule was good, we had definite hours, though long, we knew when we'd be expected to be up and ready and other than surprise inspections in the middle of the night, we got a full night's sleep, three healthy meals and plenty of exercise. We ran the obstacle course and cleaned our weapons. We polished boots and Boondockers until they sparkled black. Boondockers were low boots that had the nap of the leather on the outside, but we made them glisten with our newfound "spit shine" technique. Our rifles were our lifelines and we learned to clean and assemble them in seconds. How not to suffer "M1 thumb" which was when you got your thumb smashed by the bolt closing as you attempted to put dummy rounds in the rifle.

One fine day we were all put on busses with our sea bag full of everything we owned, except the clothes on our back and about a fifty pound back pack full of whatever didn't fit into the sea bag and our rifles slung over our shoulders. The busses took us out to La Jolla, where they dumped us off at the edge of town and we put our sea bags on a Marine Corps truck. We kept our rifle and backpacks and marched the afternoon away, going up the hill to the north and arriving in the late afternoon at Camp Matthews where we were reunited with our sea bag and assigned to a tent. This would be our new home, no heat, cold-water showers and living in a tent with about six of us together. The tents were built on a wooden platform, so we had a floor under us. In the middle of the tent was an oil stove that had never seen oil and never would. But it would have kept us warm if the Marine Corps thought we needed to be warm.

We had mess duty for a week, which gave us all a chance to learn the workings of a kitchen and how to keep it clean. The cook asked if anyone knew how to work a sewing machine and I thought that would be better than peeling potatoes so I raised my hand. That got me in charge of the laundry. I counted everything to make sure the contractor hadn't miscounted, then, with a needle and thread, made repairs where possible. Most of that consisted of sewing on buttons. I also handed out the clean laundry and took in the dirty and counted the pieces and sent it to be washed. When I wasn't busy, I helped scrub the kitchen and dining area. We ate well, but these were very long hours. We arose at three in the morning and were not in bed until ten or eleven at night.

The best part of boot camp was the rifle range. We had to get up early, go to chow, march to the range, which was over a mile away. There we were taught how to fire our weapons. No ammo, just practice and more practice. There were four firing positions, standing, kneeling, sitting and prone. All of us practiced these positions for days, then they gave us ammo and we got to fire at the targets for half the day. Then we marched back to a safe area away from the range for a bag lunch, back to the range and pulled targets all afternoon while the other half fired away at the targets. We march back to the chow hall for dinner. After dinner we spent the evening cleaning our weapons. An inspection would follow and we'd then have an hour or so before "lights out," at twenty two hundred. (For you non-military types, that's 10:00 PM.) This was our free time in which to read and write letters, smoke in a smoking area, wash clothes and cold shower.

We also learned to throw grenades, fire mortars, shoot with the pistols; carbines, submachine guns and the Browning automatic rifle. (BAR) These were fun-filled days for most of us, but tragic for some. One heavy guy, not the brightest bulb in the box, had been passed down from platoon to platoon, after he repeatedly failed to meet standards of the Marine Corps, regarding his weapons training. He should have been discharged, but no Drill Instructor wanted failure on his record, so they passed him backward to the next recruit platoon.

Our DI decided to have some of the bigger guys, make him just disappear, on our way to the rifle range. Normally the taller recruits were in the front and the shortest in the back. The appointed day, we marched at double time out to the range. That is we did a slow jog. The ranks were also reversed with the shortest in front and the tallest in the rear. I was midway down the file. We got about half way to the range and the poor guy had to drop back as he couldn't keep up the pace. When we got to the range he was no longer with us. We thought it odd that the DI didn't get someone to retrace our steps and bring him back to the range. Since our day was so busy, we soon forgot about him and concentrated on our weapons lessons.

That night as we marched back to the tent camp, which was the barracks for the rifle range troops, we heard a moaning from over a bank and the DI told us to ignore it and march "Eyes Straight Ahead" home. Some of us fell out of line and found the poor guy in a bad way. He had been beaten and laid out there just over a small embankment, but out of sight, all day in a very warm sun. We helped him out and got him back to the tent camp and somehow to the sick bay. I never saw him again, but our Drill Instructor had also disappeared. I did see the DI again a couple of years later. He was in a prison detail at Camp Pendleton, as a private, picking up cigarette butts and waste near the prison on the main base. He was with other prisoners and an armed guard, who was watching them while they performed menial tasks to keep the base clean.

Our Assistant Drill Instructor finished out our schedule with us and nothing was ever officially told to us about the change of DI's, or any disposition of the obvious crime that had been committed. We eventually graduated from boot camp and were assigned to our future destination. Ronny went to Camp Pendleton, the main base and I went to Camp Delmar, a subsidiary base of Camp Pendleton, which was the Amphibious Battalion's home. This time the Marine Corps put us in trucks, with all our gear, and drove us to our destinations. That first move was to get us all to Camp Pendleton. Some went off to other assignments in the following days.

I was to be mechanic in the Third Amphibious Battalion. This was just after the finish of the Korean War and the First Marine Division was still overseas, so the result was there weren't nearly as many Marines at Camp Pendleton, or Delmar, as would normally have been the case. Our barracks were newer than the WWII ones and the mess hall served family style with table clothes and meals were of the best quality and variety.

My place of work was down on the beach. There were probably a hundred, fifty LVTP3's (Landing Vehicle Tracked, Production 3) there that were tracked landing craft from the latter part of the Second World War and some from the years before the Korean Conflict. There were a couple of large warehouses and a shop that had next to nothing going on in it. Basically we went to the shop and smoked cigarettes and went to lunch. Once in a while we drove a tractor out onto the beach or into the pond in front of the shop, but mostly did nothing productive. Everything seemed to be in a holding pattern awaiting the return of the First Marine Division.

Near Thanksgiving 1954, I was given ten days leave, and told I would be sent to Japan. I went home on leave and wasted ten days trying to repair a couple of bad relationships and stirred up a new one, which went nowhere either. Perry got me to go for a ride with him and a girlfriend and her cousin. He had a 1935 Ford Convertible Coupe, with a rumble seat. The cousin and I rode to the Russian River in the rumble seat. I felt like I would freeze to death before we got home, but fortunately the cousin knew well how to keep a young man warm, so I survived that. That ride caused another rift with the high school girlfriend and brought my relationship count back to zero, before the ten days were over. Even the cousin had been disappointed that I was such a dull boy. (But I could have been taught, if they just had the patience to do it.)

Transferred From Delmar to Delmar

BACK AT CAMP DELMAR, I found myself being transferred to the Receiving Barracks on the main base at Pendleton. At the Receiving Barracks I was given a pile of orders about an inch thick that essentially told me to go back to Camp Delmar and report for duty at the Test and Experimental Unit, of the Schools Regiment, and I was to live in a barracks probably a quarter mile from the one I had moved from. While all this took place, the leave and transfer, the First Marines came back from Korea, Okinawa and the rest of Japan. No more meals family style, table clothes were put in storage and the price of beer in the Gee dunk went up a nickel, to ten cents a glass. I didn't mind, since I hadn't taken up beer drinking on any regular basis. What I missed the most was the service at the table and the family style meals. Our barracks were the type that had been thrown together to house troops during WWII. Walls were 1 ½ X 2½ inch wood, with plasterboard on the outside, and a button board inside that had some plaster thrown at it and scraped around before being painted. Most of it needed redoing by the time we were there.

So at the Test & Experimental Unit, I was assigned a toolbox and was put into the Maintenance Unit. There we retrieved and repaired what others broke. I had no training and so one day the Col. in charge saw me and asked my name. I told him and he asked about my schooling. I didn't have any to brag about so the next morning I was sent to a barracks a few hundred feet away and spent several weeks in Tank Mechanics School. I excelled there as it really did interest me and I was top of my class in the electronic and automatic transmission sections of the school. I believe I was second over-all when we graduated. We had also spent several days driving the Marine Corps M42 and M48 tanks. So I knew a lot on paper but didn't have any practical experience with the real world of mechanical things. Unlike the majority of the kids raised on a farm or ranch, I hadn't had a lot of experience with fixing machinery because we owned none that was powered by anything but our team of horses. I went back to the T & E Unit and was immediately put on mess duty for a month.

My first high school girlfriend had decided to join the Navy. The Navy sent her to Nurses Training in Virginia. Her plan was upon becoming a nurse, to get herself transferred to the Camp Pendleton Hospital, so we would be close together again. I think the marriage talk had come up again, probably brought on by me, but maybe by her. I can't remember the details but I'm sure the ultimate goal was that we would be together. After I had been in the Marines for a few months, that didn't scare me half as badly as it had before. But it still seemed a long step over hot coals.

After the mess duty I went back to my unit and worked on such things as breaking spark plugs and over tightening bolts until the heads came off. Eventually I got where I was of some value and earned a stripe, Private First Class. Shortly after that I did something else correctly and got another stripe. Now I was a Cpl. That would have been a big deal when I was in boot camp but by now the Marine Corps had lost some guys in Camp Jejune and the respect for rank had taken a real hit. Also, in the unit I was in, almost everyone was already promoted and most of them were Sgt. or above. Only a few test drivers were of a lesser rank than mine. But that didn't matter to me. I loved the work and being a part of a team that took equipment from a factory and tried to improve it or break it.

Somehow I found that my sister, Dolores was living in Chula Vista. I took a train down to San Diego and a city bus to Chula Vista. I had learned from Nellie to just show up, so it never dawned upon me to call first and see if it was okay for me to come visit her. I would just drop in and stay the weekend. Then I'd take the train back to the base. Dolores would show me around and take me places close by when she could, but, she had two kids in school and her husband was still at sea, so things were pretty tight for her and I didn't usually have much money, so I just bummed off her. We did enjoy our times together though and she was always very kind to me. I visited often, maybe three or four times a year, almost always for a Saturday overnight and go back Sunday afternoon to the base.

While I was taking the train back to Oceanside one Sunday night, I met a nice lady about my age that let me sit on her suitcase, as all the seats were taken. That was her idea. I sat there a while and then noticed that the nice lady was alone, no husband or kids in sight. We struck up a conversation and I found that she lived in Oceanside, a few short blocks from the train station, and had no family or friends there yet. Before the night was over, I had carried her suitcase home and learned that she had a daughter that she desperately wanted me to meet. The daughter was three, and she was about eighteen, shopping for a "daddy" for the daughter.

A few days later Ronny and I took her to the show and then I took her home. She wanted me to take her and her daughter to Knott's Berry Farm. I didn't have an automobile, had little money and so I told her I had guard duty that weekend. By the time pay day rolled around and I could take her to Knott's Berry Farm, she had already made enough friends to keep her busy for months, so another strike out.

My First Trip to Monterey Bay with USMC

MY FIRST TRIP TO THE Monterey Bay took place in late fall, or early winter of 1955. I was selected to go to Marina Beach, near Fort Ord, to take part in some extensive testing of new Amphibious Tractors, P5's, that the Marine Corps had received from Food Machine in San Jose. I was a PFC. A Marine; fresh out of the mechanics school the Marine Corps had sent me to, and bursting with energy. It was time to prove myself out in the field. Our small detachment was told to put some essentials in our sea bags and board a truck that would take us to North Island, in San Diego Bay. There we would be taken aboard an LSD, Navy speak for Landing Ship Dock. Our tractors were already there, having been trucked there in the last couple of days. The Marines had a few Lowboy truck and trailers to move the tanks and amphibious vehicles over the highways to be shipped or just relocated. We could also have driven them aboard the LSD near Camp Delmar, just out to sea and drive right into the ship, but this time the decision had been made to truck the vehicles and men to North Island and proceed on our journey from there. That probably was the more efficient way to get us all loaded at the time.

I had never been to sea before, so I was looking forward to this trip. We left San Diego in a cloud of diesel smoke that filled the deck where the tractors were. We all went below to make sure that all the tie downs were fastened appropriately and nothing would move as the ship got out into the sea. The LSD is a big ship with a flat bottom, has a large door in the rear that opens to the sea, as that portion of the ship is flooded to allow equipment to be driven into the Well Deck.[7] This had all been done a day or two earlier and we tightened the many tie downs and made sure nothing was able to move around when the ship got under way.

i

The above picture I found on the internet, and shows of Navy LSD, similar to the one that took us to Monterey Bay.

As the ship began to maneuver out of port and head for the open water, it continued to billow black smoke into the Well Deck, which is open to the sky so that smoke from the ship's stacks blew into that area. We were

---

7 The Well Deck is that portion of the rear of the vessel that holds the equipment to be transported. When the vessel is flooded that portion is lowered into the sea to allow access to amphibious craft to be driven aboard. Once that has been accomplished the water is pumped out and the well deck is again out of the water and the vehicles rest on the steel deck. That was how some sailor explained it to me.

allowed to remove ourselves, come up to the main deck where we could sit and enjoy the ride north. This would take us all night and in the morning sometime we would be in Monterey Bay. I was not feeling real well after breathing all the ship's smoke, so I took a seat forward of the stacks to avoid getting another whiff of that obnoxious odor. Then like the fools we were, most all of us lit up cigarettes and settled back to look at the scenes unfolding before us. Some went below for the dinner meal, but there were a few sissies, including myself, who stayed topside, in the fresh breeze. The weather was pleasant and the seas fairly calm, so the initial part of the trip north was uneventful.

Once out of San Diego harbor our ship began to pick up speed. That caused the ship to react more to the wind and waves, which then had the ship pitching into the waves and making groaning noises as we passed over one swell and rode up onto another. With the flat bottom it seemed that we never cut into the water, just bumped across the top of it, pitching and swaying from side to side. The wind seemed determined to bring the smoke our way wherever we tried to hide on deck. The thought crossed my mind to go below and find a bunk to try to sleep through this, however reality told me I'd be sick in a minute if it weren't for the breeze, so I remained at my little corner of the world, sort of in a corner, but where I could see the shoreline and also the ladder that would take me below, if I ever decided to venture that way. I didn't venture below all night except for a quick trip to the head*[8] and then I was back huddled in my corner, warm enough, snuggled up in my field jacket, a beautiful coastline in a bright moon and sometimes I was entertained by dolphins doing their dance in the waves, off the bow of our ship as we plowed forward. I was surprised how effortlessly they seemed to be able to keep up with us, playing in that bit of churning water we created.

As morning came, sailors and Marines began to appear on deck. Several of them guessed that we few were there because we had been sea sick, or on the verge. They laughed and made quite a sport of us, then lit

---

8 Head was a bathroom

their cigarettes and had their morning smoke. One of our Sgt's from Waco Texas, was particularly tough on me with his cutting remarks, so I got up and said something like, "Let's go down below and sample some of the Navy's greasy pork chops." That sent him running to the rail and I didn't see him again until we were ashore.

We landed at Marina Beach by driving off the LSD after it had taken on enough water to have the well deck submerged and our tractors, which had been unfastened from their bindings to the ship, to float. The ride to shore was uneventful and smooth in placid seas. We drove up high onto the beach and were met by Army guys from Fort Ord and some Navy guys from the little Naval Air Station at Monterey. We set up a tent and a guard rotation for the week and then were trucked to the NAS Monterey, where we were billeted.

Huskie Helicopter, picture taken by David Mc Arthur

This was a Marine workhorse helicopter of the Korean War era and was used in this instance to provide transportation for dignitaries and some of the high-ranking Officers from the Test and Experimental Unit and guest Officers from Fort Ord. They often flew out in the morning to make sure that the operation was going smoothly and to assess the tides, hoping to not miss out on being there when the surf began to rage with high waves, which was why we were in Monterey. We were to test the vehicles behavior in the surf under the worst conditions we could encounter. This helicopter was from Camp Pendleton and had been assigned to our Unit for the duration of our maneuvers. It also was always airborne with Navy Frogmen aboard whenever we had vehicles in the water, to provide immediate help if and when it became necessary.

Bell Model 47 A, picture I took from the Internet.

This was similar to the one that the Navy brought to Monterey as an observation post and was use to record photographically the reaction of the vehicles as they were brought into the sea and also when brought back ashore during high surf conditions.

Our workdays started with a breakfast at the NAS Monterey and a ride by truck to Marina Beach, all the way down to our tent. The prior night's guard detail was relieved and they returned to the NAS for their breakfast and they would return to the beach when the Navy trucked our noon meal out to the troops in the field. The rest of us sat around awaiting high surf to run the tractors into and out of the surf zone. We had Frog Men from the Navy there and a Marine HH 43 Huskie Helicopter for observation along with a small Bell Helicopter that was from the Navy. The Bell Helicopter was a really small affair with a large bubble of Plexiglas with room for only a pilot and a photographer.

At the end of the day, a new guard detail would be assigned and the rest of us would again board the trucks and be returned to the NAS for the evening meal and a good night's sleep. We could walk into Monterey or catch a local bus, as our time was our own until the following morning. For several days we mostly sat on the beach and watched the surf lap at the sand. Little birds entertained us running in and out with each wave, grabbing at the sea life that made up their diet.

CHAPTER 44

Watsonville Disaster

ONE EVENING, WHEN I WENT to supper, I became friendly with a sailor who was serving our meal. He had a 1940 Ford that he was asking $25.00 for and when I inquired as to its running, he threw me the keys and told me to try it out. I had a friend in Aptos that I had maintained a loose letter writing campaign with and explained to him that I would like to drive up there to see her. He told me to buy some gas and check the oil and I should be good to go anywhere. That was a big mistake on both our parts.

I had liberty on Friday night and no set time to be back until Monday morning, so I fueled up and dutifully checked tires, water and oil on the old Ford. The car ran rather well as I left the NAS and headed north for Aptos. I checked all the gauges which seemed to all be working well also. I had a general idea where Aptos was located, as I had looked at a road map someone had shown me while I bought gas. I drove to Castroville and took the turnoff toward Santa Cruz and Watsonville. I was driving by fields of artichokes and Brussels sprouts. To me the artichokes appeared to be related to thistles and I had never seen thistles that size anywhere. A few miles later I was passing the PG & E Power plant at Moss Landing. I had seen a large power station near Carlsbad, but this one dwarfed anything I had seen anywhere. Another surprise was the beauty of the Elkhorn Slough and the birds that appeared to make that waterway their home. This trip was becoming educational.

Soon I had passed Watsonville and when I arrived in Aptos, I asked a few questions at a grocery store beside Hwy One. I found out that my friend lived a few miles out in the country, so it took me a while to find her house. I arrived there just as the sun was setting in the west and there was a gorgeous red sunset. I hadn't called, but her parents were good enough to call a girlfriend she was visiting and let me talk to her. I met the girls and we went to have a bite to eat, the three of us, she and her girlfriend and me. We drove to a spot in Watsonville that the two girls thought had the best hamburgers and fries in the area.

The girls were cute and bubbly; the night warm and there was still that romantic, now nearly full moon shining down on us as we drove off to Watsonville, which was but a few short miles away. Every one of us was having a very nice time and the talk was about how the girl I knew and I had met at a church retreat near there. Everything was safe and everyone well at ease, looking forward to our dinner and then perhaps a movie. Though the girls hadn't agreed which one to see, they had agreed that we'd all go to a show and some other boy was to join us to make it really two couples instead of the two girls and me. I was hoping that he had a car and we could then be alone for some private time. We had passed a drive-In movie on our travels and I was thinking that would be my choice, whatever was playing there.

After we ate, I tried to start the car and found the battery had lost its charge. I had left the lights on and we had listened to the radio. Well, so much for conserving the battery. I used gravity to roll the car down a slight incline and out onto a one-way street, just below the main street in town. I tried, and failed, to bump start the car. A car loaded with some young guys passed us as I rolled to a stop. When we were all stopped, the guys in the other car asked me if I needed a push. I answered that I did, so they backed around to the rear of my car and then drove up beside me to tell me that I had no bumper on the rear, so they would push me backward and I could bump start that way. I agreed to that and thanked them in advance for the help.

The old Fords that I had driven all seemed to start real easily with a bump start, and they also all seemed to make so much noise when first started that talking was useless for a few seconds. My new friend, Jose, pulled up to the front of the '40 Ford and after checking that the bumpers matched started to push me backward like we were in a reverse drag race. This caused us to be going the wrong way on a one way street. The car immediately started, the engine raced as I pushed the clutch in and waved Jose off. My new friend misunderstood my signal and pushed me faster and faster, until I couldn't control the car and we hit a parked car rather violently, then came to a stop. The girls began to cry and the one I had known a bit told me that she hoped her boyfriend wasn't the cop that would come to investigate. This was the first I had any knowledge of the boyfriend or thought about cops. Now I might be faced with both.

By good luck it wasn't her boyfriend that appeared, but a rather efficient fellow, none-the-less. Jose and he knew each other from prior run-ins. He read Jose, and me, the riot act, gave us both tickets for unsafe operation of a vehicle, wrong way driving on a one way street and driving without lights. I got the added blessings of the law because all I knew of the owner was that his name was Greer and he was in the Navy. No license tags and no title to be found anywhere. Also there was a small matter of a totaled car that I had been pushed into. My ticket was so long I was afraid I'd be an old man before I was released to drive again.

I had some good luck though. The car started right up when the police officer told me I could leave and I did that in rather a hurry. I took the girls home and drove out of the area and back onto Hwy 1 as quickly as I could, having kissed off the idea of joining the other guy and the movie, I was thrilled to not be sitting in jail, or beat up by some jealous cop.

I went directly back to the NAS and to bed. The next morning I saw Greer in the chow line, I gave him his keys and told him I had bumped the back of his car, but that I couldn't see any real damage. I gave him some money to buy himself some gas plus an extra $10 for letting me use the car. He seemed quite happy and also told me he had a buyer, since I was no longer interested. I thanked him and hurried through my meal.

Back at the beach I had a long private talk with my Sgt. I told him the whole story, honestly, and explained that I had to go to court on a certain day the following week. I was afraid that I would be in jail and didn't want to be AWOL. I asked that I be granted emergency leave, if that became necessary. I would do my time and return when my sentence was over. The Sgt. told me that he would see to the details and he also warned me to not show up late at the court hearing. I promised I would be early and be very polite to everyone.

When the time came for me to go to court, I hitchhiked to Watsonville and found the courthouse. I went in and sat where I was told to sit and a bailiff informed me that it would be awhile before I would be called. I saw that Your Honor looked like an ornery old cuss. I feared that I wouldn't have enough leave time coming to avoid being AWOL. The bailiff called a Hispanic name and Jose leaped to his feet and approached the Judge. His Honor greeted him as if they were old friends and he asked about Jose's brother and how he had been keeping himself. Your Honor then proceeded to read our charges, which seemed to me, would put us away for some time to come. Jose agreed we had done these foul deeds, saying how sorry he was to be back here in court. He was fined $10 and then some for court costs. He thanked the Judge and hurried away without even a look in my direction. I feared this had not become a lasting friendship, but I still had other things to worry about, so I made no move to renew our acquaintance.

After Jose left, my name was called. I approached Your Honor, hat in hand, and, I'm sure, trembling. He read the charges, which made no mention of having hit a parked car. I followed Jose's lead, I didn't feel the need to mention the oversight of the wrecked parked car, and admitted I was guilty of all His Honor had just read. He asked about the license and registration and I told him, truthfully, that I had heard the car had been sold. The Judge appeared to like that, and commented about the sale having taken care of the issue of title. Then he fined me the same $10 plus costs and I was dismissed to the care of a deputy that showed me where and whom to pay. I followed him to the hall and he pointed to a window and gave me some papers for the clerk. I paid her about $17 and hightailed it to Hwy. 1, and I hitchhiked back to the NAS, counting my blessings.

My Sgt. told me he hadn't mentioned to anyone why I hadn't been there all day. Since I had returned, he was assigning me to guard duty that night, so all the bases were covered. He advised me to talk to no one about any of it and to stay near the NAS as much as possible. I was whistling Dixie as I walked through the sand dunes that night. I just couldn't believe my good fortune, and I never heard from the girl again or anything about the car I had smashed into. I also never tried to renew that friendship.

Following my return to the Marina Beach from my court experience in Watsonville I did the night of guard duty. The next day I was off duty until the truck took lunch, and me, back to the Marines on the beach. When I arrived there the scene was of turmoil and a lot of fast action. I didn't witness all of it, but helped with the aftermath and got every detail from my Sgt., who was in charge of maintenance and vehicle recovery. In reality, I was his driver of the LVTP5R that he had assigned me to, and he ran the rest of what the mechanics did.

He told me that the surf had began to churn and grew higher by the hour, as the Marines rejoiced to finally have some real waves to put the tractors into. There were several successful runs into the ocean and back onto the beach made by a radio controlled P-5 Amphibious Tractor. This vehicle was brand-new and a big brute of a thing, about 25 feet long, 11 feet wide and eight feet tall. It had an Allison cross drive transmission, being driven by a 1790 Cubic inch Continental V 12 Aircraft engine that had been modified to be water-cooled. It was capable of about 50 to 60 MPH on the beach; right down close to the water, where the sand was the hardest, but in the water it did at most 5 MPH. The tests were to determine how a number of lubricants held up in the high waves. The bigger waves carried much more power and more sand and silt with each cycle than did the smaller waves.

The tractor was driven out into the ocean, well past the breakers and made a long slow turn to return to shore. The idea was to get the tractor up to the speed it would normally reach in the sea while coming ashore from a ship, then drive it onto the beach and do a quick check of the lubricants. The going and coming was radio controlled to avoid putting Marines' lives in danger. All of this activity was observed by a small Bell helicopter, which had a photographer and a pilot aboard. They would follow the tractors every move and film the entire entry, turns and the run to the beach and dry land. That was overseen by, a pair of Navy Frogmen, who were swimming right at the breaker area. Overhead several hundred feet away was a Marine HH 43 Huskie helicopter, which was much larger than the Navy Bell Helicopter. This one carried a few officers and engineers to also observe operations.

The Sgt. explained to me things went well for several drives out and back while the waves were gaining in height, but things took a near tragic turn as the last cycle was nearing its end. The tractor had gone out to sea fine, made a long sweeping turn and got up to speed from about a mile out and as it got to the shore it was slowed so as to not jam it into the sand, but to drive gingerly from the breakers to the dry land. As it slowed near the point where the tracks would be contacting the beach, a much larger wave than normal overcame the machine and hit it with such force the water from the wave shot straight up in the air for twenty feet or more. Unfortunately that was where the small Bell helicopter was, and the water brought it down like a fly being hit with a flyswatter in midflight.

As soon as the chopper was down, the frogmen raced to it and pulled the pilot and the cameraman to shore. The helicopter was just fragments and neither occupant had been hurt badly, but everything else was a total loss. The tractor foundered in the surf and the wave action began to bury it in the sand. Initial efforts were spent saving the pilot and photographer.

As the tractor foundered in the breakers the engine was immediately flooded by seawater and the whole machine began to bury itself in the sand. The waves coming in would break over the top of the tractor and pass it by, but when they retreated back to sea, they ran under the tractor and removed the sand from under it. The Frogmen were there and quickly got a cable from our retriever hooked to it. This was where I earned my pay, as that was the point at which I had gotten back to my retriever and my Sgt. and I pulled the downed Amphibious Tractor up onto dry land. Sand and water drained out of the louvers that covered the radiators. The tractor was then pulled onto a Low Boy truck and delivered to the maintenance yard at Fort Ord. There it was carefully taken apart and examined by the Engineers to determine what harm had been done by its 15 to 20 minutes in the breaker zone. There was fine sand in everything that was examined. Even the servos inside the transmission and all the bearings on the wheels that the tracks run on were full of sand and silt. Likewise the engine was destroyed, with sand in every part of it. I would never have wanted to do a real wartime landing in any type of high surf. I was not part of the team that did the disassembly, as there were still tests with other tractors being run in the few remaining days of high surf.

David K. Mc Arthur and LVTP5R at Monterey Bay

After the tractor was out of danger the Frogmen searched for whatever was salvageable of the helicopter. That amounted to some mangled metal that had held the Plexiglas body together, some bent long arms that had been the rotors and after some serious searching by the Frogmen a line was fastened to the engine and we pulled it ashore. All parts were scooped up and trucked to NAS Monterey. We found pieces of Plexiglas scattered along the beach for several days after that fiasco, and all of them also went to the NAS.

We got back to Camp Delmar in time for another disaster for the whole Camp Pendleton body of Marines. There was a large Navy and Marine, joint venture type night drill. The Marines were to land and attack the beach approximately three miles north of Oceanside. The invasion force should have all come ashore just north of Camp Delmar on a very nice smooth beach that has shallow water for quite a distance from shore. The trouble was caused when somehow several tanks and trucks were driven off the Navy Vessels in water that was too deep for their snorkels and those machines instantly had no power and were in much too deep of water. Several of the men in tanks, including the base adjutant of Camp Delmar were drowned.

Also as the vehicles that were in this mock invasion were coming ashore, they were to be guided by a red flare on the beach. There is a seawall that is on the south end of Camp Delmar that runs out into the sea for about a quarter of a mile. On the end of that wall, which was loosely stacked boulders, was a red-lighted buoy to warn boats away from the seawall. Several of the drivers of the invasion vehicles mistook that light on the buoy for the red flare they were to drive to and as their vehicles crashed into the rocks they, overturned, killing or injuring more Marines.

I had guard duty that night and there was a great commotion as MP's and the base Fire Department all came driving past my post. I had no inkling of what the problems were until some MP asked me if there were any lights on the seawall. I was able to turn some switches and some lights came on for the rescue effort that was taking place a quarter mile away. I could not turn off the red light. Unfortunately that light was controlled from the Port of Oceanside. I wanted to take part, but in the Marines you do not leave your post without being properly relieved and no one was interested in some poor sentry at that moment. My relief came and I was taken back to the guard shack and the excitement was all over. I still didn't have a clue how many we had lost, but later found it had been in the teens drowned and missing, and probably twice that many with significant injuries. And still we do win battles.

I don't remember the number lost to that incident though, seventeen sticks in my mind. One of them was the commander of Camp Delmar. It was a very bad day for the Camp Pendleton family of Marines. Many had lost good friends over a miscalculation of the attraction of a red light and not getting the depth of the water right before leaving the ships,

CHAPTER 45
Walter returns from Japan

WALTER CAME BACK FROM JAPAN and took part in the nuclear tests out in the Mojave by Las Vegas. He was all Gung-Ho Marine, spit and polish. Eventually he went to some school at Camp Delmar, close by my barracks. We got together and travelled home to the Bay Area in his '50 Cadillac a few times. Not much had really changed. He conned me into giving him my paycheck one time, and he was to bet it on a sure thing at a racetrack in the south called, "Delmar." Guess how that turned out for me. Our horse won, but was disqualified for bumping another horse at the starting gate, so another month's pay down the drain.

In our travels home, Walt and I would have a few riders to help with gas money. Often I would just hitchhike home and he might just pass me on his way back to the base. It did upset me when I could tell he had room for one more, but had left me standing in, say Tulare, in 108 degree weather, (not that he had air-conditioning), but any ride was better than standing out there in the heat of the day, three hundred miles from where I absolutely had to be sixteen hours later.

Perry got remarried, this time to the lady that lived across the street. Then he got a job in Fallon, Nevada and moved there to work on the building of the Naval Air Station bring built here. He said that was some of the best times of his married life. I had tried to arrange another date with her cousin, who seemed quite willing, but she wrote to cancel, as she was getting married the weekend that our date was to be. Dang girl didn't even invite me to the wedding.

Walt met a lady that worked for a Foster's Freeze in Oceanside. Donna was a great catch and they eventually got married. After he was discharged he also found work in Oceanside and attended Oceanside Junior College studying architecture and business. I went to their wedding and later would visit when they had a little place of their own just up the hill from the Foster's Freeze on Hill Street in Oceanside. Donna had a younger sister, Lynn, who came to stay with them after a tough divorce from some Marine that she told me treated her badly. Lynn had a small baby and Walt and Donna would take care of it while I pursued yet another dead-end relationship.

While in the Marines I also worked for a time on a farm in Bonsall, out east of Oceanside. I bought a car and then I could drive down to Chula Vista, visit awhile and go back to the base. Dolores asked only that I, "Bring no Jane's." I was afraid to even ask what she meant by that. One time I did bring a girl that lived near where I worked in Bonsall and she was very pleasant to the girl but a little cool toward me. I couldn't imagine what I had done wrong.

Just a bit later the, above mentioned girl and I had a bit of a spat and were parked near her home discussing it when a guy shined his spotlight on my car. Not to be outdone, I shined mine back and hit a white door on a black sedan. This was the California Highway Patrol. He was not pleased and explained that to me in very convincing tones. Then asked the girl how old she was. That was something I had never done. She told him fourteen and I thought he was going to take me to jail. He told me to take her straight home, which I did. We didn't go out much after that, but I had to know why she had been upset enough to tell him fourteen. She explained that she was fourteen. I had given her a ride to what I thought was her High School in Vista, and she had walked into the school and out the back, to her Jr. High, which she hadn't bothered to tell me about. So, chalk that one up to another strike out.

CHAPTER 46

US Marines in Monterey, February 1957

IT WAS A WONDERFULLY CLEAR, calm and sunny day in Monterey Bay, mid- February of 1957. A Navy LST lay at anchor about a mile out in the bay from Sand City. The surf barely lapped at the shoreline as the shorebirds darted in and out gathering their breakfast. There was only a slight westerly breeze and no hint of clouds anywhere to be seen. This was just another perfect winter day in the Monterey area. Shirtsleeve weather for the Marines disembarking from the LST in their LVTP5's this bright morning. They were arriving to conduct some testing of new amphibious vehicles in the high surf that had been predicted to come to the Monterey Bay shoreline soon. Their mission at Sand City Beach would be concluded in approximately three weeks.

Those Marines in the "know," whispered amongst themselves that our Commanding Officer had been told by his girlfriend that her, career Navy husband, had shipped out on a Mediterranean Cruise. She would now be alone and lonesome for several months, patiently awaiting his return. Poor thing would also be about ten miles from us there in Sand City. She lived in Carmel. They seemed sure this was the real reason for the "high surf" prediction that only our CO appeared to have become aware of.

I took my tractor down the ramp and into the ocean first. My job was to get to shore first, as I was driving an LVTP5R, the "R" being for a retriever. I had just been promoted to Corporal and given this tractor to drive and I was very proud to have all that responsibility, though I also had a Sgt. with me at all times, whose job was to oversee anything to do with maintenance. I was to position my tractor well back from the breakers and to watch for any tractor that got into trouble. I had all the equipment to get a foundering vehicle out of the surf zone and up onto dry land in the event of a problem. That was provided it was within 250 feet of my tractor. That was how far the tow cable on my power winch could be played out.

With the calm weather and surf conditions all of the tractors and equipment were brought ashore with no mishaps. Within an hour's time we were positioned on the beach to await the coming of the high surf. We had a large tent for the enlisted men and a smaller one for the civilian employees and the officers. These served as a place to keep equipment dry and out of the blowing sand if the wind came up. Also there were tables and benches for our noon meal, which would be brought to us by the Navy. There were no beds, as we would be spending our off-hours at the Naval Air Facility in Seaside, which was about a mile from the beach location. The Navy would furnish us with meals, transportation by truck and a place to call home away from the ocean until our testing was over. (Or as some said, until the CO got tired of the girl friends demands.)

But, and this turned into a big "but." Marines and Sailors seem at times to clash. This apparently was to be one of those times. During one of our evening meals at the Navy chow hall, one or, more of the Marines didn't like their treatment in the chow line by the sailors that were serving them. A couple of them exchanged some heated words with the sailors. I was already seated with my meal, so I didn't hear what it was all about and a Staff Sergeant soon had everyone seated and quieted down. I thought that was the end of it. I ate my meal and began to have the onset of a cold or sore throat, so I retired to the assigned barracks early and was in bed by 9 PM.

About eleven in the evening the lights came on amidst a lot of loud talk and shouting, then a small Marine Captain came hurtling into the room, backwards and collapsed in a heap in the corner, just by the foot of my bunk. I was in the top bunk asleep when all this started so it took me a moment to have it register what was going on. The little Captain had been punched fully in the face by a very large and very drunk, Guamanian Sgt. The Sgt. followed up his punch by coming into the room after the Captain, but the Captain sprang back to his feet, wrapped his two hands behind the Sgt's. head and yanked it down like Mighty Mouse, while bringing his knee rapidly up to meet the face of the Sgt. as it came down. There was a loud sound of cartilage breaking. As the Captain stepped aside, the Sgt. fell like Goliath, unconscious onto the floor at his feet.

This little encounter was followed by a stampede of footsteps in the hallway outside, sounds of several more blows being struck, grunts and cursing, then there followed the tweet of whistles being blown and MP's and Shore Patrol were everywhere. I saw that the Captain had lost a good part of one ear, which I found out had been bitten off by the Sgt. The Sgt. was still out cold as the Shore Patrol and MP' separated the combatants and told me to get back in bed and not to move. Under the circumstances I followed that good advice and everyone else was removed from the room. The Sgt. was dragged out of the room and I never saw him again. When I saw the Captain next morning, he had a large bandage covering half his face and over the torn up ear, two black eyes and was wearing the smile of victory, though at what cost?

I went to sickbay the following morning, which was a Saturday. I was admitted and advised that I would be in there for the entire weekend. I protested that all I had was a sore throat and I was looking for something to take for that. I had thought I would be given some throat lozenges and released so I could then go on liberty. I was hoping to hitch a ride to Oakland. Orders were that any Marine that came into sick bay that day got the same treatment, a private room and was confined for the entire weekend. The Navy wasn't having any more drunken outbursts.

I was stuck there for the weekend and had nothing to do. I got over the sore throat but wasn't even allowed out of bed, so I slept a good part of the time. Meals were brought in on a tray and they were a welcome diversion from the boredom. I found out from the sailor bringing the meals that all the enlisted Marines were now stationed in the big tent on the beach. No beds, but good down sleeping bags and soft sand to lie on. All meals were brought there now, and no more Marines were on the Navy Base, except a couple of us in the sickbay and the Marine Officers.

Sunday morning brought the usual breakfast on a tray. At about ten o'clock there was a cute little nurse with a single gold bar on her shirt collar which indicated to me that she was a Lieutenant, JG, and probably new to the Navy. She was about my age, twenty, or just slightly older. She took all my vitals and brought me some APC pills, which we called all-purpose capsules. After I had taken those she told me I would get bathed. I told her I could go shower, but she wasn't to allow me out of bed except to use the bathroom, Doctor's orders. She left and reappeared with a pan, towels and washrags. I was told to lie on my stomach, naked, under a sheet and then I would be bathed. She left the room and I feared some big sailor named Bubba, with a lisp, would be in to bathe me, but she came back. She took a nice warm washcloth and rubbed all over my back and even places that no one had rubbed since I was in diapers. Then she told me to roll over and she started at my chest and worked her magic with the washcloth. Well you can guess the result, I was twenty, looking up at a cute little girl with the scent of some provocative perfume wafting about me, with her hand and a warm wet wash cloth going over me. I began to rise to the occasion and daydream. Suddenly she lashed out like a maddened witch, or a nun, with a pencil that had been behind her ear, while giving me a loud order, "At ease." I just about died of humiliation and didn't have a chance to apologize as with a parting swoop she had taken up everything she had brought in and she stepped out of the room like it had caught fire. I lay in anguish and agony until I was sure she wouldn't be coming back in. Then I did a quick assessment of damage, got dressed again and continued to be bored out of my mind until the Navy released me on Monday morning. I was then whisked off in a Jeep to the tent in Sand City.

Monterey in 1957 was mostly a working fishing village along the water's edge with large canneries scattered along the beach. It was also a spot where a lot of well-to-do folks went to retire, a bit farther inland. Residents and visitors could watch the sea birds and the ocean swells from the beaches or bluffs along the shoreline. There were quite a few boats tied up at the Wharf and built onto it were some nice restaurants and an art gallery or two. A couple of bars and one large curio shop were right as you came off the street to get onto the wharf itself. Along the old downtown, which was just a short distance inland from the wharf, were a couple of theatres and a few of the stores usually found in a modest-sized town. It was a nice town, proud of its heritage. It kept the streets clean and when the stores were open, had a bit of hustle and bustle to it, but in a laid-back sort of way. Things were happening, but people also had time to talk and visit as they went about their daily business. The town was also decorated with a lot of potted plants in front of most every doorway of any business. Nearby, on the beach at Sand City, was a small contingent of the USMC, a Test and Experimental Unit, part of the Schools Regiment, at Camp Delmar, Camp Pendleton, CA. They had come to test their Amphibious Tractors in the surf of San City. These Marines had been stationed at the Naval Air Base at Monterey for a week, had overstayed their welcome, having done dastardly deeds to Naval Personnel and themselves As a result, all of the enlisted Marines were banished from the Naval Base and removed to a large tent in Sand City. Only the Officers were welcome on the Navy Base. The enlisted men were to remain outcasts until the testing was completed and they would again be taken aboard an LST and delivered to the beach just north of Oceanside, to make their way back to their quarters at Camp Delmar.

I was one of those Marines and was allowed to go home on the weekend to Oakland. I hitchhiked to Oakland and when I got to my home a few hours later my brother Eugene lent me a 1938 Ford roadster until such time as I didn't need it anymore, which meant until we Marines were to debark for Camp Delmar. I had a marvelous weekend and on a bright

Sunday afternoon, I drove back to Sand City and parked a hundred yards from our large tent on the beach. I had known I would have Guard Duty that night so I wouldn't be going to town until the following night.

One of my Marine friends asked me if he could use the little car to go into town and see a show or whatever, with a buddy or two. Since we often shared cars at Delmar, I saw no reason to object now. They left and I wandered my post for a four-hour stint, plodding through the sand around the perimeter of our camp and all of our equipment. At midnight I was relieved and went to bed and slept like a baby. I awoke a couple of times to some giggling and laughter and the sound of the little Ford going away again. That seemed odd, but I was tired from walking in the sand for four hours and almost immediately dozed off again. I wanted to get some sleep as in the morning we would have some tests to run in whatever surf there was and we would also have some dignitaries come out to the site to observe what the Marines were doing there.

In the morning I got ready to go receive our breakfast from the Navy truck that would be delivering it. I found that our tent and the walkway to it had several potted plants placed neatly around so as to make the place look lived in and a bit more "homey." Matter of fact it looked like something out of a travel guide, except for the Marine Corp Insignia prominently displayed near the road end of the path to our large tent. There were even a couple of small palm trees that had been placed on each side of the entry to our tent. Quite a lovely touch to a barren wasteland covered in sand and a fringe of ice plant. With the mildly pounding surf in the background, it made a wonderful picture.

After we had our breakfast, the officers began to show up. Not all of them laughed about the new décor and when the Colonel showed up, accompanied by his friendly dignitaries and photographers, I began to feel uneasy. The photographers took lots of pictures and then we all went to work for several hours running our tractors in and out of the surf, which wasn't very high, so nothing spectacular took place and eventually all the spectators and the Colonel left. The photographers did a final sweep of our little base of operations and took a picture of everything in sight. Nothing was said of our decorating the campsite.

The following morning was entirely a different scenario. The Colonel arrived just as we were finishing eating breakfast and it was plain to all he wasn't in a jolly mood. He had a newspaper with him and called our little Captain and a couple of Staff Sergeants into the Command Tent. The Colonel got very loud with the discussion in the tent, all of it was one way, no replies solicited or offered. After a very short time the Colonel stormed out, got in his girl friend's car and left for the day.

The Captain called us all to attention and then showed us that the Monterey News had some lovely shots of our premises and half the plants from downtown. He ordered a truck from Fort Ord, and we all were assigned to load flowers, trees and decorative plants onto it. Then the truck and several Marines were sent to Monterey to return the borrowed decorative items. The culprits weren't identified and the means of transportation remained unknown. Marines, who had no idea which plants had come from where, returned the plants to town. Even the culprits couldn't remember, as they had been drinking the whole evening. Though I thought we'd be grounded for the rest of our enlistment, no action was taken against anyone. I believe the Colonel didn't want anyone to bring up his absence from our camp, so the fun was over, as the saying goes "No harm, no foul."

CHAPTER 47

A Short-Timer

A SGT. IN MY UNIT had gotten married and lived in LA. He liked my 1947 Studebaker six, with overdrive, and he offered to trade a 1935 four-door convertible Ford for it. I balked, as he had paid $25 for the Ford and I had paid $75 for the Studebaker, so we made a deal. I would buy the parts and he would rebuild the engine, a 59AB block. For those of you that don't know, that was a sought after engine from the Mercury line and had 100 hp instead of the 85 of the Fords. So we did the trade and he even rebuilt the transmission, putting in Zephyr gears. This actually made the trade lopsided in my favor. The Ford was rather rare and was in pretty much the same or better condition than my Studebaker. Parts had cost me $50.

After a couple of weeks we consummated the trade and I drove to LA with him. That was the first time I saw my new machine. I was well pleased. It was the first four door convertible sedan I had even noticed. It was shiny black and had a white top. What a magnet for girls this should be. Much better than a sedate Studebaker sedan. So I drove off with my new purchase.

Back then the road from LA south went almost directly through Long Beach and pretty much followed where Hwy 405 goes through the LA area now, but it wasn't a freeway, just city streets. I believe Sepulveda was the main one. I drove to San Juan Capistrano and it began to pour down rain. My wipers couldn't keep up and so I followed a car, trailing him very closely. I knew we were real close to the ocean and that the visibility would only get worse, so I kept fairly close until we were on gravel and his lights went out. I stopped and had to roll down my window to see out. We had pulled off to the favorite necking spot where the street ran into the Coast Highway. By now the guy was wondering what I was doing so close and I apologized and backed off and waited until a truck went down Hwy 1, then pulled behind it and continued on to Oceanside. By the time I got to the base I was soaked, it had also quit raining and I was wondering if my trade had been such a good idea. It wasn't. I don't believe any girl ever even sat in it, let alone go for a ride with me.

I did drive my newfound toy over to Escondido. That was a town of maybe 5000. It had a skating rink and that meant girls and guys might actually mix a bit there. So off I went and learned that I wasn't really cut out for roller-skating. I had done okay on ice, once or twice, but roller skates had a way of making me find the floor rather rapidly, so I mostly just stood around and watched. All of the girls appeared taken, so I got back in my car and headed back to the base.

There was a smaller town on the way to the base, San Marcos. Nearby was a gas station that did some repairs on cars, sold tires and odds and ends. I found that my car was overheating and drove in there to see if the man could help me. He checked over my car engine and thought that I should have the radiator rodded out and cleaned. I asked the cost and he asked me if $10 would be okay. I checked my wallet and pockets and told him that all I had was seven bucks. He told me to help him remove the hood and we'd be getting me going in a bit. I had to pump gas and clean windshields when he had a customer, but he pulled out my radiator, unsoldered the top and bottom tanks and rodded the core tubes with a long flat bar made for that purpose, then soldered it all back together, painted it black and reinstalled it. I helped put the hood on and gave him my seven bucks and was about to leave, when he yelled, "Hold it!"

I couldn't imagine what the problem was now, but he stood in front of my car and told me I can't go anywhere on that tire. I got out and looked and the tire was just beginning to show the inner tube. I probably couldn't have driven a block before it would have blown out. He inspected all the rest and looked at the spare. He told me the spare wouldn't get me very far either and that I had to get a decent tire before I could go anywhere. So he went and found a fairly good-looking used tire and came back and told me I could have that for five bucks. I explained that it was mid-month, payday fifteen days away and I had given him everything I had in cash for the radiator job. He told me to pull onto his rack, so I did.

He took my wheel off, dismounted and remounted the tire, bad one for good one and told me to come pay him when I got paid. I guess he thought he had donated to the unfunded Marine car club, or some such. But I did come back and pay him two weeks later. He thanked me and I bought a tank of gas and never was out that way again. About fifty-five years later I told that story to the wife of Cleo Stover, a guy I went to school with in Idaho, who now lives in Rancho Murrieta, CA. She informed me that the nice guy that helped me was her father. He was the owner of the only fix-it shop and gas station on that road. Strange how things happen sometimes, isn't it? What would the odds be that I would meet the anyone that had ever heard of that shop, or even San Marcos, let alone that I should meet that fellows daughter and she would have married a guy I went to school with in first grade

CHAPTER 48

Minnesota on Leave

WHEN I FIRST WENT TO work at the Test and Experimental Unit I met a man from Minnesota. He had lived on a farm near Fulda and even in a Marine uniform he looked the part of a big happy farm boy. His name was Reiner Bruns, but everyone called him Tiny. He was well over six feet tall, I believe six four, but never asked. He must have weighed about two hundred and fifty to three hundred pounds, but was quick as a cat. He was a mechanic and worked in a big shop that had just the two of us assigned to it. We had a Sergeant, Delmer Starrett, that was our boss and he was more like a father figure to us than a boss. Our fathers had raised neither Tiny, nor me. His had died early and you know my early years were with an aunt and uncle. Sgt. Starrett has returned from the Korean conflict and decided to make the Marines his career. He had been a mechanic in Kansas and felt this would be a better life for him. He is the one that traded cars with me.

Tiny and I hit it off well together both on the job and during our time off. We went to town together often, liked the same people, the same shows and the same foods. We would get a couple of other guys and go to Tijuana Mexico, eat tacos from the street venders carts despite the food being heated by a little candle, or lantern, and therefore having moths all over it in the evenings. We would stay together, at least Tiny and I, looking but not touching the local women. I know we both had been warned, repeatedly by, the older women in our lives, of what these little vixens were up to.

Also the Marine Corps had shown us countless movies about the effects of VD that any female for a hundred miles of a base was apt to be spreading.

We would go to the strip joints and listen to the music, watch the girls dance and ply their trade with the Sailors and Marines. Sometimes we would have to buy them a drink to keep the owners of the establishments happy, but neither of us was tempted to try our luck. Aunt Nellie and the Marine movie folks had convinced me no good would come of it. We didn't have much money so we went to the cheaper spots that had a few topless girls, but none of the "dog and pony" shows stuff that folks always talk about.

One of the other guys was from Minnesota also. He seemed to have a real thing for one of the girls in a place we frequented. Anytime we were going to Tijuana he would beg to go with us and he'd get drunk and sentimental before too long. I didn't drink much, a couple of beers and I'd switch to coke or iced-tea, like the drinks we bought for the girls. The girls would come out and do a strip, each taking off a tad more than the one that had just preceded them. His friend was the finale. She would appear on stage half-dressed and end the show naked, doing some crazy dance to get every eye on her before she left. I guess that was why he was so enthralled with her. Then she would sit with us and talk dirty until the next show. He would spend all his money on buying her drinks, more iced tea.

Tiny and I also worked together for a civilian engineer on our free time. He worked at the T&E Unit and had married a lady that owned some property on the edge of Bonsall. Bonsall was just a wide spot in the road then. There was a restaurant that may have been the post office, but nothing else that I knew of. The property had a hill on it and at the top of the hill there was a man-made pond. Most of what I did was to help Tiny and sometimes, another Marine place pipes around the property, so as to form city sized lots, with a water pipe to each one. This was done under the guise of being an irrigation system for his alfalfa field. We also irrigated the alfalfa and put it up when the time was right.

The engineer had a daughter and there came a day a friend of hers came to visit her and she and I got acquainted. She rode a tractor with me and I asked her out. She agreed and I guess told her friend that I had asked her out. I don't know if that had anything to do with anything but from then on I didn't have that job.

Tiny was about to get discharged in the late spring of 1957, several months before I would be discharged. He asked me to help him study for his GED. I didn't know what that was and when I found out we both studied and we both passed it. I was told I had done real well on it and should probably take that as an incentive to go to college. I was not interested at the moment but did discuss it with some engineer from Michigan. He told me if I was serious he thought he could help me get into a program with General Motors. I'd go to school for six months then work for six months until I got my degree. I never followed up on that either, so I don't know if that program existed or if he was pulling my leg.

Tiny invited me to visit his mother's farm with him and spend a ten day Christmas leave with his family including his mother, brother and sisters. I said I would go. He told me that Minnesota was not at all like California and we would never see a girl in pedal pushers. There they all wore dresses and that it would be cold, so they'd be all bundled up in coats, hats, scarves and big boots. I was really excited, as I hadn't dreamed of traveling anywhere like that on my own. The Marine Corp appeared to like me where I was, so this would be a fine adventure.

We made our plans, got our ten days leave, Tiny invited our friend from the Tijuana trips to join us, and a few days before Christmas we were on our way. We all had the weekend off and had our leave start on Monday morning. That gave us two extra days to spend driving and still have most of our leave days at his family farm.

Friday night we left through the back roads to get out of Oceanside, through Palm Springs and Blythe, then up to Flagstaff and over to Tucumcari, New Mexico where we would jog up to Mc Pherson, Kansas and drive about straight north to South Dakota, then finally east to Fulda,

MN. Both of the men from MN were reluctant to drive through the mountains, so I drove most of the way to Flagstaff. Then we took turns sleeping and driving and not too much into Sunday morning were in Fulda. We dropped our stuff off and had lunch with his family and took our friend another 100 miles north to his home. By the time we got to the farm it was time for dinner and bed. We were pretty tired from all the driving.

We left Pendleton on a Friday afternoon and arrived in Minnesota on Sunday morning. We said "hello" to Tinys' family, then drove our friend another couple of hours north to his home way out in the woods. The following days we drove to a couple of towns close by and visited some of Tinys' friends and relatives. An uncle owned a theatre in Pipestone so we went there and saw some movie that had just come out. There was a lot of snow on the ground and the temperature was fairly constant for the entire time of our leave. The days were normally ten degrees F and the nights were minus ten.

Tinys' mother owned a dairy farm and they milked about 15 head of cows twice a day. Every other day a truck came by and exchanged the full cans for empties. The girls all helped with the milking and there was a mentally disabled brother that also did the heavy lifting for the mother and girls. Tiny and I were guests and were treated like royalty.

Breakfasts were farm fare; eggs, ham, bacon, biscuits and gravy with milk and beer to drink. The beer with every meal struck me as odd. I don't know if that was a cultural thing or if this family just liked their beer. I usually just had milk and coffee, not that the beer was bad, I just couldn't get into beer with my breakfast.

Tiny got a date with a young lady he had been writing to and he wondered how I would manage. He felt strongly that I should go with them and I felt as strongly that I would surely be out of place. I convinced him that he and Hilde should go out and have fun and that I could stay home with the family for one night and that would be fine. So I spent a night with all of the girls, mama and Lester, the mentally challenged son.

We played some board games and some cards and they told me about their school and they wanted to know everything they could find out about me, and life in California. They were all nice people and very pleasant to be around. There was one girl about my age, whom I recall was the oldest girl, that spent the whole evening dwelling on my every move and I felt a bit uncomfortable with her and that much female attention around the rest of the family. There was no hint of too much closeness, so I just made a point of talking to all of them and as the first of the family made moves to retire for the evening, I made my way to my room as well.

The next day Tiny and I went to some small village and had a late lunch in a café, just as school was letting out. A young girl came in with pedal pushers on and I made some comment to Tiny about how the times must have changed. We both talked to her and I found out her father was the postmaster and Tiny knew the family. Eventually she and I took the car and I gave her a ride home. We did exchange addresses and a bit of cuddling and smooching until I decided I better go get Tiny, so she went in the house and I went back to pick up my friend.

The rest of the visit was spent running around from farm to farm, and calling on Tiny's friends and acquaintances. We met the girl I had met a couple of times and sat in a booth drinking coffee, tea or cokes. Tiny always drank beer. Generally it was a very pleasant time and the ten days was over in the blink of an eye. Our friend from farther north in Minnesota met us at Tiny's mom's house and we all said our goodbyes. The oldest girl asked if she could write to me and was pretty teary that we were leaving. I felt really badly for her as I had done nothing to encourage her and frankly she reminded me too much of Tiny for me to have been involved.

Our drive back to the base was as fast as our drive to Minnesota, there were no storms and the roads were clear. Albuquerque was all lit up in blue lights. It seemed every house had put up the same color lights for Christmas, outlining the roofs of the houses along the highway with blue lights and a Christmas tree with the multi colored lights in the front room windows. There was a lot of snow beside the road all the way to Williams Arizona, where the snow vanished as we dropped down from the higher elevation to the Colorado River Valley and worked our way across the Mojave Desert to California and home to Camp Delmar.

Later on in life, after Nelda and I had been married a while, I believe this may have occurred as we were picking out Christmas lights for our home, I mentioned having been through Albuquerque when all the houses on the highway were decorated with blue lights. Nelda had been through there the same Christmas season, visiting her grandparents in Oklahoma.

CHAPTER 49

Discharged From USMC, Now What?

I WAS HONORABLY DISCHARGED, THE second of July, 1957. I went to Walt's and stayed a day or two with them, then bought his car for $300 and I left my 1935 Ford four door convertible sedan there for him to use, but not to sell. I planned to come get it a little later as I knew it was a rare car and had a good engine and transmission. He promised me he'd look after it and I could come get it anytime, he'd find other means of transportation. So I drove home in what had been his 1950 Cadillac. It was a very pretty hardtop convertible, light pink with molded front and rear. That was quite the fashion at the time.

Upon arrival back on Auseon Avenue I found our little world there had changed significantly. Most of the old neighbors had moved away, or wished they could. Blacks were in the house next door and people were getting cautious and beginning to lock their doors and they didn't leave the keys in the cars at night. Kids came by and invited me to join them in a jaunt up to Castlemont to "Rumble with the blacks." I had never heard the expression, outside of it being used in some movie. I wanted no part of that.

Another change was that Perry had been in a car wreck and was recovering at my father's house. He and his wife and a daughter, had moved my father out of his bedroom and into the one that we kids had used when I first came back from Idaho, bunk beds and all. There was also another baby that was going to be there real soon. I was relegated to a couch in the front room. Things were somewhat like the first time I lived in that house where everyone seemed a bit tense all the time.

I called my Oakland girlfriend and talked to her mother. I asked if she was there and the mother told me that she and her husband had just gone back to their base at Oak Knoll Naval Hospital, which was in east Oakland just below where I had caddied. Perhaps I should have been a bit more diligent in answering her letters.

Next I called my friend in Citrus Heights and made a date with her. She was now living and working in Sacramento and she gave me explicit instructions as to where, when and how to meet her. I went to the appointed spot and waited. Nothing became of that either, she didn't appear and I eventually went back home. I had waited until it was dark and I was clearly stood up.

I found out that Aunt Nellie was someplace in California and Angus was recovering from another stroke, at a sister of Jess Mathews' little farm out toward Garden City, or maybe even Meridian, Idaho. (For some reason this portion is pretty much a blank spot in my memory.) I went to Idaho and do remember that I had my own car there. I drove to where Angus was and found him standing out in a pasture that was real close to the road I was on. We talked over the fence and he told me how he was doing, which at that time wasn't real good, but he was okay enough that he was out in the evening with a shovel in his hand and he had been changing the water in that pasture.

He told me that he had his second stroke, and he couldn't move at all. He had been lying on the couch reading or napping and when Nellie came in and found he hadn't stirred in a long time, she got after him to get up. He told me she had a fit of anger when he told her he couldn't move and that she had taken the little fire shovel and beat the tar out of him with it. But he still couldn't move, so she left and got one of the Ourada boys to come over and help him. They took him to the hospital and she went to California. I was unaware of any of this, except that she had left Idaho again without him.

I felt really sorry for him and gave him a couple of cowboy shirts I had bought just before I got discharged. Beautiful shirts with pearl buttons, fake I'm sure, but real nice and I was very proud to be able to give him something that I thought was so nice. I hope he liked them and wore them some, though I never saw him again. I know that I felt so bad for him that I cried. I think that I may have tried so hard to erase the sight of his plight from my mind that instead, I erased everything about how and when I got there for that final visit.

When I left that fence I must have wandered around some old haunts in Boise. John Henson, eldest son of my seventh and eighth grade school teacher's, Lola Henson, told me he heard I was scouting around in the home neighborhood of the Culver girls. They had lived close to his parent's home in Boise. I have no recollection of that, how or when I returned to California. I know that I didn't go to the Toll Gate, as I had read a Statesman paper that showed the fire department burning the buildings, with the blessing of the health department, so that squatters would not take up residence there. I'm also sure that I didn't go to the Ourada ranch or to Spring Valley. I believe that the only person I saw that I knew was Angus, and I visited him for less than twenty minutes, all of the time standing on opposite sides of a fence from each other. How sad is that? Not even a hug for the old gentleman.

Back in Oakland, I had no job and no prospects for a job. I had almost joined some other Marines in taking a test for the Riverside, CA Fire Department before I was discharged. Since I still had six months to serve before my discharge date, I found that I didn't qualify to take the test. My civilian-related occupation, listed on my DD 214, was Tank Mechanic. Now I wasn't really up on things, but I was fairly sure that I couldn't make much of a living as a tank mechanic, outside of one of the services that used tanks. That left the Army or Marine Corps, so that didn't look too promising either.

I went to some summer camp again at Mt. Herman. I met a few girls and I had this cute car to travel about in, Walt's Cadillac, so I took a load of them to Santa Cruz and we had all kinds of good times. There was even a girl I had seen a couple of times at Elmhurst Baptist and there was another pretty blonde that looked strikingly like my Citrus Heights friend. The blonde and I got real cozy and did a lot of hand holding and a few smooches here and there until she told me she was engaged to marry some minister from Richmond, CA. I had flashbacks of another girl that was engaged to a minister, so I took my leave of her and went in search of greener pastures. That search took me right back to the girl I had recognized.

Nelda Rodgers was the girl from Elmhurst Baptist that I recognized. She had just graduated from Castlemont High School, eighteen and seemed to be alone. I tried to get her attention by snuggling up close to her at one of the outdoor sermons. This same tactic had met with very little success years before, but this time we seemed to be a lot more on the same page. I didn't offer to smother her in my leather jacket, as I had done before. She hated coats but she didn't seem to mind if I held her hand, so I did at every opportunity.

Nelda's brother, Bill, had driven up to the camp from Oakland with his wife, to give her a ride home. She declined his kind offer, as I had also offered her a ride home. So once again I was making some progress. That made me think there was some real hope here and she wasn't engaged, nor getting over some bad relationship or well, one could go on and on. It seemed she was a very nice girl and came from a stable family that led a normal life. She had plans to go to a Dental Assistant Program at Laney College, in Oakland, when finished she had a job offer waiting for her with Dr. Rooney, DDS in San Leandro.

I now had to make plans for finding a job. My separation pay from the USMC was about used up. I asked Eugene where he thought I might look and he took me to Sunshine Biscuits in Oakland and introduced me to the night manager who immediately hired me. I was in perfect shape, strong and healthy and he needed someone strong and healthy, to do the heavy lifting that the ladies weren't allowed to do. Brains didn't play a part in that position, they needed brawn and willingness to work. I had that covered.

At the beginning of the following week I reported to work and was shown where my job was. The shift manager introduced me to my foreman. I went to work in the packing department, which was at the outer end of the ovens where the cookies and crackers came off long steel belts and went onto cooling belts. This allowed the material to cool enough for ladies to handle them. These ladies put the crackers and cookies in boxes and they went off on the belts to the shipping department.

Some of the products were taken off the belts and put into tins boxes to be processed for restaurants. The ladies weren't supposed to lift the full tins as they weighed more than the labor laws allowed a woman to lift. So that was my job. I lifted tins of crackers, stacking the tins on pallets and pulled away loaded pallets with a hand truck, to a place of storage between the ovens. I also provided the ladies with empty tins as they needed them. Not brain surgery, but a good workout, which I got paid to do. It was about 120 degrees between the ovens, and more like the 80s at the end of the belts. I was constantly in motion between the two places, so I never got too hot, but I sure did sweat a lot. The nurse gave me salt pills and told me to drink water at every break, which I did.

I got over a lot of my shyness there as a few of the ladies took an interest in me, and talked the whole shift, nonstop. They never missed a beat of their work but chatted constantly about everything under the sun. They talked mostly about family, but with me, about who was doing what and with whom, along the line. They tried to embarrass me and it took only a week or so for me to get over a lot of my inhibitions They talked about literally everything and wanted to know everything about me, my girlfriend, past girlfriends and anything personal they could get me to let slip. I rather enjoyed working with them and never did get into mischief with any of them. Some did want to, but I was still a bit afraid we would lose our jobs, or worse, so I didn't do anything more than go to lunch with some on paydays, so we could cash our paychecks.

Eugene and I lived in a rented room in a house close to High Street in Oakland. I think we each paid a few dollars a week and we shared a bed.

Then he went somewhere, got married I think, and I took a room at 92nd and East 14th Street. Sunshine was on 85th Avenue and I had lost my drivers' license for a year, so I walked to and from work, and took the bus if I had to do any real distance. I spent a lot of time at Nelda's home and we walked a lot.

The reason I had to give up my driver's license was that I had traded in the Cadillac for a 1947 Lincoln Continental Convertible. I bought insurance and found that I didn't have liability coverage, when a lady ran into the rear of it and then a few weeks later another guy ran into the driver's door. The state didn't care that I wasn't at fault in either accident, just that I had to have insurance, so they took my license and I walked. How I survived that for a year is beyond me. Well, it wasn't really a year. The state had waited about six months to notify me of the suspension, and the year was from the date of the first accident, so I got my license back in the middle of August 1958.

Nelda and I were getting along well and she introduced me to all her relatives and friends. She already knew my brother Eugene so I introduced her to the rest of my family as well. This was getting serious and I knew that we were meant for each other. Her sister's husband was a fireman in Oakland and he told me to take the uppcoming test. He introduced me to a guy that had an evening school for guys interested in learning how to pass the test, but since I worked nights, I had to pick up the material and study it on my own. It was a lot of questions that had been asked on past tests so I studied hard and when the time came for the test, myself and another guy, Stan Daily, Perry's wife's cousin's husband, went to the University of California, in Berkeley and took the test.

This was a two-part test. The first part was to take an Army IQ type and the second part was more of an Oakland-specific type test made up just for Oakland recruiting. The first section was graded while we took the second section. If you had failed, the proctor called your name and you left the room and went home. You were through until the next test for fireman was given, probably two years later.

I took the first test and started into the second one. I had felt intimidated by my friend Stan. He was a big man, bright and looked the part of a policeman or fireman. He had a job selling printing equipment for Pitney Bowes. I just assumed he would beat me out, but as we sat there taking the second part his name was called. That shocked me badly, and I felt certain I would be called soon, but the tests hadn't seemed too hard, so I continued on. Eventually I finished and handed in my papers and met Stan for a strange ride home. I couldn't believe that he had failed and didn't really know any words to say that wouldn't sound out of place. So we went home rather quietly and I don't recall ever seeing him again.

A couple of weeks had gone by, and I was invited to an oral board testing. I put on my best face and went to that with no idea what might be asked, except that the instructor of the class I got information from had told me the oral board members would like Catholics. The examiners seemed to ask questions that I knew the answers to. I think they were just trying to get to know me and whom I was, not trying to trip me up in some way. They asked about the schools I had attended and I told them I went to school in Idaho. I knew they were looking for young men that had gone to a good Catholic school, but I didn't, so I avoided telling them that I had gone to Elmhurst and Castlemont in Oakland. One of the examiners asked more questions about my girl friend than anything else and wondered if she was pretty and if we would be getting married. I answered yes to both, adding, "If everything goes my way." That seemed to tickle the whole board and I was dismissed having no feeling for how I had done either way, good or bad. Evidently I did well, as in another couple of weeks I was told to report to the drill tower for a physical agility test.

This consisted of running an obstacle course, lifting some weights and carrying a dummy up a ladder. We also had to climb a one hundred foot aerial ladder, touch the top rung and return to the ground. I knew I wasn't a fast runner and worried about that. Part of the obstacle course was getting over a wall, then through a tube and then running for a hundred yards, all timed. As I came out of the tube I began to fall and I ran as hard as I could, just to get my feet back under me. I never did fall and set a good time, probably the fastest I had ever run in my life. Nelda's sister had shown me how to pick up the dummy. She had picked me up onto her back several times to demonstrate the lifting technique. I had real trouble with it, but when the time came I did it and climbed a ladder with the dummy on my back. She had also told me not to throw it on the ground when I got through, just set it down, so I laid the dummy down carefully and had passed the test. Candidates lost serious points if they threw the dummy down when finished.

I placed thirty-third overall, out of about 2500 that took the test. I was very pleased with myself, but there was still the matter of a physical examination at the Kaiser Hospital. That would be the last step before I could be hired. For the time being I had to continue working at Sunshine. One of the cooks on the ovens talked to me a lot about the fire department. His father had been a tiller man,*[9] on the back of a hook and ladder, in San Francisco and he told me to be sure to take this job, that it was the best job in the world for someone young and strong. He had failed because of poor eyesight but he insisted I must get this job. The poor eyesight thing frightened me, as that was why the Marines had cancelled my orders to go to Japan. I had a "lazy eye" and at my age that was not fixable.

By this time Nelda and I were engaged and planning on getting married October 17, 1958. That was fast approaching and the City of Oakland had told me to come in for a physical exam. I was afraid of the eye chart, so Nelda's sister got one for me and I studied it. The 20-20 Line read DEFPOTEC and I still remember it. Another chap, just ahead of me at the hospital asked the nurse where the eye chart was and she told him. Then he asked her for a pen and paper and she gave it to him. I thought we'd get kicked out. When I went to take the eye test, that same guy was just in front of me and read off the chart while hardly looking that direction. The lady called me and when she asked me to follow her pointer, she didn't

---

9 The tillerman steers the back section of the articulated ladder truck, enabling it to make sharp turns that are required by the congestion in the downtown, and the narrow roads in the hills.

point to lines, she pointed to specific letters and I had to quickly calculate that the fifth letter was an "O" and so on. She passed us both and he eventually became the Chief of the Oakland Fire Department.

I was accepted and notified to report to the Drill Tower on the 28th of July. I went to the union office of the Bakers Union to ask about my vacation money. They assured me that I qualified and though I hadn't been at Sunshine for one year, by the time I would be hired I would have that year. I asked about just quitting a week ahead of time and if that would affect my holiday pay. They assured me that I had earned it and that nothing could change that, so I went to Sunshine and told them I would be leaving in the week before August 28. That was settled. When I went back to the Union Hall, to get my vacation pay, they told me that I no longer was qualified for it as I hadn't completed my one-year at Sunshine. There started a lifelong distrust of the union leadership, that claimed to be there to help us. They appear to be there to help themselves.

A City of Oakland letter told me to go to the Hub in Oakland or the Fashion in San Francisco and buy my uniforms. Also I was to go to Globe Supply on Broadway in Oakland and purchase turnout gear. These were approved vendors that sold to most of the Fire Departments around the San Francisco Bay Area. I was to tell them I had been hired in Oakland and the store would know which gear I needed. The store also would arrange for credit for me if I didn't have cash to pay for it all. I went shopping and picked up about $450 or $500 worth of uniforms and equipment from the Hub and Globe Supply. Both had all the required things in stock and were thrilled to have me in there being outfitted, so they made sure I got everything I would need, except for leather gloves. The City furnished the required gloves and a bronze hose spanner, used to make and break hose connections. Our starting pay was $483 per month, so I could make this back in about one month of recruit firefighter pay. At Sunshine I had been taking home about $54 per week.

The City sent me a letter and told me to show up at the Drill Tower on Mac Arthur Blvd. at 8:00 AM on the 28th of July, 1958, which I did. They had also told me to wear my uniform pants and a Navy blue sweatshirt and my boots. I also had to bring all my turnout gear, which consisted of heavy canvas pants, a coat and helmet. I showed up and at some point we all were sworn in and given a badge for our shirt and uniform cap. We received a leather badge for our helmet, which had our badge number on it also. Then the drill instructors read us the rules and regulations that would apply and we started drilling with hoses and ladders.

We were divided in two groups and each group had ladders to hoist in the morning and hoses to handle in the afternoon. The following shift it would be the other way around. We started with short one-man ladders and the worked up to two-man ladders, then the three or four-man ones on up to the 50 footer that required six men to throw and extend it. We worked hard and got the knack of spotting the base of the ladders so that very little, if any, moving was needed. The ideal angle was 70 degrees for climbing and we soon learned how to judge that. I seem to recall that I was on the A Shift and our first day was a B Shift day, so I got to go home at night after the first day and the B shifters had to go to their assigned firehouse that night. The next day they were off at night and the A Shift went to the Fire Station. We did that for two weeks and then reported to our station ready for duty.

For the first several shifts that I worked, I had to get a ride to the Drill Tower with Nelda's mother and the next morning I would take the bus home. This was not how I had it pictured, but it was how circumstances had found me. I would hope no one asked me for a driver's license because I didn't have one and that was one of the requirements of being an Oakland Fireman. You had to have a valid California Driving License in those days. Fortunately no one checked until after I had received mine back, which was about the middle of August. In reality I had only been without it for about seven months, but that was a long time for a twenty-two-year-old.

As new kids, we were drilled all the time at the better firehouses, and basically ignored in some of the less busy houses, except while the Battalion Chief was due to come around, then somebody would have the new kid putting a nozzle on a piece of hose, or some menial chore. The good houses had us out learning things most of the day. Some of them even overdid it, but I never complained and loved it all. Besides the work was fun and the pay was double what I received at Sunshine Biscuits. The days off were just wonderful.

I did vacation relief*[10] in the downtown area of Oakland and got to know the streets pretty well and went to many large fires and lots of small mattress fire in the flop houses around the poorer sections of town. Also there were still a lot of sulfur dioxide refrigeration units around. If they sprung a leak it was impossible to breathe in the gas cloud. (It was physically not possible to breathe; your lungs will shut down.) That was the one place that even the old timers thought it was proper to put on breathing apparatus. Not anyplace else though, or you were a "Jake," and would soon find that you didn't work downtown anymore, and your evaluations were very poor. You would find yourself out working where the owls were romancing the chickens, the old timers told us.

I liked going to work at the fireboat, which was a part of Engine 2. We were just getting a new foam system and to test that, we spent several shifts making piles of foam on piers and docks and seeing how well it covered. We didn't get to set any ships on fire to try to put them out, but I guess that would have been a bit over the top. On a smaller version, we set pans of gasoline and oil on fire and played hand lines of foam over them. They went out rather nicely, but it left a mess that took a while to dry up. Also the Engine Company (2 Engine) ran as a land company, running a two-piece company. That means we had a hose wagon followed by a pumping engine and we were on call for alarms just as any other firehouse.

While working at 2 Engine, the first few weeks I went to at least three large fires of multiple alarms. At a couple of those we were the first on the scene and had the whole fire to ourselves for a minute or two until the other units showed up. That was always a fun place to be in, and always a bit frightening when I look back on it. But we worked hard and got water flowing on the fire. Usually those multi alarm fires are a lost cause before

---

10 That is I went from station to station replacing the member that was on vacation from that assignment.

we were called, but it was a good feeling to know that usually we had prevented other properties from becoming involved.

Firefighting can be a dangerous job. While at a large fire, another fireman, Marty Gaylord, and I were told to take a large line onto the roof of a small garage and play water onto the building next door from that vantage point. I was a bit larger than Marty and had the nozzle and he was lightening up the hose for me to advance it to our spot of operation. When we got the hose and nozzle into position we yelled to have the line charged and I gingerly opened the nozzle to let the air out of the line and let the water advance. This was a big fire and the engineer had the "Big Fire, Big Water" mentality take hold of him and gave us more pressure on the line than we should have had. As I opened the nozzle the pressure pushed me backward and we were eventually able to brace ourselves against a high wall that stopped the hose from receding further.

With both of us sort of braced in a corner I hefted the nozzle up pretty high so I could play the water down onto the fire next door. I thought we were doing real well and decided to move forward a bit. I turned to look at Marty and note that he was helplessly pinned to the wall with the big line across his throat. He was just on the point of passing out when I had turned. I pulled the line hard and he staggered out from where it had him trapped and took a few minutes to regain his breathing and strength. Then he gave me an earful about not doing him in or some such, which was mostly lost in the noise and confusion that accompanies these large events.

At another large fire in a foundry that was close to 2 Engine, third and Broadway, Marty and I were taking a set of "Baby Lines," into the building. I had heard the Lieutenant ask for a second alarm, so I knew this was a big fire. I had the thought in mind to attack it so aggressively that Marty and I would have it out before help arrived. One of the lines appeared to be caught on something so Marty and I pulled just one line, with him just behind me and. We were making fair progress advancing the line and putting out fire on both sides of us as we advanced. Marty gave the line a couple of tugs and I turned to see why. He pointed down and I looked down instead of ahead. I had crawled out onto a girder over the basement and there was no floor, just the girder. We backed out and hours later the fire was extinguished.

From 12 Engine, I went to a fire on the top floor of an old hotel downtown. Most of the fire was in a room and part of the hallway, but some had come out the street-side window and Bob Comella and I took a set of baby lines up the aerial ladder and worked on pulling the cornice apart and putting out the fire to keep it from extending into the attic. My friend Bob was aggressive with his axe and got off the ladder onto a ledge that was a couple of feet wide. As he pulled more of the cornice loose, I followed him and carefully hung onto the window frames, looping the hose into the windows as we passed them and working the nozzle along, but careful to advance the hose so it didn't fall off the ledge. Eventually there was no more fire in the cornice and Bob told me to go back to the ladder.

I looked behind me and this was the first I realized how far we were from the ladder. It was about 20 feet away and we were seven or so stories off the street. I told him I couldn't go back; I had to go into a window that was just past Bob. He ducked into it and pulled me in. There, sitting up in bed, was a startled young lady, naked to the waist at least. Bob turned to her and told her to "Hide your eyes." She quickly raised her hands over her eyes and we left her room and went into the hallway.

We went back to another room where the ladder truck was spotted just outside and carefully retrieved our hose lines and backed them down the ladder to the street. Once on the ground, I was scared as never before, when I looked up and saw how tiny the ledge really was that we had worked off. I vowed to never do that again and I have kept that vow. I had confidence in the aerial ladders, but not in anything stuck to the side of a building. One never knows how it is held on and some of the bric-a-brac is just tacked in place for looks.

I had liked all the excitement of the downtown and decided I would put my name in for 1 Engine or 2 Engine. The administration did what they could to satisfy my request and gave me 21 Engine, which was out in the safest residential part of Oakland. A big fire there was a cigarette butt falling through a crack in a porch and smoke coming back out of that crack. We delicately poured about a cup of water on it and the problem was solved.

One morning, an old timer named Frank Kenna, came to work and told me that, "This is just like the day that the Big Berkeley Fire of 1923 happened on. Wind from the hills, blowing toward the Bay, hot and everything is all dried out. You watch kid; we'll have another big one today. That one burned right to the Bay before it stopped."

He had been a fireman in Berkeley before he came to Oakland, way back when. He had told me his job in Berkeley had included riding with the Engineer on the old steamer and throwing coal at the cars, when they got too close, so they wouldn't scare the horses.

We ate our breakfast and the weather got hotter, the wind picked up and by noon, there was a reported wildfire miles away off Skyline Blvd, about as far up in the hills of Oakland as one could go. Almost immediately other companies were sent to assist and we were moved to 19 Engine to be closer. We never made it to 19, dispatched to the fire scene and so we wound our way up Tunnel Road and proceeded east on skyline. There was a huge cloud of smoke from the ridge all the way to San Francisco and we couldn't see where the fire was. The Engineer and the Lieutenant were pouring over maps in the driver's seat, every few blocks they would stop on the shoulder of the road and discuss the maps, the radio worked sometimes and we were to go to some street none of us had any knowledge of and try to assist 19 Engine, which was already there.

The street was found on the map and again away we went, this time with a real spot in mind. As we passed on of the streets that went back downhill, toward the fire, a ladder truck from the East End came toward us. They stopped and the Officers and drivers all looked at maps again and away we went, the ladder truck turning around in a driveway and following us. About a half mile further we took a road down toward the fire and then we found we were past where we should have been and a bit too far east, so we took another road back uphill and came upon the head of the fire. We still had to find 19 Engine, so I took off my turnout coat and held it like a blanket to protect myself, and the Engineer, as he drove through the blistering heat and came upon a tank wagon in the road.

Fire was racing up the hill toward us, and the E19's wagon. Just past it was 19 Engine and we were all in the path of the bulk of the fire coming up that hill. 19 Engine was trying to reel in the hose from the tank wagon. My Lieutenant, Jerry Mokma, told me "Chop that dang hose loose and get on, we have to get out of this gully."

So I took a couple of swings with my axe and resumes my station covering the Engineer so he could see and we followed 19 Engine and it's tank wagon out of danger and eventually we all got some lines on the fire from our rigs, and a water supply from a hydrant. By then the wind had died down and the fire became much easier to extinguish. Within a few hours it was just about all over. Patrols were kept for the next several days to prevent a rekindle.

We were sent back to 19 Engine to cover their district until they got back late in the evening. Our Engine had some scorched paint, but not nearly as badly as the paint on 19 Engine and their tank wagon. They had lost the 200 feet of hose from the tank wagon, but the only injury to men had been some first degree burns and some of us got poison oak. It could have been tragically worse, as we saw in the fire of 1991, where 25 civilians, one Police Officer and one Battalion Chief, lost their lives on just such a day. Over three thousand people also lost their homes.

CHAPTER 50

Firehouse Characters

THESE ARE SOME OF THE characters that were firehouse fixtures, though they were not firemen. Generally they were from the neighborhood of the station where they first started showing an interest in things fire-related. The ones I mention here, were not firebugs in the sense of ever becoming arsonists, though the thought struck most of us, at one time, or another, that they could have been. Almost all of them were harmless simpletons, that were just trying to find someplace in the world where they could fit in for a while each day, and have some type interaction with their heroes.

The first that I met was an exception to the above, as he was a sailor that would have too many at a local bar and then find his way to the main fire station, One Engine in Oakland. The firemen all called him Chief, though I don't know what his rank was. He was a small man, very clean and dressed in civilian clothes of blue jeans and a short- sleeved shirt, no matter how cold it was. He never wore a hat, always had his Navy dress shoes on with a brilliant spit shine. I am sure he looked real good when he had left the Naval Air Station or his ship. I never did know where he came from.

By the time he got to the firehouse, he was quite drunk, a little disheveled from having been in a fight during his ejection from his favorite watering hole of the night. He usually came to the front door and then some fireman would invite him in for a cup of coffee and attempt to patch any obvious sore spots, sober him up a bit, then see him onto the bus at the corner, which would return him to his base. Often he'd argue a bit, tell a few sea stories and then get on the bus.

I was a new kid at the station and one night he showed up and I was out front so he asked me if "George" was there. I knew whom he meant so I got George for him and they went into the kitchen/dining area, which was just off the apparatus floor and next to the street. There they sat down to some coffee and a dessert. Things got a bit loud while the old boy was telling some wild sea story and a few of us were listening.

Soon one of the firemen left the group and disguised himself as a Native America with a pillow to create a huge hump back and a rubber mask that looked like Geronimo. He had some long flowing wig and garb that made him appear wrapped in a blanket. He came into the kitchen and stood behind the sailor. Someone introduced "Chief" the sailor to "Chief" the Native American and then things went from good to bad to worse rather quickly.

The Native American said, "Me want Tobak."

Someone told the sailor, "The Chief is in a foul mood. You better give him a cigarette or he'll start a fight. He comes here drunk and goes wild if he doesn't get his way."

The sailor said something like, "Tell him to go to Hell."

There was a louder, "Me want Tobak, NOW!"

The fake Native American slammed his hand down on the table making us all jump from the noise that caused. Then he made a move as if to throttle the sailor. That didn't sit well with the sailor who was visible shaken, but wasn't about to back down. He grabbed the side of the table, which was a huge and sturdy affair, capable of seating about 10 to 12 men comfortably and lifted the whole thing off the floor and threw it at the "Indian."

You can forget the "Tobak." We all ran to get out of sight. The crash of that table back onto the floor was enough to awaken the dead. Our Fire Chief for the downtown district liked his rest and had retired at exactly 10 PM, as that was when the book of Rules and Regulations said firefighters could retire for the night. Not a second before. We knew the commotion would bring him out of his room, bent on firing who ever had been the cause of this unnecessary awakening. Most of us ran to the dormitory and didn't see whatever followed.

Early the next morning we found that the sailor had left just as quickly as we had fled. The "Indian" got caught by the chief and had he not been one of the old time fire fighters, would have found himself suspended at best and at worst fired. He was soon transferred from the Truck Company to the Snorkel, which was supposed to be a demotion in status, a common type of discipline. I think he loved the change of assignment. As for our pal the Navy "Chief," I never saw the man again. He probably had horror stories to tell on his ship.

Dale Freschi had been hanging around firehouses for many years when I first was introduced to him. He had black wavy hair, a ready smile that showed a mouth full of teeth and his face was full, but it seemed like his tongue was too large for his mouth. He was the victim of some brain damage caused by forceps during his birth. He had noticeable indentations in the temple area of both sides of his head from the forceps, which gave him a distinctive look, that was all his own. He was clean, dressed in an old Navy pea coat and black jeans. He never wore a hat, even in the rain. His clothes looked a bit too large for him, giving him a bit of a disheveled look, but they were clean. His shoulders were not wide and he carried some extra weight in his hips and legs.

It appeared that he had some mental problems and after very little conversation, that became quite clear. Though he did seem to be quite functional at menial chores, his whole interest in life was centered on the firehouse, the apparatus and discussing the, "Big fire in Oakland, boy!" He was polite and well mannered. I was told Dale started coming to the firehouse before he was in his teens.

I found him to be most pleasant. He surprised me when the gong system rang for a box alarm in North Oakland. He knew the location, what apparatus would respond and the names of most of the men that manned them. He knew several of the box numbers by heart and knew the first alarm assignment to most any box alarm in the city. For North Oakland and the downtown, he knew all the assignments, through the sixth alarm, which is to say he knew the entire assignment for that alarm box. That was something very few, if any, of the fireman could boast.

Dale was mostly cheerful and just happy to get to spend some time at the firehouse. He was about thirty years of age, lived at home with his widowed mother. He was slow in his movements, awkward, and very predictable; he was deliberate in all his actions. He could get his feelings hurt easily by one of our mean spirited officers, who seemed to delight in running him off from the station. I never liked one particular officer for that very reason.

Dale also knew of any big fires that had taken place in San Francisco or the Bay Area. I don't remember him being able to read, but he would study the pictures in the newspapers and would make a very astute evaluation of what had likely taken place. I found that a lot of his knowledge had come from riding with the District Chief that worked out of 8 Engine. "Roaring John Burns," who would tell Dale, "Get in the car, Dale. We have to go on the route now." In the late 50's, the Chief and his Operator would drive to all the houses in that district, which was 6 Chief's at the time. They delivered whatever mail came out from headquarters and picked up any outgoing mail from each station. While they drove, the chief would discuss any and everything about the fire department, good or bad, purchasing of apparatus, costs, what type, where it was being purchased and anything unusual about it. Dale often knew more about what was happening, or going to happen soon, than all of the Lieutenants and Captains. He even knew more than several of the Chief Officers about things to come. That didn't sit well with those left out of the loop. A gripe we often heard was, "He finds out before I do."

Dale also went to any emergency that 6 Chief responded to, while they were "out on the route." They often arrived first or second in, and Dale sat in the car and watched quietly until things settled down. Then the Chief or his Operator would tell Dale where there was a good spot for him to watch from, and he would go there until they came and got him. If it was a big fire and they were going to be there a long time the Chief would call Dale's mother, or have a policeman do so, and tell her where he was and that they'd bring him home when the time came.

As he got older, Dale learned all the bus routes and ventured around town some. He was allowed, to go only to the downtown, west of Lake Merritt parts of Oakland, as he wasn't to go into east Oakland, mom's orders. When he visited the firehouses he came around about the same time every day. His mom had chores for him to finish before he could go, but once they were done he could be on his way. This was where he had a problem with the one Lt. I have mentioned. We often would find he arrived right at lunchtime, and we'd invite him to stay for the meal. He never turned that down, and the Lt. felt this was costing us too much money. I thought otherwise, and often secretly gave Dale fifty cents to throw on the table to show that he had paid for his keep.

After lunch Dale would go to the apparatus floor and inspect the rigs. If we had a spare rig, he knew where it had been, when it was first line equipment, what Engineer had driven it, if it had been in any wrecks and whose fault they were. He also knew how much hose they carried and how much water, along with about how long that water would last at a car or grass fire if the rig wasn't connected to a hydrant. Dale also knew what all the different colors of the tops of the hydrants and caps meant. (They depicted, at a glance, how much water to expect the hydrant to be capable of delivering and the average pressure of the water from the hydrant.)

Dale's life ended while he was visiting his favorite firehouse, 8 Engine. He got up from lunch and took a few steps toward the door to go home, when he was struck with a fatal heart attack. Even though by then we had EMT trained personnel on hand and the right equipment, he was dead by the time he hit the floor. That is exactly how he would have wanted it, tragic as it was. His mother was very pleased with the life the majority of the firemen had provided him with, and we never told her about any of the bad apples.

Jerry Morretti was a bit of a sadder case than Dale. Jerry knew there was something wrong and could reason things out just a bit better than Dale, so it seemed to me sort of sad that he hadn't been just a bit lower on the intelligence chart, or a few notches up. He was situated where he could do some things and he even had a bit of a part time job that gave him some money of his own. But he was well aware that there were things he couldn't do and a lot of things just didn't make sense to him, though he knew they should. Jerry's job was at the Tuscany Bakery, cleaning up the floors and emptying garbage cans and wastebaskets.

Jerry had a car and became fast friends with Dale. This made them both able to get to all the fire stations and they did, even to all parts of Oakland now that they didn't have to travel on the bus or streetcars. Like Dale, Jerry lived at home with his widowed mother.

Jerry was about six feet tall, with short, sandy, thinning hair, and wore little round glasses that always needed to be cleaned. He was overweight, but not much worse than some of the firemen. He was nervous and talked in spurts of words. Sentences seemed to shoot forth as a thought went by, then there may be a long pause, or another subject entirely, brought forth. He was usually clean with his clothes in order when he got out and about early in the day, but that would fall apart as the day wore on. He was a person that was prone to sweat heavily and his clothes, especially shirts, paid the price. By afternoon he would look rather rumpled and his t-shirt would be stained around the neck, arm pits and down his back.

Jerry knew many of the firemen by name and which houses they worked in, though he had none of the in-depth knowledge of the apparatus and equipment that Dale did. He fell in love with all the ladies that got hired. He didn't say much to them, but he could tell us how each of them was doing in the drill tower and later at the stations, what fires they had gone to and if they had families. He seldom came around without Dale, after they had met, unless to visit a station where his favorite fire lady at the moment, was working. He wasn't a real bother to them and would sit in his chair or out in his car for hours until they said a few words to him, then he would get all flustered, break out in another heavy sweat and go home.

Jerry and Dale got the nicknames of "the Chief and his Operator." They always told us, as they were leaving, "We'll see you next time we're on the route." Then they might go home or go visit another station. Both had to be home before it got dark. They never came around before 10 AM, as they both had things they had to do before their mothers would let them go.

Jerry learned how to make a pineapple upside down cake and took great pride in preparing one for the firemen. He would show up well before dinner, after selecting the day for the cooking session, then he would get all his ingredients together and become a nervous wreck as he mixed the ingredients in a bowl and poured the batter into a large round cake pan or a cast iron skillet, if the station didn't have exactly the size pan he needed. The preparation was something to behold and he became covered in sweat flour and sugar. Then his glasses would get so fogged up he couldn't see through them. He would huff and puff as if he were hand sawing a large redwood log and he'd be trying to wipe off all the sweat with a tea towel.

When the cake went in the oven he would be paralyzed with fright for fear he had left out some ingredient. Mostly the firemen reassured him that once again he had gotten it right and we'd hear, "Boy I hope so."

He would pace around like an expectant father until it was time to remove the cake. Then there was another fear that would grip him. "What if it sticks to the pan?"

I never saw one fail, though I'm sure he would have been mortified if anything were to have gone really wrong. We almost always had someone that had watched the whole process that found they were suffering from some malady such as diabetes, which made eating cake out of the question for their survival. I always thought the heat in the oven probably killed anything carried in the sweat that had dropped from his brow into the batter, so I politely ate a piece and never suffered any ill effects. The cake may have been a bit salty, but good none-the-less.

One afternoon they dropped in late and we invited them to stay for dinner. We found out it was Dale's fiftieth birthday so our cook ran off to the Merritt Bakery and bought a wonderful birthday cake with, "Well wishes for a Happy Birthday" and a fire truck on it. We sang Happy Birthday and let him blow out the candles, just five. He cried and said it was the best birthday he could remember. They stayed until well after dark and Dale's mom called us to see if we had seen them. We promised her that they were fine and that we would send them home right away. As they left, Jerry turned to us and quietly, so Dale couldn't hear, said, "You'd think when you turn 50, you could stay out until nine o'clock."

Firemen were good to them both, but the firemen also could be out of order. One day the pair of them came in 23 Engine while I was working. They both looked frazzled from diving through some of the worse traffic in Oakland on a Saturday morning. I guess they had almost been in a couple of wrecks and had seen a wreck or two on their travels, that morning. They almost ran for cover within the firehouse, as Dale said to us, "A lot of dodos out there today."

The Lieutenant spoke up and said, "I just saw a couple out front."

Thankfully that went over both of their heads, as they looked back to see if they would see the same dodos.

Not very long after Dale died, Jerry's mother also passed away, probably within a year. One of the Captains at 8 Engine took him under his wing and kept him out of trouble. It so happened that a few of the ladies of the night were trying to get his money and it took a lot of the Captain's time and a tremendous effort to keep Jerry from having a permanent house guest or two. Jerry had inherited the house and a few dollars and the girls figured he would be an easy touch. He was rescued often from such goings on. He died of natural causes within a few years of Dale and his mother.

There were probably a hundred other characters that I met through the years, most of whom the firemen had given nicknames to, that were seldom used in their presence. The Suit, The Tie, The Shirt, Mattress Back Mary, The Nun, Chicken Little, Jimmy Jet, all of them examples of these characters. We'd see them on the street; or in the flop houses and shabby bars so often that the nicknames would stick in our minds and if one of them died or was treated by our Medics, we had to find a relative to give us a name for our reports. Some begged for money and some got run off by the Oakland Police when they became suspected of petty theft or repeated drug problems.

Some came to us with good acting ability, and one took a friend and me for the few dollars we gave him to help out with his situation. His story was that his wife had suddenly died in LA and he had to get down there to identify her and get her released to the funeral folks. He had only a small amount of money, which he showed to us, probably $13.00 and change and it would cost him $25.00 to get to LA and see everyone he had to meet. My friend and I each gave him $6.00 and he went on his way, a happy soul.

A few months later he came to the same station, but on a different shift, with the identical story. I happened to be working and of course everyone knew of the prior goings on, so the first fireman he had approached called me down to the watch-room to hear this poor fellows story. When he saw me he said something like "This isn't going to work, is it?" With that we threw him out and he never came back.

CHAPTER 51

Nelda and I get Married

Nelda Rodgers, just became Nelda Mc Arthur

NELDA AND I HAD A medium-sized Wedding at Elmhurst Baptist Church in the evening and after the ceremony went to her folk's house, on 94th and Walnut, changed clothes and left on our honeymoon. The first night we stayed in a motel in Rancho Cordova, near a nice motel Nelda's boss, Dr. Rooney, DDS, had recommended to us. That one had been full, so we took a sort of cheap dive nearby instead. It was scary to spend my first night in a motel, which was also my first night in a bedroom with a girl, which was also my first night with a wife. Wow, all that in one night.

We went on to go to church in Carson City the next morning and then went to Reno for a day and night. I found my bride very lucky at the slot machines and both of us had our pockets and her purse full of coins when we finally got back to our motel room. I don't know how much money we had exactly, but our brother-in-law, George Drennon, had asked me if I had enough money as we were leaving her folk's house and had given me fifty dollars as a loan. This we paid back and we also had enough to pay a month's rent on our apartment on Estudillo. Seventy-five dollars and we still had over a hundred dollars left to last us until payday, which was twice monthly. I'm guessing, we combined had won three hundred dollars, or close to it.

Nelda and I then left Reno late the next morning, were driving to Drennon's cabin at Camp Meeker, CA, to spend a couple of days there. That took us the rest of the day and into the evening. As we arrived between Sebastopol and Camp Meeker we saw lights coming rapidly down a road to our left and could see that there was a very narrow bridge about 500 yards ahead of me that the car belonging to those lights would soon have to cross, so I pulled almost off the road, and stopped.

The car had to make a sharp right turn just before it crossed the bridge and as it made the turn it slid across the road and righted itself enough to get across the bridge but then went into another slide and managed to be almost past our car, but not quite so that he hit us just behind the driver's door and continued down the road a couple of hundred yards before he stopped. I got out of my car and could tell that it had been hit but little damage done and we were not hurt at all. I thought that the other car would come to us, but they looked at their car, got back in and drove away at an even faster rate of speed. I didn't want to chase them, so I drove over to Drennon's cabin and we went inside.

Immediately, fleas attacked me, and they were hungry. I got into a shower and washed dozens of them off and we went to bed. I didn't sleep well as the fleas ate me up. The next morning I took another shower and washed another dozen or more down the drain, got out of there and went to get some breakfast and go home to our apartment. I looked at our car and it had a small dent in the side and a roll of tin wound into the rear bumper. The bumper had taken a swipe out of the other car about five inches wide and three feet long. It wound up like the tin did when you opened a coffee can with a key, if anyone can recall doing that. Not knowing what to do about the collision, we got in the car and returned to our apartment in San Leandro without any further problems.

I bought a motorcycle to get to and from work. A NSU 250 Max, as I recall. I had never ridden a motorcycle, but decided this was the right transportation, so Nelda and I drove down to a motorcycle shop on East 14th Street, Nelson Brothers, and I looked at a nice Harley which was too expensive so I was shown this pretty little NSU. One of the Nelson's took it out the door and told me to get on behind him. We drove two or three blocks and he took me back to the shop and then had me ride it a few yards up a side street and back to his shop and I came home the proud owner of my first motorcycle. No motorcycle license and no insurance, just dumb luck that nothing bad ever happened while I owned it.

Nelda and I began a family on March 26, 1960 with the arrival of our daughter Janette. Nelda was working for Dr. Rooney and I hadn't dared to take on a steady day off job yet. I did work for a moving company one day and was warned by my Lieutenant the next shift at the fire station that recruits couldn't work on their day off. Nelda went back to work after a short recovery break and I babysat. I found that the only way to keep Janette happy without her mother was to lay her on the seat beside me and drive.

She would immediately go to sleep and stay that way until I stopped, then she'd yell bloody murder and I'd drive some more. When I picked Nelda up after work she'd be just a perfect angel and Nelda wasn't sure that I wasn't exaggerating her screaming.

Janette was a beautiful baby. Nelda and her folks took her to Oklahoma when she was a little over three months old and when they stopped for a meal, the waitress asked to take her into the back to show the rest of the family what a pretty little thing she was. She was always very happy and good-natured as long as her mother or her grandmother was in sight. Not so with me.

On the day we were given shorter hours I was transferred again, to 12 Engine. That was a two-piece company at 9th and Alice Streets, right in the center of Chinatown. We had an Engine that pumped water and a hose wagon that naturally carried hose. The best of all worlds, we went to any fire in Oakland if it got big enough. We were one of only two companies that did that, the other being 16 Engine. We also didn't have an inhalator, thus saving us from thousands of useless medical calls. The firehouse itself was a tall two story concrete building, built in the teens to house a horse drawn fire apparatus. It was comfortable, but not like the present plush station houses for fire people. (We can't say "Firemen" anymore.) We didn't have all the amenities that the modern fire stations have today.

We also didn't have computers and all the modern dispatching technology. We had a bell and tape dispatch, similar to a telegraph, with a paper trail. Punch marks in the paper made a coded message that informed us where we were needed and other messages that announced deaths, payday, what apparatus was out of service, and why. There were boxes on street corners that transmitted a four digit code to identify the location. We compared punches in the tape to a card file, called running cards that gave us the location and what companies would respond.

Once we learned the basics of the ticker tape dispatch system it wasn't too hard to keep the status of all the fire apparatus in the city straight. It could get complicated only if there were more than one multi-alarm fire simultaneously. I believe it was quite reliable and had the citizens had respect for themselves and their city, it could have remained a viable means of dispatch. As with many large cities, Oakland changed demographically, and the reliability of the box system went out the window, as the moral decay of many of the populous of Oakland took over. The last year that there were street boxes in Oakland, they were pulled 11,000 times with no justification and not once did they announce a fire that hadn't previously been reported by some other means. So all the street boxes were pulled out and the dispatch was by CAD, which is Computer Aided Dispatch.

On September 4, 1961, which was Labor Day, our son Robert was born. He was a fine lad and sturdy. He ate well and got to crawling about, getting into things and became good pals with his sister Janette. He didn't show much interest in learning to talk. He and Janette had their own little language and it worked fine for them. Then one day Janette was at her grandparent's house and Rob was home with us. He wanted some cookies he knew we had, but had no real way of telling us that and ran around frantically looking for Janette and then trying desperately to make us understand what he wanted. Finally he got Nelda to the cookie drawer and she opened it and got him satisfied with a cookie or two. That put him in a frenzy to learn to talk to us. Within, what seemed like just days, he was able to talk quite well, another crisis nipped in the bud.

March 26, 1965 brought us Darlene, the last of our brood. She was another individual that differed from the others. She had a great sense of humor and was very bold with the neighbor's dog. The dog was a German shepherd and was the watchdog for the family next door. If someone came to the front door, the dog didn't like it and barked and snarled something fierce. Darlene walked over there and the dog met her at the screen, teeth bared and barking loudly. Darlene opened the door, pushed the dog aside and went right in the house. Nelda had seen all this happen but was unable to stop it. She was sure the dog would really hurt Darlene but the dog didn't at all and after that when Darlene was over there playing, Nelda would have to call the lady to get her to bring our kid home, because the dog liked Darlene and wouldn't let anyone bother her, even her own mother.

Darlene also would hide when her mother called her and she wasn't ready to come in. She was the only one of our children that did that. She would make us laugh and that would ruin the chance to reprimand her, thus she got out of a lot of trouble by diverting our energy. Really all three were pretty good kids and when I saw the troubles other's kids got into that ours didn't, I was always very thankful. It had to have been good parenting on the part of their mother that did it. I really had no idea how to be a good parent, having been raised as loosely as I had been by Nellie, and somewhat abandoned, or so I felt, by my parents.

CHAPTER 52

Another Promotion and Builders Concrete Pumping

AT 12 ENGINE WE WERE subject to a steady flow of officers on our shift. After we had been together for a year or so, there was a new Fire Station completed across the street, facing the old one. I never saw the need for that change. Later we found out that a relative of a chief had owned the property, so it became imperative that the city buy it and build a new station. I was just then beginning to sense how government worked. Now instead of turning right to respond to incidents along 8th street, we had to turn left. Obviously that made it worth the expenditure of a few hundred thousand dollars. The citizens were never told the truth regarding the chief's relative having a hard time dumping a poorly kept piece of property.

We moved into the new station and with the new house, we got another change of officer. Our old Lt. was claustrophobic and after we pointed out that the only hazard in the new house was the electrical panel, located conveniently near the only exit to his room, and that he couldn't see out of a window in his room, he told us he'd never work a shift in that house. He never did, as he got his wish to be transferred the day it opened. We were very happy for him and set about getting used to a string of new officers awaiting permanent assignment. That made, a few of us start on the road to promotion. I was deathly afraid of how some of these new leaders thought and was certain they would lead us into disaster. Three firefighter deaths at a grass fire at Mills College, just a couple of years later, proved that our fears were well founded. Common sense didn't count toward a good score on the testing process anymore.

We eventually got the best Lt. I ever worked for, even though it didn't last very long. He got promoted to Captain after a couple of years and we got another Lt. that was not equal to the task of leading. He could pass tests, so eventually he was promoted as far up as Deputy Chief and was remembered as a disaster in all of his positions in the department, by all who worked for him. This pushed us further to study and get promoted to save ourselves. I believe that 12 Engine probably produced more officers and engineers than any other house of its size, through the sixties and into the seventies.

I also got a day-off job driving a truck for a tire-casing dealer. I would drive all over the San Francisco Bay Area picking up used tires from Standard Stations along with some other retail tire sellers and after grading the casing, I would haul them either to the dumps or to a yard off Hegenberger Road that was behind Bruce's Tires. There the casings I kept would be stored and sold to re-cappers. The best casings went to Bruce's and on down the line to some pretty poor quality cappers out in the suburbs of Lodi and such. I also hauled many loads of tires to Fresno to a couple of tire cappers there.

My boss and owner of the company was Whitey Reschert, a fun-loving and friendly type that always spent more than he earned and was constantly just a tad behind in paying his bills. Bruce's Tires couldn't let him go broke, as the owner, Bruce Alexander, had loaned Whitey money so often that Whitey would hurt Bruce's financially if allowed to default. I had a sound job there, as well as with the City of Oakland. I was sent to LA a lot, when my days off would allow for the time. We firemen were now working a sixty-three hour week, one day on and two days off. There were extra days off to make it come out with the proper number of hours and about every five weeks, I would be off Monday and Tuesday on my regular shift off and also off Wednesday because of the extra day off, then off Thursday and Friday again on my regular shifts off. When this happened I would fly to LA and work the week there, coming back Friday night with a load of tires that were saleable and then I'd go to work Saturday at the Firehouse. Sometimes Nelda would fly down and drive home with me. That always was a welcome change of pace.

While I was doing this, I had also been studying to take the Engineer's test. The Engineer is the guy who drives the pumping engine and he is responsible for getting the apparatus to the scene of the emergency safely, but quickly. When at the fire scene he is responsible for delivering the proper amount of water under the proper pressure to maximize the effectiveness of the company's attack on the fire. He also has to maintain the apparatus in such a manner that it is ready constantly to respond to an emergency and that all the tools and accoutrements aboard are in first class working order. Needless to say that also means keeping things filled with fuel, oil and water, as well as all the air bottles and the inhalator O2 bottles ready for service. The Engineer also needs to know the streets of the city, main thoroughfares of the surrounding cities and the county roads.

One day I was working my day off job, unloading casing at Lutz Brothers, which was a recapping company in Benicia. I had an awful nagging feeling that there was something that I needed to be doing that day, other than rolling tires into a bunker for storage. When I got home I remembered that this was the last day to sign up for the engineers test and by now it was much too late. The City Hall was closed and there were no valid excuses for missing a deadline in those days.

Fortunately there was a Lieutenants' test a couple of months following the Engineers. I had never considered myself to be an Officer candidate, but went anyway to take that test and I passed all phases of it. Though I didn't do well on the oral part, my written was good enough to get me on the list. I was disappointed that I had done so poorly, but happy to have passed and when I went to work just after the results of the test came out, I was sent to 20 Engine to act as Lt. That was my first official acting Lt. stint and though I had to learn a lot in a hurry, I did enjoy the job and had only the Captain and the District Chief to answer to. They were both very helpful to me, and the crewmembers made me look like a good leader at all the incidents we went to. I mostly kept my mouth shut and let the crew do their job, assisting where I felt I would be the most help. I finished that period of acting Lt., after thirty days, and I was hooked, I wanted that job.

Also at this same time I was friendly with a fellow Hoseman on the B Shift at 12 Engine, Paul Taylor. Paul was building a home on a lot on Exeter Drive in the Montclair area of Oakland. It was a steep lot and hard to work on, so the contractor had hired Hank's Concrete Pumping to come pump concrete into their forms. Paul told us all about it and I was intrigued and before very long he and I were the proud owners of one Azar Concrete pump and were operating as Builders Concrete Pumping, licensed as a San Leandro Company, because Oakland business license cost more than I felt we could afford. This was an exciting and scary business. We handled a lot of value and if we couldn't deliver, our fame and fortune was put at risk daily. We did all of our own work and made it through the first year showing a profit, which meant taxes and partnership filings and all kinds of new things to me. But we got through it and we even grew the business.

So from then on I studied harder and took a lot of practice tests, bought all the study material I could afford and watched the officers that I worked with. I learned a lot of things about what I didn't want to do, probably more so than what I did hope to do, if I got to be a Lieutenant someday. I also was told by our Assistant Chief to ride in place of our Engineer, to do all the driving and hooking up to the hydrant and all the hose lines before I came to the fire, leaving the Engineer to mind the settings I had made. I still can't believe that the Chief had me do all that and let the Engineer essentially take a free ride, while in reality if he was that incompetent, or disabled, he should have been removed from the job. But no one had the brass to stand up to that responsibility and we worked as outlined above for over a year.

The end date, of the list for Lt. was coming up. A swarm of activity took place to encourage those who were eligible, to quickly retire. I got a call in the middle of the night that I was now on the top of list. My friend Paul Taylor had talked to almost everyone that was eligible to retire. And he had found out what would convince them that now was the time. His interest in doing this was, Paul was a few places ahead of me on the list, and he wanted a Lieutenant's job also. I thought about this for a while and felt it would be unethical to approach someone to retire and I sort of laughed at Paul. He told me to come down to the firehouse, which although it was midnight, I did. We discussed the situation and the possibility of reaching the top of the next list and he convinced me that it would be more detrimental to my family, for me to pass up this opportunity, than it would be to follow the established practice of "buying a job." That is for those down the list to pay someone a stipend to retire, so they could get the opening. So I made a deal that I would help some poor chap make up his mind and he would leave the job. In those days there was no skipping over because of race, religion or sexual preference, as has become the practice just a couple of years after this testing period was over.

The Fire Department allowed us to work on our day off; as long as we requested, and were granted, a "work permit." When I accepted my Lieutenant's badge I in turn requested a work permit, I believe that to be the first one ever requested, until then. I received the permit to operate Builders Concrete Pumping, as did my partner Paul.

The day we got our badges we were given a long lecture in ethics from the Chief of the fire Department. We also had a job for a contractor that afternoon and I began to feel the pressure mounting as the Chief dragged on and on with his speech/reprimand for our "buying a job." He then rambled off how proud we would have felt had we been like the Battalion Chiefs he was about to appoint, and how they had honorably earned their jobs. Little did he know that Paul had found jobs for both of them; as he had found a job for himself, and for the rest of us on that Eligibility list. We did get to our jobsite and got set up to pump concrete just as the mixer trucks arrived.

So in due course I had been promoted and I was determined to excel as a new Lieutenant, which I did. I found men worked for me, whether old timers or new kids, all seemed to believe I would always take good care of them. I tried my best to do that and let everyone that worked for me enjoy the job and rise to their highest potential level. I tried to be fair and even in work assignments and to give credit whenever it was due and avoid the sense of disciplining when I had to alter some behavior.

I had been sent to 4 Engine/2 Truck and worked there for about five years before I took and passed the test for Captain. No more searching for a job, I finished high enough that I was guaranteed a job and my friend Paul had been kicked off the list, having failed the oral examination. He was a "marvelously at ease" sort of fellow in any situation and I couldn't believe the oral board had failed him. I had told him before he went to the oral that I thought he should get his haircut and he had said he would. As we talked after, I found he hadn't had it cut and that had been the basis for failing him. He appealed and we all wrote letters telling of our experience at the oral exam and what we thought of the process.

I explained that when I went into the oral board portion, I was introduced to a black gentleman that was introduced as a Chief from San Francisco. I believe they told us his name was Chief Dennums. However, we all knew he was a Hoseman, not a Chief. I added to my comments that this was confusing to us and unfair. We had all been trained to lie to the oral board about how good we were, and about all the things we knew about the fire service, but here the oral board was obviously lying to us. Evidently a lot of shenanigans had gone on in the scoring of a written question that we had to write, a long explanation of our thoughts and why we would act the way we did.

The end result was after a hearing before the City Council, the test was certified with Paul Taylor on the bottom and he had no score attached to his name. All the rest of us had some score above 70%. We were given a written and you had to pass with 70% or better, then we had to get 70% or better on the oral. Had they given Paul 70% on his oral it would have moved him ahead of a black guy on the list and how would that have looked? So Paul received no score, we all were promoted off that list and so it was settled without the threatened lawsuit.

I took classes at Chabot College, San Mateo College, Oakland's Merritt College and Cal State Hayward. Most of them were Fire Science and Municipal Management, or something to do with city governing. To break it up I also took a couple of creative writing classes and art history, but obviously no English. While I was doing this I got involved with the Girl Scouts and Boy Scouts. There was a program offered by St. Mary's College that would allow me to combine all my credits and complete another year of classes with them and I would end up with a Bachelor of Science degree in Municipal Management, so I signed up and completed that. The GI bill paid for a lot of those classes and so the time in the USMC had paid off in a way I had never anticipated.

Paul and I sold the Concrete Pumping business to a competitor who had more customers than equipment to service them and we were about the opposite, we had equipment that sat at our yard sometimes for want of work, so he needed our machines and we had been getting burned out with all the hassles with unions and the unsteady pace of the building industry. So we sold and kicked back for a while. Paul took a job as the Fire Chief at Meeks Bay at Tahoe, near his house at Homewood and I stayed at Oakland Fire for several more years, working at 1 Engine, then back to 23 Engine for a year or two then about four years at 16 Engine and about eight or so at 18 Engine on the Truck and finished out my career at the foot of Grove Street back on the Fireboat. I was retired for disability, due to a number of on duty injuries, in October of 1991.

CHAPTER 53

Austin Healey's

BY THE END OF 1974 Paul Taylor and I had sold Builders Concrete Pumping to Bruce Cunningham. He had a business in Larkspur that was in need of more customers and another large pump. Our business filled his need and his buying us out filled our need to kick back and have some fun without a lot of pressure on us daily. We were both happy that it was Bruce Cunningham that bought us out as he did have a good business and was located in an up and coming community. It didn't hurt that his wife owned a large piece of property that was slated to become a ferry terminal and the surrounding area that would become a shopping center. We just couldn't see a down side to this sale. Paul's brother, Wayne, was our lawyer and did the paperwork for us so we were protected and Bruce was happy. I would run our big pump for him for a month, or until he trained an operator, whichever happened first. He got all of our pumping machines, equipment and our pickup truck.

The day everything was going away to Bruce Cunningham, it dawned on me that the pickup truck had been my second car and with Nelda now working again, I had to find a way to work. I had always liked MG and Jaguar cars so now that I was financially flush, or so it seemed at the moment, I began to read the car ads listing the British cars for sale. Jaguars were a bit too pricey, MG's a bit too small for a family man, but the car that really caught my eye was an Austin Healey 3000, 1965 Mark III, roadster. I went to look at it and was surprised to find that the trunk lid had been smashed, but otherwise, it was a fine running machine with a lot of power. I bought it and took it to the fire- house the following morning.

At the Station, the firemen told me what a piece of junk it was and how all of the British cars were plagued with problems with their electronics and their carburetors. I was used to that type of treatment of any new purchase from the firemen and though it bothered me some, I wasn't going to let it show. I got a guy to commit to fixing the trunk lid for me and he pointed out another spot that needed attention. He had a body shop for his day off job and to keep his sons employed. I had seen their work on other cars and trusted them to fix my machine to top-notch condition for just a couple of hundred dollars. I even made an appointment to bring it to them when they had time for it, a week or so away.

The next morning I drove home from the firehouse and just as I turned off 14th Avenue, onto the 580 on ramp, not a mile from the firehouse, I heard a definite sound of a piece of metal that had just snapped. As I mashed down on the gas pedal the engine revved right up to the red line, but the car barely moved. The metal that had snapped was the diaphragm spring that applied pressure to the clutch disc to force it toward the flywheel, thus providing the power from the engine into the transmission and on to the rear wheels. I am a bit mechanically inclined so, I recognized the problem and knew that racing the engine would not do any good. I let the engine slow down until all the parts were turning at about the same speed and gradually increased the engine speed. The clutch held enough to get me going with traffic and I knew I could get the car home.

After a long circuitous route to my house, so as to avoid any steep hills, I got the car in my garage and sheepishly went in to tell my bride that my new shiny toy was broken already. I had to swallow some pride and go get a repair manual from the British Motors store near me. I read how to change the clutch spring and proceeded to get to work. Some of the tools to do the job were Wentworth, a British size, some were metric and some were the American size. I had to go beg tools here and there to finish up my job. A few days later I drove it to the body shop.

When I retrieved it from the body shop, it was primed and ready for me to paint. The bodywork was very nice and I decided to paint it the same color as a car in the neighborhood, so I went to the lady that owned that car and asked what color it was. It was Mallard Green and I purchased the paint and went to work on taking the car somewhat apart to paint it properly. It took me a week or two to get it painted with several coats of synthetic lacquer and get the finish rubbed out to a high gloss. I was very pleased with how well the paint job turned out.

Nelda and I joined the Austin Healey Club of America, Pacific Centre. The President made us feel welcome and we went on a road trip to Pinnacles National Monument, near Soledad, CA. Mr. President and his better half seemed to be battling the entire time, so we chummed up with some of the others and found that this was a way of life with those two. We avoided getting too close to them, but had a lot of fun with the others. We took the car to San Diego and showed it to Rich and Dolores. We also drove it to many events with the Austin Healey Club in Yosemite, Tahoe and Santa Cruz. There were others I know, as there was some type of tour almost every month and we attended as many as we could.

We also teamed up with the Morgan Club for a road race in Marin County. This was an unsanctioned event, put on by the clubs. We drove from the outskirts of Novato over a winding back road to Marshall. We were timed and surprisingly, at least to me, one of the best times was set by a club member that worked with me, Mike Kelly, but not in his Austin Healey, this time he drove the family Chevrolet sedan. That took a lot of the starch out of more than a few collars. I forget if we ever got any type of trophy or not, but it was sure a lot of fun for all of us. And the ride back I had time to admire the beauty of the Marine County back roads.

I bought a few other Austin Healey's over the next several years. I usually had one that ran and one I was working on. I traded the first one I had owned in on a 1975 1/2 Jensen Healey. This was a more modern car with a bit more comfort and could travel farther on a gallon of gasoline as well as holding the road better than a lot of the older Healey's. It also was faster than most cars I had ridden in. Mike Kelly and I drove it to Long Beach to watch the first Gran Prix race held there. The race was September 28, 1975, though we went two days early to see some of the practice runs and visit the pit crews before the actual race took place. On our way to the race we were closing in on our own land speed record when close to Avenal we decided we were traveling too fast, we had caught up with the California Highway Patrol aircraft that was watching for the likes of us on Hwy 5. We still arrived in Long Beach within less than five hours of leaving San Leandro, approximately 385 miles driving distance.

I purchased a BN 1, Austin Healey, which was similar to the first ones to come to the USA. The engine was a 2660 cc four cylinder, mated to a three-speed transmission and an electrically activated overdrive. That gave me the equivalent of a five-speed transmission and it was a lot of fun to drive. I took it to Fresno with the A/H club and Mike Kelly and I drove it in some parking lot races, where all you did was try to beat a clock. For safety reasons only one car at a time was allowed on the track. We did rather well and had a lot of fun. On the way home, the engine quit in the middle of a bridge and I had to make a quick repair on the electric fuel pump, to get home. I hit it with a lead hammer and that freed up the points so it would again pump fuel.

I found a few days later, that the repair hadn't totally cured the problem. I had just had surgery on my right knee and took the car to my therapy in Castro Valley. After therapy, for an unknown reason, I took the freeway home. On one of the long bridges the fuel pump again ceased to work, I was pretty much in familiar territory so in order to not stop on the freeway, I made an abrupt right turn at the end of the bridge and drove down an embankment from the freeway to a surface street where I had to abandon the car and walk a mile and a half home. Hitting it again with the hammer didn't work this time. There is nothing like walking that far to exercise a torn up knee.

When I got home, there was no one there so I got to work making a "jury rigged" auxiliary gasoline tank from an empty quart brake fluid can. I soldered a short pipe to the top of the can and soldered a long pipe right next to that one. One went just into the can the other went to within about a quarter inch of the bottom inside the can. I filled it with gasoline and attached two flexible rubber hoses to the two pipes. Now I had a one quart gas tank and a man powered fuel pump. By blowing into the hose hooked to the short pipe I would force gasoline out of the long pipe, which I hooked into the little car's fuel line. All I had to do was keep blowing into that hose and the car would run. I hooked it up and drove home, only to get caught by my neighbor, a mechanic, and my wife, a worrier. I got called a few things that amounted to not too bright, but even with all that, I had managed to get the car home and could now repair the fuel pump properly, Someone, even made a smart remark about a reusable Molotov Cocktail.

Sometime while we were in the Austin Healey Club, the club had some extra money and decided it would be a fun thing for the members to get a chance to meet the man that made the cars. I had just bought the 75 ½ Jensen Healey and was going to make sure that he saw it, so I signed up for the tour. We would all drive our cars up Highway 101 to Eureka, Ca., close to the Oregon border, on the coast. It is an absolutely lovely drive any time of year, but this was late summer and all the roads were clear and the tourist traps open for business. The drive-thru redwood in the Avenue of the Giants and the house made from one tree were both open to impress us. Of course the best and most impressive part of any of it is the trees themselves. They were magnificent and the weather was perfect for sightseeing.

We left the overcast of the Bay Area and were in bright sunshine as soon as we reached the San Rafael Bridge and headed past San Quentin Prison for Hwy 101 to take us north. I had my Jenson Healey glistening, as I wanted it to look its best for Donald Healey. We made a stop along the way and as several of us had met the parade of Healey's at different points along the way, this opportunity was taken to introduce our guest to all the members and he had a few words of appreciation for the members having honored him with this trip to California. The handshakes and salutations over with, we again drove north. The little cars all behaved well and there were no fears of troubles this trip. Everyone appeared in a splendid mood, and the road was good, light traffic and clear weather for the entire 275-mile trip.

At our next rest stop, Donald Healey approached me and said he had never seen a Jensen Healey with spoke wheels. He was curious if I had put them on or if it came that way from the dealer. I explained that the car stood just as I had purchased it new from British Motors in Oakland. He told me that he liked the look and so I asked if he'd like to ride a bit in it, or he could drive it if he would like to. He declined my offer with a laugh and asked me something to the effect, "Why would I ride in one of those bumpy little cars when I can ride in a most comfortable Chevrolet sedan with air conditioning and a radio I can hear?" I really didn't have an answer for that, so he rode on in the comfort of the Chevy and I bounced along in my Jensen Healey.

Donald Healey was a great sport. Most of us were a bit tired after the long drive in our little cars and after a family-style dinner at the Samoa Cook House, a bit of a poolside party after and perhaps a glass of wine or two, we were ready for bed. He wanted to go dancing with the ladies and have a little fun. I was told that he was up past midnight drinking and dancing with any who would participate, then had a midnight swim and retired for the night. He was also up early the next morning and trying to find anyone interested in finding some breakfast. Not bad for an 80 year old gentleman.

Nelda and I left the group after a couple of days and drove to Hwy 5 at Reading, spent the night, then drove down the Sacramento Valley, stopping in Orland to visit her cousins, then we continued home. It had been a busy long weekend, but we enjoyed meeting Donald Healey and hearing his stories of starting his car companies and failures and successes. Most all the nuts and bolts for the Austin Healey's were left over's from the war effort. He was Knighted, Sir Donald Healey in 1972 for his contribution to the UK export business.

People began to offer me serious money for my Austin Healey's and all the spare parts I had accumulated, so just before we moved to Danville, I sold the last one and all my spares. Big mistake, the prices have gone so high that I can't justify buying any toy that costs that much now.

CHAPTER 54

Change of Day Off Job and Vacation Scheming

ONE DAY IN 1977, MY friend of many years, Bob Comella called me and asked if I was interested in building a house with him. He had built a few before and I thought this would be perfect opportunity for me to learn a useful trade. He had also driven and operated concrete pumps for me for a while, besides building the framing on the addition to our house in San Leandro. He had also often called me to assist in some remodel job he had. I had called him to help me with a lot of things about my house also. We knew how we both worked and were happy to work together again. He told me he would have his brother Tom and another guy I didn't know, Brad Vincent there to help, along with Don Parker, whom I did know. All were Oakland firemen.

So we went to work in Danville building a house for Don Parker, also a fireman. We started out by digging the foundations, boring pier holes, placing the steel and pouring the concrete. Though we all knew how to finish concrete, Bob had hired a guy to finish the garage floor. That gentleman showed up a little drunk and did a foul job of the floor so that when he declared it done and left, we took a broom to it and after toweling it again and broom finishing it, the floor turned out okay.

Bob's uncle Joe would come out to check out our work. He told me one day while I was doing something, that "You do that just like I do." I told him I knew that, since he had taught Bob, and Bob had taught me it should be obvious in reality since Joe had taught me, and everyone else on this job. He thought that was quite funny since he now had a whole bunch of firemen he didn't really know that were doing things the way he had done them as a young builder himself.

I worked on Parker's house until it was almost done, then I went on vacation and when I came back it had been finished. I wasn't out of a side job for long, as Parker had a friend, Jack Parent, who owned a lot in Bollinger Canyon and he wanted us to build a house for him. The same crew went over there and did the same thing, dug all the foundation and built the house from there on up. This one had a lot of trim around the windows and Bob put me to work on doing that. I told him I wasn't sure I could do it but he was sure I could and told me to just take my time and measure everything twice before cutting. So I did and I thought he would be upset with how long it was taking, but he wasn't, and the trim looked great. There was one piece that was a long bull nose on the top of a step-down into a room. That one piece of Oak had cost a lot of money and I measured that one about four times before I made the first cut. I was sure that would get me fired if the cut was wrong, but it was correct and then I had to repeat that operation for the room just opposite the one I had just finished. It had the same step-down. I thought I was pretty good when I got that done. I guess Bob did also, because he called me later to help him with a house that had lots of wood trim everywhere, but he didn't get that bid. I was still proud that he felt I was good enough at it to be on the job if he did get it.

In 1977, while I was assigned to 1 Engine as a Captain, I became a bit bored with the pace there. It had changed so much downtown that over the years we had started to respond to more medical calls and car fires, than building fires. So to get some excitement into things, I wrote a letter to the "Captain, One Engine, London Fire Department," something to the effect that I would like to exchange homes with any fire people that wanted to visit the States and we could save a lot on hotel costs if we just exchanged homes. I wanted to visit London in the coming year or two.

After a month or two went by, I got a reply from a man that informed me that he was the Editor of the Fireman Magazine for the London Fire Brigade and that he would publish my letter if I gave him permission to do so. He also informed me that there was no "London Fire Department," that it was a brigade and he mentioned that his new magazine was shared throughout the country and also went to Australia and several other countries, including France and Germany. So I told him to publish it if he would and sat back to see what the response would be.

Out of that I got a number of responses. Interestingly, none came from a promoted person. All that responded were the bottom rank of Fireman. Also my timing was bad, the London Firemen had gone on strike and it didn't go well for them. Many of the older guys were very disillusioned with the fire service and were looking for any excuse to leave with a disability and the younger guys were just hoping that it would get better if they could find another line of work.

I also got responses from Australia and New Zealand as well as the Channel Islands. Basically they all followed much the same pattern. They had no money for travel and that they still would like to put me up at their place so I could have the experience of seeing their country. Most of the British Firefighters seemed to badmouth their country quite a bit. That was mostly due to their strike, I believe.

I also heard from a Korean lady, married to a German Fireman. She had traveled through Alaska for a day and learned English while there. He spoke no English. But we were welcome to come to Bremen and visit. They wouldn't mind coming to the US if they got where they could afford to. Right then wasn't the time for them to do it as she going to have a baby.

So I culled through all the letters and tried to make a decent response to all of them. I told them that I would like to visit with the ones in the London Brigade that had expressed the desire to someday come over to the USA. There were only about four of them and after a few exchanges of letters, one guy volunteered to be my contact. He even had booked a visit to the Bay Area and would be staying with another Oakland fireman, Bob Strohmeier, for a few days then come stay with me. I had arranged for the other fireman to meet him on a quick trip to London and they had gotten on well together. That person was Les Williams who was working in the London Brigade and living in Earlsfield, near Wimbledon, with his wife Sue.

I was now back at Engine 23, and had a young crew that seemed interested in my scheme for a trade of houses, though none of them wanted to be involved, save Bob Strohmeier, the fellow that was on his way to visit Les in London. When Bob got back, he was full of good cheer and stories of the good times his wife and he had with Les, even if it had only been a day or two at their hotel, but they both were anticipating Les' visit to Oakland and the Bay Area.

Then Les and Sue Williams came to visit, in the late summer or early fall of 1977. My friend Bob Strohmeier took him to a cabin on the Russian River, all over San Francisco and I had to almost beg them to make time to come to my house for a while. They finally did and I found Les and his wife to be having a wonderful time here and looking forward to the time I would bring Nelda there. We spent only a couple of days together here as he had spent almost his entire vacation with the Strohmeiers'. But we determined that in the spring I would come to London and we'd see a few people and stay with them for a few days each. He would set it up there and I would just be passed around from home to home and there would also be a week trip to Scotland that he'd book for me on a British Tour, much cheaper than if I booked it as an American.

We made all the arrangements and I had talked to the lady in Germany through a German-speaking fireman in Oakland, Fred Schreiber. The reason I did that was that we had a breakdown in language along the line. I had written to inform her that we couldn't come to Germany and she had written back to tell me how excited they were that we were coming. She and her husband had both gotten off work for the month of April so they would be able to accommodate us any time we got there. So Fred assured her we would be there in Bremen and that I would have a German speaker call her from London and inform her of exact time of arrival. I picked out a tour from some brochures Les had sent me and we sent him some money to book it for us.

CHAPTER 55

1978 European Trip

WE FLEW OUT OF OAKLAND and arrived, by way of Bangor, Maine, in London the following morning. Les Williams met us at Gatwick Airport and asked if we wanted a drink. I declined, thinking alcoholic drinks, but learned he meant coffee or tea, which I would have loved. It had snowed and all of southern England was covered in several inches. Les drove like all taxi drivers, that had been his day off job and we surrendered to the thought that this was probably our end, here we were flying down the wrong side of the road, (in our mind) in snow and ice at breakneck speed in a car the size of the trunk in many American cars with a driver who was extremely difficult to understand. He had a Cockney accent and stuttered badly, so that and our unfamiliarity with the British accent made him hard to follow.

But get to his home we did and met his wife Sue again and we went to Wimbledon, Southern Carburettors*[11] and then over to Hampton Court Palace. A couple of days with the Williams' and we were delivered to another couple, the Murphy's, Les and Madelaine. They along with the Hall's, Bill and Allison, took us to several places in London and up to Cambridge. We toured the area of the American Cemetery and along the River Cam to King's College and drove back to London.

The following day we were taken to Houston Station and boarded a train for Carlyle. There we boarded a coach that took us on a seven- day

11 I was restoring an Austin Healy and found that Southern Carburettor's was one of the places to buy parts, thus my interest in visiting this firm.

tour of Scotland, which was wonderful. We met a lot of stuffy people who couldn't laugh at the coach driver's jokes, because he was Irish. After a couple of days they got over the stuffiness and began to enjoy themselves. We went out to Mallaig and over to the Isle of Skye, to Dunvegan Castle, home of the Mac Leods of the Islands and then to Loch Ness, Culloden and up to John O'Groats. From there, back to Edinburgh and then back to Carlyle, where we boarded a train to London. Les Williams met us at Houston Station and took us to meet Doug and Pat Smith. We stayed with them a couple of days and then they took us to Heathrow for our flight to Bremen.

Our flight to Bremen was short and when we got there, Soon Hai Ahlbrecht, and her husband, Helmut met us. Her English was not terribly good as we got into their automobile, however, by the time we reached their home, her English had come back to her and she was quite easy to understand. Helmut and I poured over pictures and conversed with gestures and laughter, sometimes having to call Soon Hai in to interpret to get us back on track, but all was good. The following morning I got up to the smell of fresh bakery goods and found that the person that had made the call for us in London had been told that I liked bread and jelly, so Helmut had purchased several breads from a nearby bakery. They had also bought several jellies for me to choose from. They showed us around for a while, and then they had to go to a funeral and left us to enjoy a nice hot bath and a little peace and quiet.

When they came back we went to Helmut's uncle's farm, a few miles out in the country. It was also a dairy and they made cheese and wine. So we had a bit of all that and had a wonderful time getting to know Jon Lüchen and his wife. They had a typical German farmhouse with one end of it connected directly to a barn. Under the stairs to the upper floor of the house was where they hung meats, such as hams and sausages to be smoked. A small peat fire was kept below the stairs for that purpose. Strangely there were no obvious odors from all that.

Jon Lüchen took us out to his fields and proudly showed us his crops of hay and grains, which had just started to come up nicely. We also were shown where he digs the peat for his fire and which layer he uses to cure his meats. He also showed us the wooden shoes that he used to use in the bad weather.

The Ahlbrecht's took us to meet his family. His father had been in Holland during the war, a big kid, he was put into the SS and admitted that they did terrible things there. He said they had no choice and that he hoped that we didn't hold that part of his life against him. He had been very young then, and now would like to visit the USA, but felt as a former SS member that was out of the question. They introduced us to their daughter and her husband, a Jewish man. So now he has a Korean daughter in law and a Jewish son in law. Not what you would expect of an old SS Trooper. We all had a fine meal together and it seemed everyone got along quite well.

After our meal we went to see the fireboat and the fire station. We were given quite a nice ride up the river on the fireboat and told all about it by one of the firemen who had worked ships in the San Francisco Bay, before becoming a fireman. I was also treated to a ride up in a snorkel that went about 50 meters into the air, stopping beside the steeple on a church. We saw the station Helmut worked in and his apparatus, a Volkswagen Ambulance. Much of this was very familiar as they did a lot of things very much like we did them in Oakland.

During that visit we also saw the very thin houses of Bremen. The properties were taxed on the street frontage of the house so it turns out that the smallest one was, if I understood correctly, just one meter in width; however it was two stories tall and about thirty feet deep.

Early on our fourth day in Bremen, we boarded a train that would take us through Belgium, all the way to Ostend, there we were to take the ferry to Dover and return to Strood, near Rochester, which was where the Smith's home was. This turned into quite an adventure. All went real well and was a very pleasant journey through Germany. We crossed into Belgium and noticed that the train seemed to be running slower than it had been and several people seemed concerned. One pretty lady in particular seemed to be talking to anyone that looked in any way to have some authority. By the time we got to Brussels we gathered that we were not going to make our connection with the ferry in Ostend. The pretty lady and a couple of other ladies seemed to have joined up, and were planning something together, but they were speaking in German and I had no clue what it was they said. I was sure it had to do with the train running slowly.

I finally spoke to one of them and she told me there was some labor problem. Some man told Nelda the train was going on strike. The pretty lady confirmed that and talked to us quite a bit in very good English. She was a tour guide that was to pick up a bus the following day near London and take a busload of American tourists some place in England for a week or two. She had usually flown from Germany but thought the train would be fine since she had the time and it was much less expensive. Her mother had told her to just fly and forego the train, but she was a tour guide. "What could possibly go wrong on a train?" Now she knew.

When the train got to Brügge, it stopped and after a bit the engineer walked off across the tracks and disappeared. We talked with the ladies again and the pretty one told us to watch her bag and she would be back after a bit. So she left the train and I didn't see where she went, but a while later she ambled back and told us to get off this train slowly, like we had no place to go, but to go to another train on another track and to bring her luggage there with us. "Don't be in a hurry and act like you have no idea what you are doing," she told us. That wasn't hard to do because we didn't have any idea what we were doing. We did as she told us, got off the train and wandered about a bit, then got on the other train.

We sat on that second train for a few minutes alone. The other ladies slowly joined us and we all sat wondering what would happen next. I had the pretty lady's luggage and Nelda had ours. We all hoped we had done the right thing. Then the pretty lady came back and sat next to us and told Nelda that she would need me at the next stop, which was Ostend. She had made some flirtations with a Belgium Marine and talked him into driving this train to Ostend. I was to be the reason she couldn't go with him when we got there. Jealous husband and all, she just couldn't get free. I was hoping that this didn't end as poorly as I could have imagined was possible. Sure enough the train began to pull out of Brügge and was headed for Ostend, which is only a few kilometers away, but still we were too late to catch the ferry we were scheduled to be on.

As we pulled into Ostend, the lady stuck real close to me and we all got off and walked over to the ferry terminal. I never did see any Marine, but I felt really lucky once we were in the ferry terminal. I asked the lady how the phone worked, as I had to call Doug Smith and tell him we would be late, if we got there at all tonight. So she asked to see my money and we went to a phone. She told me to put some of my coins in the phone and I asked her how many, "just some.' was the answer and I heard a dial tone after a few coins went into the slot. I dialed Doug and explained our situation and told him I would call again whenever we got to Strood.

The ferry took us to Dover and after we got through Customs the lady again asked that I watch her bags. She would leave the ferry terminal and we were to stay inside, so that I could let her back in, as the doors were closed to entrance from outside. She was going to find us a ride to Strood and herself a ride to London. A few minutes later she rushed back in and she told me she had a lot of offers for a ride for herself to London. Seems most of the truckers were quite willing to take her on as a passenger. But, there was nothing for us to Strood tonight. I asked about a hotel and she grabbed a phone and made a couple of calls and told me to come with her. We did and we were told to get into a taxi and he would take us to our room for the night. I asked her, "What about you?" She said, "Oh, I'll accept a ride to London." We went to a nice hotel that was reasonably priced and she went off into the night. We didn't even know her name. I had to tell Doug it would be next morning before we would be back in Strood.

We got up, had breakfast at the hotel and caught a train to Strood the next morning. Spent another day with the Smiths and the following day, Les Williams took us back out to Gatwick and we flew back to Oakland.

We had survived our first real trip out of the states and had a wonderful time. We had made new friends, many of whom later came to our house and stayed a while, except for the folks in Germany. They never did come over, but we stay in touch with them.

The Murphy's and Hall's came over together and we had a great time with them. Bill Hall seemed to have read a lot about the Donner Party and the history of the west in general, so I took them to Reno and Tahoe. We stopped at Donner Lake and went to the Donner Party Memorial. We also took them to Disneyland and San Diego Zoo as well as meeting my sister's family in Chula Vista. They spent several days going about San Francisco, Russian River and any other spots they showed an interest in. I know we went to Yosemite, because of the wonderful mispronunciation Allison did on its name, calling it, "Yoe's a Mitty." They also rented a car and went to Las Vegas for a couple of days. I arranged a ride on the fireboat for the men, and then they spent a night at the fire station, though we had no responses that night.

I thought they must have had a wonderful time and though I heard that Les and Madelaine had divorced and he has remarried and moved to Switzerland, we soon lost contact and they haven't ever gotten back in communication with us. We certainly enjoyed getting to know them and still have wonderful memories of all the places we went together, both in London and here in the States.

Pat and Doug Smith came over with their two boys, Terence and Roy. We all went to Disneyland and San Diego. They became friends with my sister and brother in law in Chula Vista as well as with the rest of our family in the Bay Area. We visited the Drennon's*[12] cabin in Camp Meeker and spent time with the Smith's at Lake Tahoe. They seemed to have a great time and we enjoyed showing them around all the places we could think of that they might enjoy. Doug spent a shift with me at the fire station and we had a run in the evening that took us to an incident near where the wife of one of the Assistant Chiefs' had a store. He hap-

---

12 George Drennon was married to my wife's sister, Elizabeth, better known to most as Jane.

pened to be there and came over to see what we were up to and noticed a guy in a made up uniform that he didn't recognize. He asked me where that fireman came from and I told him, "On loan from London." That seemed to satisfy him and I was never reprimanded for having a guest fireman on the apparatus.

CHAPTER 56

Meeting the Lützel's

ONE DAY IN THE SUMMER of 1980, while assigned to 16 Engine, Nelda and I happened to be in Alameda, for what I don't remember. We were driving back toward Oakland on Webster Street and I saw a sign for Mexicali Rose. The owners ran two restaurants, one in Oakland and one in Alameda. I had heard that they had excellent Mexican food but had never been inside either place. I asked Nelda if we should stop for a meal and she agreed, so in we went and sat down to a fine meal.

Just as we got settled in and were having our salsa and chips I noticed a guy and girl come in. They appeared a bit odd, not strangely attired, but they appeared cold and sort of lost in a way. I also noticed that they ate like Europeans. They held the knife in their right hand and fork in the left, but they didn't switch back as Americans do, to take the bite to our mouth. That got my curiosity up and eventually I went to their table and made enquiry as to where they were from. The gentleman said Morro Bay, in a mildly German accent, very understandable though. So I said that I meant originally, before Morro Bay and he explained that they were from by Stuttgart, Germany, were on a bike ride to stay with a BMW Club member in Alameda, but hadn't been able to contact him. They had tried for a couple of days and no answer, so they didn't know just where they would go tonight. I asked them to come to our house after dinner and that they could stay there, and that we'd take them around to San Francisco this evening. They agreed and as we left the restaurant later, he asked me if it would be okay for his wife to ride with us and he'd follow us home on his motorcycle. We did that and arrived home a half-hour later with Fritz and Madeleine Lützel.

We asked them if they would like to take a bath and get warmed up, as they were obviously freezing cold, and then we'd take the car and we would go to San Francisco. I would show them the sites to visit the following day or two, whatever they liked. So we went for the 49-mile drive through San Francisco and over the Golden Gate Bridge to Sausalito. They took in all the sites and were very pleased that we were so nice to them. Both of them spoke very good English. Madeleine had worked as a domestic in Nottingham, England and Fritz had studied English at the University in Heidelberg.

We also found that Fritz worked for Lufthansa Airlines and that he had a friend he had spoken with in LAX about his trip and the fact they both had full leathers and planned to ride up the coast to San Francisco area, then to Tahoe, to Las Vegas, go see the Grand Canyon, then on to San Diego and sell the bike and fly home. The friend told them to leave the leathers at home, it was ninety four degrees at LAX and Tahoe and Vegas would all be warmer, so they had come away with light clothes and had been okay as far as Morro Bay, but when they left there, they followed Hwy 1 to SF. The fog was close in and the temperature never got much above sixty degrees. No wonder they were frozen.

The next day we loaned them some warmer outerwear and they went to San Francisco and did all we had shown them, and more. They came back and had made a full day of it. I had to go to work the next morning and made a map for him of things I thought they would enjoy and put in such things as Hwy 4 and the Big Trees, Yosemite, Death Valley and a couple of the passes through the Sierras. I also gave them a small map and address of 16 Engine and told them to come by for breakfast. I told them that I worked with one of the finest cooks I had ever come across in my whole fire department career. His name was Bill Reeves, and he was up to the task. He did his level best to make that breakfast the best one that could be found in the USA.

After breakfast at the Fire House of fruit, omelets, hot cakes, hash browns, toast, fruit juices, bacon and hot coffee; they were off, following my map toward their eventual destination in San Diego. After a week or so he called me and said they had made it to San Diego, "no worries" and they had gone everywhere I had mapped out for them, they were just now soaking in somebody's hot tub and would be flying out in a couple of days. The only problem now was that they still had to sell the bike, but the ad was running and he had his hopes up. I found out later that the bike sold just before they left and they were happy for that. It would have cost a lot of money to ship it home. I also found out the cost would have been his own fault, because part of his job with Lufthansa was to set the rates for all airfreight they carried.

CHAPTER 57

Our First Harley Davidson

I BOUGHT A 1975 HARLEY Davidson Sportster, 1000 cc motorcycle, from a fireman I worked with. He gave me the key and told me that if I'm ever drunk, trying to remember which way the key goes in, the notch is up. I told him if I'm drunk, I certainly hope that I have lost the key. So now we had a machine to tackle the winding roads of the coast and the Sierra's. We took our first long ride down to San Diego to visit Richard and Dolores. That is about a 600-mile trip from here and we thought it would be a good way to get our feet wet in motorcycling. So we bought a couple of long strapped bags, threw a few spare clothes in them and tied a tent and two sleeping bags on the back and took off down Hwy 1, which is the Coast Hwy in California and is a beautiful ride. This road seems made for motorcycles as it winds its way along the coast with some places climbing the side of the cliffs and other spots it is flat and smooth. As one drives south, the ocean is always on your right side. Some of the cliffs are sheer drops for several hundred feet into the ocean. This is not a road for the timid.

We had a smooth ride into Morro Bay and I had to fuel up and check my oil, which was fine, but the guy behind me was getting anxious to get to my pump so I just pushed the bike forward and Nelda went in and paid for the fuel. She came back, jumped on and we took off for Santa Maria and our KOA campground for the night. We hadn't gone a quarter of a mile when Nelda tapped me on the shoulder to inform me we had an oil leak and it was pumping hot oil onto her leg. I pulled off the road and her pants leg was soaked in oil. I hadn't put the cap back on the oil bag when I had checked the oil and the motor was now seriously low on oil. Luckily we were still close to stores.

We went into a 7-11 Store and bought a quart of oil, which filled the oil bag and we used some paper towels to dry off Nelda's pant leg and continued to the KOA where she changed pants and washed her oil covered ones and I set up our tent. We had some type of dinner that I can't recall, but I do recall the couple next to us. Full dress Honda and a trailer, reclining lawn chairs and a barbeque and the lady began telling us what a hard day they had just been through. Heat and cold, all kinds of depredations had come their way. I thought they must have ridden a thousand miles, but no, they had covered about sixty-three miles, a little over an hour and eleven minutes, not counting stops. They had started in Santa Barbara. From then on we ignored her sad stories.

The next day we arrived in Chula Vista and spent the night there with my sister and her husband. We had planned to go to Ensenada, Mexico. We drove down to the border in a mild drizzle that turned to a downpour as we went through the border check, so bad that water was over the tops of my shoes and the bike was pumping water all over us with its front wheel. We made a fast retreat back to my sister's and dried our clothes and ourselves, then went to lunch with them, in their car.

A couple of days later we rode up Hwy 395, which is the east side of the Sierra Nevada's. That is another beautiful ride. At Bridgeport we headed west into the high passes on Hwy 108. Just as we passed the Marine Cold Weather Training Center, I pulled off the road to look at the beautiful view. Wheels in the air, gravel on the road and I was under the bike, it was idling nicely as the rear tire shredded one of our bags, exhaust pipe burned my leg and I was laughing too hard to realize that I was in pain. Fortunately Nelda had landed clear of the bike and me as we all fell in slow motion.

I crawled out from under the bike and turned it off, to discover we had bent the chain guard badly and that was the only real damage. I stood the bike up and we taped up our luggage, thank goodness for duct tape, and soon were on our way. Evening caught us close to Long Barn or Strawberry, somewhere thereabouts and we found a campground. I borrowed a hammer from another camper, took the chain guard off and beat it out straight on some flat granite I found. With that done we set up camp and had a pleasant night.

Our trip home, the next morning, took us close to a New Malones Reservoir, a large beautiful reservoir on the Stanislaus River. I thought this would be a nice place to pull onto the parking strip and get a couple of pictures. That would have been so if the parking strip hadn't been covered with gravel. We repeated the wheels in the air trick, but this time the motor was already shut off, so we didn't lose any more baggage to the grinding of the rear wheel. Again Nelda was lucky enough to have fallen free of the bike and me. I had just a little road rash, didn't hurt the bike this time. Nelda told me to tell her the next time I had the urge to leave the pavement she would rather just jump off and hope for the best. That was the last time we fell. It seems that someone must have been watching over me as the only two times I have fallen with a motorcycle, it was stopped or at least nearly so.

CHAPTER 58

"Goldwinging" It

FOR OUR NEXT MOTORCYCLE, NELDA and I bought a 1976 Honda Gold Wing from a fireman, Martin Rinne. He was retiring and had bought a new one. He sold it to me for what the dealer would have given him on a trade in, which was a great deal for me. We had a condo at Lake Tahoe and made several trips there, to get used to the bigger bike. Then we did trips to Chula Vista and Reno with the Goldwing. We also rode it up to Bend, Oregon to see my brother Walter. He wasn't there to meet us, so we spent the night and went to Salem by way of The Sisters. I had a lot of urgency to urinate so at The Sisters, I went to a drug store to get something for that urgency and a back pain that seemed related to it. The druggist told me to go across to the street to the grocery store and buy a bottle of cranberry juice. I did that and after a while that seemed to be helping and I could ride a little longer without having to stop at a restroom.

We spent the night in Salem. About midnight I was in real pain and told Nelda I was going to the hospital, wherever that may be. So I left her in the motel room and went to the hospital. I saw a doctor and was informed that the pain was most likely from a kidney stone and that I should pass it soon. By then I wasn't hurting and went back to get some sleep. A few hours later we were on our way home.

The following day I worked at the fire station and had a relatively good day of it. Then about midnight I awoke and had a desperate journey to the bathroom and had pain urinating like I had never had before. Then I could feel something passing through me, and eventually there appeared a large greenish-yellow crystalline object about twice the size of a grain of rock salt. I washed it off and really looked it over. There was no part of it that didn't appear jagged and sharp. No wonder they hurt so terribly bad. I showed the stone to my friend Sid King and he made the suggestion that I should go pass another one and make some ear rings for Nelda from them. Bad idea, I never want to go through that again. I have heard that pain is similar to childbirth. It may be worse. Many women seem to not give up having children after one, and will try for a second one. I have yet to meet a man who is looking forward to passing another kidney stone.

Now that I felt so much better, we decided to try another little longer trip. We would go to the World's Fair in Vancouver, BC. After that we would continue on to Chicago and eventually down to Oklahoma City for my fiftieth birthday party. Some of Nelda's cousins were putting that on for us, so this would be a really good time. So we took off one morning with all the above in our plans. While on our way to BC we were passed, or passing, a lot of other Honda Goldwing motorcycles. When we got to a viewpoint at Lake Shasta, we stopped by a bunch of them that all appeared travelling together and I asked where they were headed. They said they were going to Grants Pass, Oregon for a club function. Several of them invited us to join them for at least the coming night. We did and joined the Gold Wing Club.

The campground for the night was right next to the Rouge River and for a small fee to join the Goldwing Motorcycle Club; we had a great dinner and were given a good site for our camp. We took a walk down to the river and Nelda told me I looked like I had a cloud over my head wherever I walked. Mosquitoes were everywhere. So they drove us away from the beauty of the riverbank, back to our tent and had a restful night's sleep. The next morning, as we left the group, I asked about whom should I contact about lodging near the venue in British Columbia and there seemed to be just one united voice that I should contact a couple that would tell us of any openings. I have to confess that I have forgotten their names.

Then another lady gave me a roster of all the Goldwing Club members, worldwide. I didn't need to use it, but it was reassuring to know there were people across the country, willing to be called anytime by Club members if they needed assistance along the roads.

We went on into Oregon and spent a day or two, with another of Nelda's aunts, Verla and her husband Lloyd, on their farm near Wilhelmina, Oregon. We called the lady in BC and told her what time we would be taking the ferry from Vancouver Island over to her city of Vancouver. She told me we would be getting off the ferry first and that she would honk and wave at us and we should then follow her to her home. Things all went according to plan and she made us very welcome in her home. She had dinner prepared, and told us where our room was. I told her we could camp in her yard, but she wouldn't have it any other way than we take a room and enjoy our visit. We thankfully agreed as it was raining quite heavily.

The following morning she fed us a good breakfast, took to where we could catch the train right to the fair and told us to call when we were back at that station, so she could take us back home. We did all that and spent a full day at the fair and another night with her and her husband. They were wonderful to us and I made them promise they would call me when they came to California the following year for the Wing Ding, which they described as a Goldwing Club meeting, on the National level. It was to be in Santa Clara the following year. They agreed to call us and we departed to take a new toll road northeast that would take us to Revelstoke, Lake Louise, Banff and on to Calgary. It had rained most of the time we were in Canada so far and that day was no exception.

As we got higher in the Canadian Rockies it did cease to rain for a while, that was so it could snow. The Toll Road was free for our motorcycle because the powers that be couldn't decide what they should charge for motorcycles. Canada is as messed up in government stupidity as we are, in a lot of ways. We spent a night in Revelstoke and dried out and got warm. The next day was a bit clearer weather and we had a pleasant ride into Lake Louise.

As we approached Lake Louise a traffic jam began to occur ahead of us. As we got nearer we found the reason to be the largest buffalo bull I had ever seen was standing beside the road, pawing the ground in anger, head down and apparently ready to charge. He had crossed the highway and just missed being hit by a car and was not pleased. All of the folks in cars were slowing down to get a picture of him and that left us in a bad spot. We being exposed on a bright red Motorcycle and the only thing moving smaller than him left me wondering if we had any chance of survival if he charged us. Luckily he didn't and we were not waiting around to get his picture.

We rode to the Banff Hotel and stopped to admire it, get a warm drink and a snack. We decided to spend the night and I went to the desk and made inquiry only to find they had no rooms available. So we had to go on and spent the night in Calgary. I had mixed feelings, Banff was so pretty that I really wanted to stay there, but I'm sure the room rates would have taken away from the beauty of it all. But Calgary was nice and we had a good room and fine food.

The next day's trip was straight south to Great Falls, Montana. I have never been where wind blew so hard and so constantly as when we drove from Calgary to south of Lethbridge. There was no gusting but a constant side wind that had us leaning the bike into it in order to go straight ahead. When we got back into the mountains the wind subsided and we rolled into Great Falls and found a KOA campground for the night. This was our second night of camping for this trip. All the rest had been in homes or motels as we didn't want to camp in the rain. So we set up out tent, ate our dinner and visited with fellow campers before retiring for the night. It seemed we had just dozed off when a jet plane sounded like it buzzed our tent at a very low altitude. Back to sleep for a bit and then another jet went by and awakened us again. This time it was hard to get back to sleep and the jets continued to fly until about two in the morning, when at last they stopped going over us and we could get some rest. The next morning we found that we were at the end of the runway near a Naval Air Station and the pilots had been practicing touch and goes in the wee hours.

Our next night was the KOA in Sheridan, Wyoming. This one was near a rail yard and was just as noisy as the airport the night before. We determined that we would scout out our surroundings a bit better before camping from then on. We visited Mt Rushmore and the Badlands and after a couple of days we were across the Mississippi and on our way near Madison Wisconsin. I noticed that no other vehicles seemed to be on the road, so we went into a café and were told that those clouds outside were why there was so little traffic, there was a tornado warning in effect. We found a motel that was made of concrete blocks and booked a room.

The following day we went into Chicago and had my first experience with toll roads. Every couple of miles, it seemed, we had to stop and pay a toll. They weren't very much, but we had to have the change to pay them and we spent a lot of time digging in pockets and Nelda's purse for the thirty-five cents, or whatever it was. We did a bus tour of the city and had a pizza someplace where you're supposed to eat pizza in Chicago. Rode the El and saw the water tower, the Sears Tower, Miracle Mile and after a night in town fled for safer pastures.

We camped another night and spent a night in a motel on our way to St. Louis and the Gateway to the west. We suffered a bit from the heat there as the weather had taken a sharp turn to the warmer side. We didn't spend a lot of time sightseeing because of that and kept moving west through Tulsa and on into Oklahoma City. This was where we planned to stay a week or so with relatives and their friends while celebrating my fiftieth birthday. Nelda's sister and nephew from CA were to meet us there to join in the festivities. It was good to get settled into a house, room of our own and air conditioning, meals fit for farmers and great company. We rested well.

The next morning brought all of our plans to a crashing halt. One of Nelda's nephews, the brother of the one we were expecting to meet in Oklahoma City, had died unexpectedly during the night. We decided to ride on home as quickly as possible to be with the family as it suffered through this sad time. We loaded up our bike, and after saying goodbyes and a few good cries, headed west on Hwy 40. It is about fifteen hundred miles to our home so we thought we could do it in a little over two days, if we didn't lollygag along the way. We wanted to catch the other cousin, in hopes of turning him around before he got to Oklahoma. That was not to be. He passed us without seeing us on a section of road where we would have to go several miles to turn around and he was traveling at a good clip, so we determined that it wasn't prudent to try to catch up with him, and we'd lose a lot of time in the attempt. So we continued west.

Outside of Albuquerque, NM, we saw a large black rainstorm heading our way. We weren't wearing any more than enough to protect us from the heat so I thought of pulling over and putting on some rain gear. It did seem the storm was mostly to our south, so I kept on going. This turned out to be a serious error. We turned left with the freeway and hadn't gone a half-mile until the rain hit us. It didn't ease onto us but hit us with a downpour that had us soaked before I could stop the bike. We put on the raingear and went to the first motel we could find in Albuquerque. As we rolled into the parking lot the water on the ground was over our tires, at least five inches deep. We checked in and found a meal someplace close. Then we dried our clothes and went to bed.

Early the next morning we headed west under a rather nice warm sun, no rain and no wind. We were thinking this to be a real good day for a long ride. About fifty miles out of Flagstaff, AZ, the engine on the bike began to run on two cylinders instead of the four it should be running on. This had happened once before on the trip and I had stopped in a large Honda shop and they had found no problems. When they looked for the problem it ran on all four. We determined at that time that the miss may have been caused by some water getting into the wiring because we had been in some rain then also. But this was worse, we had been out of rain for several hours this time and it still continued to miss as we entered Flagstaff.

We discussed this and decided to ditch the bike at a firehouse in Flagstaff and get an airplane to Oakland. We would return later and get our machine, so I went to a firehouse and explained our problem and my reluctance to drive down into the Mohave Desert with a miss in the engine.

The fireman was alone and a bit apprehensive, but let me put the machine in the back corner of the station and we covered it with a tarp so his superiors wouldn't know he had allowed me to abandon it there. We were sworn to call only him when we came back and with his number in hand we got a taxi to the airport.

Flagstaff is high in the mountains and the airport has one short runway so all flights out of there are on small aircraft. Therefore we had to fly to Phoenix, then on to Oakland. The flight to Phoenix was on such a small plane I had to crawl to my seat and we sat one in front of the other. The plane was full with all ten of us, or whatever it held, but it was a pretty flight down into Phoenix where we caught a big plane into Oakland.

A week or so later we took my pickup and a ramp, to load the bike with, and headed to Flagstaff. I called the number and the fireman told me the hour to meet him, which we did. I took him some beer as a token of our gratitude and rolled the bike outside to start it for loading. Wouldn't you know, it started right up, running on all four cylinders and continued to do so for six months until a friend and I found an intermittent open in one of the pickup wires from the electronic ignition. We loaded the bike onto the pickup and went to San Diego to visit my sister Dolores and her husband, making it a leisurely journey home.

CHAPTER 59

We Buy in Danville

MY PAINTING BUDDY, BRAD VINCENT and I had worked for a realty lady, Brenda Olson. Her company had hired Brad and me to help her bring some condos to market. As I got to know her more, I thought she might be able to help Nelda and me relocate to something in a quieter neighborhood. I wanted to bring my tax base from Alameda County with me, which meant we had to buy down. I knew pretty much the value of our home in the Ashland area and felt we could work something out. When we got out to the better areas of Contra Costa County, I found that I was facing a nearly impossible task. Brenda showed us a lot of homes and I tried again to explain to her that I couldn't pay as much as the asking price of the homes she kept showing us. The law was such that I would have to sell my home for more than I would be paying for the one we planned to move into. Prices were much higher than I had anticipated in Contra Costa County.

One day we were eating lunch with the Brenda in Medlyn's, which was a locally owned restaurant in Danville, she told us there was a home about two blocks away that needed work. We went there and looked at it and it was a pretty badly neglected piece of property. It had been a crack house, a house of ill repute and then abandoned for a couple of years. There were walls and ceilings missing and weeds three feet tall in the front yard. My grandson, Max who was three or so, used to call the backyard the "woods," because it was so overgrown with trees and full of junk. The house was also full of squirrels, rats and mice. The floors were covered with walnuts and waste from all of the animals. We went on to look at other properties

A couple of days later I called Brenda and asked her to meet us at the house. I brought coveralls and a stepladder. She unlocked the front door and walked in, screamed and ran back out. I thought she had found a dead body, but it was just the animals running all over the house that scared her. I put on my coveralls and climbed into the attic and crawled all through the house. Then went under it and did the same. I could find no real structural damage and it appeared the house had been fairly well built. We then made an offer to purchase. The owner accepted and the bank refused to let him sell it to me. He hadn't told us that it was in litigation and that he had a court date coming, but when we found he couldn't sell it I went to court the day he did and watched the proceedings. He could sell another property he had on the block, but this one he had to give to the bank.

This older gentleman had been a schoolteacher and realtor in his spare time. He eventually got himself fired from the school district for some indiscretion and must have been living on some modest income from his investments. He lived in a house about half a block away. That house had no electricity or running water and there was a pool in the back yard that was full of junk and stagnant water. No toilets functioned in his house, feces in piles on floors in many rooms and there was no real furniture, but he did stay there, until after I bought the other house from the bank.

I asked Brenda to go to the bank and get the place we had made the offer on for as little as she could and that if she did, I would pay her commission based upon my prior offer, as long as that was not part of the total transaction. She agreed and a day later we had the property and had reduced our cost by about twenty-four thousand dollars. That would cover about half of what the repairs to make it a good house would end up costing me. So it turned out to be a good deal.

After a yearlong fight with the county, I also got to use the selling price as my purchase price, which they were reluctant to allow. They said I had gotten a good deal and should have paid more for this house; therefore my tax base could not come with me. I had taken pictures and I wrote them a letter and sent the pictures along to back up my contention that I should be allowed to use the sale price, which was eventually allowed. That saves me a few thousand dollars. Money the county would have probably wasted, every year.

Nelda and I had bought the house in Danville, CA and fixed it up to make it livable then moved there and eventually sold our home of 31 years in the hills just east of San Leandro. We had lived in the Ashland area. It had San Lorenzo Schools, San Leandro post office, Alameda County Sheriff for law enforcement, Castro Valley Library and Ashland Fire District. Our daughter Darlene had been living in England and when she moved back she and her husband rented a new apartment on 159th and East 14th Streets, just down the hill from our house. About the first weekend in that new place there was a murder of one of the tenant's right out front in the parking lot. They moved to a secure condo in the area of Oakland near Lake Merritt and close to Grand Avenue. Nelda and I decided to leave shortly after that as we heard gunfire a few times and decided we were too old for this new lifestyle being brought our way.

During the course of bringing the house into being a home we could comfortably live in, we would drive to Danville, turn on the heater and go to Vally Medlyn's for breakfast. That was about a two and a half block walk and the house would warm up a bit while we had a leisurely breakfast. This got us in contact with a lot of folks that were the movers and shakers in town and we got to know them and liked most of them pretty well. Some of them even suggested that I should run for some office in town. I thought about that and was a bit tempted to do it. Then I decided that if I did run and got elected, I would have immediately lost half the friends we had just made. It just didn't seem that important to me, so my political career ended before I even ran for dogcatcher.

The house was so badly neglected that one morning as we returned to it, mid -day, which was later than usual, we found that a half dozen buzzards were on the roof. They flew away as we walked up to the house as they are fairly shy birds. I got curious about what had drawn them to our roof and went up there to look around. They had come for a dead rat that was on the roof. I removed that and they never returned.

CHAPTER 60

IRS Comes to Battle
the Retirees

IRS CAME AFTER THE RETIREES of the Oakland Police and Fire Retirement System. IRS claimed that we could not be tax free as disabled retirees. That was a real change, as IRS had allowed a total deduction of wages when the member had been retired for disability. This did get my goat, and I joined with a few hundred others in a seven-year battle with them on this subject. I was on the Disabled Police and Fire Association board for almost the entire battle. It consisted of three police officers and three fire department members, all retired for disability. We hire a team of attorneys, worked with them to get them educated to our system's nuances and eventually we went to court and presented our case to the judge. He ruled against us and we were crushed, but decided to appeal.

We worked hard on the appeal and the attorney group even hired another attorney to join their group. He couldn't work on the appeal as he was the attorney for IRS that had beaten us. We finally got our date with a three-judge panel of the 9th Circuit Court of Appeals and we went over to the Federal Court in San Francisco to watch the proceedings. The lawyer from IRS seemed to rely more on her good looks than on her preparation for the case and then when an elderly lady Judge asked her to explain some bit of the IRS' logic, the young lady got into an argument with the judge and made the judge mad. She had told the judge, in a very condescending tone, that, "Oh, we don't have to get into that." The old gal got a bit red in the face and told her in no uncertain terms that, "Yes, we do have to get into that." From there on I felt very confident we would prevail, which we did with a caveat.

The ruling would apply only to those who had worked twenty-five years or less, before they were retired. I could hardly breathe when I was told of that ruling. I really thought I would pass out on the spot. But I talked with our attorney and this time the one that beat us while he worked for IRS could work on it for us and we agreed to have him pursue it for the post twenty-five year guys also. The police were very apprehensive of the cost of doing that. All of the police members of the board had twenty-five years or less on the job and thought it a waste of time and money for the few police that would be affected. I refused to accept that position and pointed out that the reasoning IRS was using for that restriction on twenty-five years, or less, was that if one worked twenty-five years they were vested in full retirement. It appeared obvious that any thinking IRS attorney could eliminate anyone that had worked twenty-five years and they also would not qualify for disability retirement. So I was given the authority to pursue a deal that would cover the rest of us.

That came about really quite quickly one day when the attorney and an IRS agent worked out an acceptable language in a "global settlement" that we could all live with. The disability pension would be for a twenty-five year based retirement, and anything over that would be taxable. That was exactly how it should have always been, as that was the language of the Oakland City Charter establishing the Oakland Police and Fire Retirement system. So I was thrilled and called for a meeting of the board to get the attorneys paid and decide what we should do next with the Disabled Police and Fire Association.

The meeting was at my home. I was the board president, at the time and centrally located for the members of the board. The police officers showed up in a foul mood and they felt the bill for the attorney's was outrageous, and they were not going to pay it. So I didn't call for a vote whether to pay the attorneys or not. Instead, I adjourned the meeting. Had I held a vote we would have had a three to three tie, and the meeting was turning ugly, so I squelched the vote. I had volunteered my phone to the police so they could call the attorneys and let them present justification for the charges, but none of them wanted to do that.

I called the attorneys and told them that I would be over the next day to pay them and I wanted an itemized bill to present for re-imbursement, which they agreed to. Then the next morning I gave the Law Office my personal check for the full amount of their bill. Then I wrote a letter to the members of the board, resigning as a member, as did the vice president also, and I requested to be paid for my out of pocket expenses, including the attorney's fees. After the treasurer paid me, I was done with the DPFA. Total time on that board was about seven years and it felt real good to have won and get the tax exclusion, and it was great to not have to go to combative meetings anymore.

The only thing left to do was to get back the taxes we had overpaid during the length of the litigation. We had made a deal, when we started, that if we did prevail, IRS would waive their three-year restriction and let us go back to when they first disallowed our claim. Seven years of disability had been taxed and the IRS had to refund that for all of us. The City of Oakland had to tell IRS how much the city had withheld from each person's check and the amount that should have been withheld under the new IRS agreement. That developed into another job for me, as the city had given a very bad number to us to represent what they had withheld. They also had no idea how to calculate the amount we should receive back for each of the seven years. I did figure it out and had to go educate the city workers how to come up with the correct numbers. I asked the auditor if they weren't just a little embarrassed that they were finding out from a high school drop out how to do their job. They just laughed and said, "No, we just want to learn how to do it correctly." So I showed them.

I even received the entire Police and Fire Department roster with all the information on it, wages, Social Security, everything the city knew about them. I was asked to audit their account and let the city know if it was correct or not. I deleted that email immediately, and called to tell them that I would audit one or two people that had asked me for help, but that I didn't want them to send me anymore of that kind of information. If I were to need it, I would have the individual get it and turn it over to me, without Social Security numbers and all. The city didn't share anyone's secrets with me ever again.

CHAPTER 61

Bob Comella Moves to Danville as I Start a New Career

As Nelda and I were rejuvenating our new home, one of my old friends, Bob Comella, from 12 Engine helped, by hanging a new front door for us. The old one was thick oak wood that had been carved with an axe, by someone, who made a sunflower in the middle of it. It was a two-piece affair that looked like a barn door, but not as pretty as when the house had been built in 1950. Now it just looked old, so I bought a nice new one and asked Bob to come out and help me hang it. As we did that he looked at all the rest of the work necessary to get the house in livable condition. He told me he thought I had lost it, thinking I was just too dang old to start on this type of project.

He hung the door and we walked downtown, two blocks, for lunch. It was one of those days when everyone we met was in a good mood and they all spoke with us, lunch was a good sandwich and a shake, he had a diet coke, but enjoyed the break. On the way back to the house he told me he really liked it out here and if I ever saw another fixer upper, to let him know.

The opportunity to tell Bob of a fixer upper in the neighborhood opened a couple of years later. The neighbor across the street from me had just disappeared one evening, and the house stood vacant for a month or two. Then I was out by my garage and saw a guy I knew to be a building contractor and some guy that I didn't know, were really looking the house over. I went over and asked if I could be of some assistance and was told that the owner of the loan, a person I hadn't known, and the contractor were trying to get an idea of how much time and money it would take to get the house on the market and sold. I told them they probably could get it sold by just calling a number, and I gave them Bob's phone number. They thanked me and shortly thereafter they left.

I called Bob and asked if he was interested in looking at a house. He said he'd be right out and within a half hour we were going around it and looking at what it would take to fix it up. It had suffered a bit of neglect and some shoddy work here and there, but was basically a good building and had good street appeal if he wanted to just fix it and sell it. Bob's house had been built by the same man whom had built our house. This one had been built for his daughter, so she would be close to him and his wife, as they grew older.

Bob, the owner, and the owner's realtor got together and Bob made an offer on the house. The owner made a counter offer, after a couple of days and Bob countered, that counter offer. I watched for any signs of activity and asked Bob if he had heard any more. He told me that the owner had countered and that was where they were now. He wasn't saying he wouldn't counter again, but I had known him long enough to know that was the case.

Quite a few days went by and I found the realtor was over there at the house, so I went over and asked how it was going. He said they hadn't heard anything back from my friend and so they were planning to prod him along a bit if they could and get this deal closed. I told the realtor that I had known Bob for close to forty years, and I felt he had countered their counter offer and I would bet big money that Bob had made his final offer. I said that I hadn't talked money with any of them, and wouldn't, but that if they wanted him to buy it they surely knew his best offer by now. I also explained that I hadn't anything to gain either way, whether they sold it to him of not. Then I went home and the realtor drove off. About an hour later Bob called me and said, "I guess I just bought a house." The owner had accepted his offer and I now had a new neighbor and an old friend across the street from my side driveway.

Part of the bringing our new found Danville house into becoming a home required the complete remodeling of the kitchen. The old one had the original dishwasher, which was so small that when it was full of half a dozen plates and the silver, it was totally full. The stove was a pull out electrical unit that had been wonderful in 1950, but was now near ruin and so dirty that we just threw it out rather than try to clean it and repair it. Also the cabinets hung from the ceiling and made the kitchen seem smaller than it was and very dark. So I drew up what I thought would look good and approached a friend, Tom Griffin, who built cabinets. He added his ideas and gave me a price to build and finish the cabinets.

We didn't get any other bids on the cabinets. We had Tom build them and told him I would do the finishing, as we had ideas of exactly what we wanted this new kitchen to look like. He said that was fine and was glad to let me finish them, as he hated doing that part. He then asked if I could do the finish on some more cabinets. So we discussed this and I found out that he was teaching school full-time, he was building cabinets part-time out of his garage, doing about a kitchen a month. He would pay me well to do the finish for him. A kitchen a month sounded perfect to me, no hard work and a little extra money coming in would be nice. I had all the equipment and had been painting for years with a friend, Brad Vincent. Painting had become our last side job while we were both firemen, so this fit us well. At that time Brad was still working for the Oakland Fire Department and sending kids to college. The extra money would help us both.

I discussed with Brad that we take on this cabinet finishing and he agreed, so I told Tom to build away and we would take on the finishing for him. He was happy and did a real marvelous job of building cabinets for people. I attended a couple of seminars to hone my skills on cabinet finishing and learn all I could about the new water base wood finishes that were coming on the market. Brad and I practiced a lot on stuff that didn't show, and brought ourselves up to speed in a short time. We went to a retired finisher, and asked him a thousand questions and he came to my house and showed us a few things.

After a few months I noticed that it sure seemed to me that we were doing an awful lot of cabinets and sometimes some furniture that didn't just seem the normal things to have in a home. Another discussion with the cabinetmaker brought out that he had quit his school teaching job and had hooked up with a design group. He was building furniture that was going into model home garages to convert them to offices in new tract home developments.

This turned into a full-time job for several years and was very good for all of us. We made a lot of extra money and Nelda ran the business for us so she got her quarters in with Social Security. We did the finish work and the design group would tell us what the theme for the tract was and what type of finish they wanted. They even showed us how to do some of the finishes that we had never done before. We got pretty good at making things appear aged, fly specked and crackled, as well as all the normal finishes. We had cabinets and furniture shipped to NY, South Carolina, Hong Kong, Nevada and Arizona, as well as all over the bay area counties in California. Not all of it was for model homes, Caroline Comella and her husband, Simon Morgan owned a lot of what went the farthest away, They must have liked our work as shipping costs must surely have been quite high.

CHAPTER 62

We Buy a Model A

AROUND THE MIDDLE OF 1992 or thereabout, my friend, Sid King called me and told me he was having "buyer's remorse" over a car he had bought. I asked what he had bought and he explained that he had gone to the Blackhawk Auction in Danville to watch the action. His wife had told him not to buy anything younger than he was. Then a 1933 Ford leaped out at him and he says he scratched his nose and ended up owning it. When he called me was the next day and he was at work at the fire station in the west end of Oakland. I asked where the car was and I went by and had a look at it. It was behind a fence, but I could still get real close and see that it looked very well maintained from the outside.

I went home and called Sid and told him if he felt that bad about buying it that I would gladly relieve him of it for what he had paid. Then he said he felt a lot better and we continued to discuss his purchase and what all owning an older Ford V8 could entail. He told me he had already been approached by a couple of people in the Early Ford V8 Club and a parts dealer, so he felt he wasn't all alone with the only one of the old Fords still on the road. With that bit understood and my offer, he felt relieved and now was looking forward to enjoyment of his purchase. I told him to let me know if he saw another old Ford somewhere, and we could travel together some time. Then we sort of forgot that subject for a couple of months.

Sid is a bit of a collector of many odds and ends and one thing he want- ed was a "one armed bandit," the old slot machine. He had watched some

Penny Saver or some such newsletter and saw that a fellow in Castro Valley had several of the slots for sale. He drove over and eventually bought one or two and in the exchange, then he asked about an old Ford near the back of the guy's property. The gentleman told him he had acquired it recently and he needed to get rid of it. Sid asked about price and then called me and told me he had a car for me.

We went over, just to look, and I returned with a 1929 Ford, Murray bodied Model A, four door sedan, pretty much in original condition, with maybe one re-spray paint job. It ran okay and was a really nice old car, but the more I looked into it the more I felt restoring it to be something I shouldn't get involved in and it was a bit too far gone to leave it as an original car. Nelda and I joined the Model A Club in Livermore and within a few months I was the Vice President, then President. Not that I was so clever, but that I hadn't protested my nomination loudly enough and was therefore the only candidate.

So now we had a Model A and belonged to a club and so we went on the tours locally. What I learned was that I had a fairly unique car, not of great value, but it would be a shame to not re-do it correctly, and it did need work. So I was determined to sell that one and buy another that was pretty much all done already, but still a Model A. And because I had always had later cars, these were challenging and fun cars to drive about locally. I watched the magazine that the Model A Club of America, the national club, put out. There I found a little 1929 Roadster being sold by Allen Funt, of Candid Camera fame. I made contact with the man selling it for him and he told me that the car had already been sold. I told him to let me know if he had any others and he told me not to give up on this one. The guy that had bought it may just want to sell it again and he would check. So we exchanged phone numbers and email addresses, while he tried to get in touch with the guy he had helped buy the car.

A couple of days later, my new friend, Paul Sund of Pacific Grove, called to tell me that I could probably buy the car from the man who purchased it a few weeks ago, who happened to live in Santa Cruz. He didn't want to get involved with pricing, so that would be between myself, and the new owner. I called a number he had given me and a day or two later Nelda and I took my truck to Santa Cruz and happily brought the roadster home. The guy had loaned me a tow bar and insisted that I should tow it instead of driving it as I had planned. So we hooked it up, put the top down and towed it over the Santa Cruz Mountains to Danville.

When I made the last turn approaching my street, the bumper fell off the Model A and it rolled ahead through the intersection and into my neighbor's high juniper shrubs. That was a total of about 300 feet from my driveway. I had watched helplessly as it buried itself up to the doors in the junipers and feared that the front end had been totaled. The left front fender had taken the brunt of the blow and that was the only real damaged part of the car. I pulled it out of the junipers and started it up and drove it home, totally bummed out by what had happened, but thrilled that it had happened there instead of going over the mountains or on the freeways. This was just bent metal and scratched paint; any other spot someone may well have been killed.

I discovered that there are two bolts that hold the front bumper onto a Model A. They are imbedded in a cast metal part of the bumper. On the cheap reproduction that was on my car, even the bolt was just a threaded pot metal casting. Strange that it had held together for the 100 miles of so I had been towing it.

I fixed the dent and repainted the fender over the next few days and got busy trying to get the car in my name. The gentleman I had bought it from had made no effort to change the title and had given me all the paperwork that he had received. I took it all to AAA and got a temporary title and registration and a list of things that I needed in order to clear the title change. I called my friend Paul Sund, and asked if I could get the title signed correctly, if I brought it down to him. He told me sure, bring it down and he would take it over to Funt's and have it taken care of. We arrived at a date and time and Nelda and I drove down and met Paul in person, nicest guy down there. He told us that he'd handle this while we went to lunch and that in an hour or so we could come get the papers and be on our way.

After a great lunch in Monterey on Cannery Row, we went back to pick up the papers. Mr. Sund was a bit solemn as he told me that the Funt's attorney had told him, "We have done all we will do with that title" which turned out to be that they had done nothing with the paperwork. The title was still signed incorrectly and there was none of the other paperwork I needed for Motor Vehicles to transfer it. This was the first of three trips to the Monterey area to get the title straightened out and the car registered in my name. I did however have temporary title that worked and insurance. I even had a personal plate that read 29 SMILE. Funt had had SMILE 29, which I had been told I could use, but was then told "No, they [the Funts] may want to use it on another car someday."

I really was stunned that there was no apparent way for me to get the title. I thought about it for a couple of months then wrote a letter to the attorney for the Estate of Mr. Funt, informing him that since they wouldn't enable me to get the title in my name, I was just going to keep driving it in the Funt name and since that was the case I would save myself the added cost of insurance. About a week later, I received a pink slip with the car registered to me, and everything in my name. No explanation ever was offered and I still have the original "SMILE 29" plates that came with the car.

My next Model A trip of any consequence was when I saw an ad for a 29 Pick up for sale in Rio Rico, Arizona. I emailed the owner and received lots of pictures, which showed a very nice little closed cab truck. Nelda and I decided that we could use it so I borrowed a trailer from a friend in Brentwood, Bob La Follette, another fellow Model A guy. Early one morning I drove off for Rio Rico, money in hand and filled with anticipation. When I arrived in Rio Rico it was so late, I found a room and called the folks I was to meet and told them I would be by in the morning, after breakfast. They said fine and I went to bed with visions of a pristine truck in my head.

When I got to their house the next day I found that the truck was not quite as nice as the pictures showed, but that it appeared to be quite good mechanically, just had a few issues with the lack of body work before it had been painted. We adjusted the price, just a tad in my favor and I towed it over to San Diego. I stayed there a couple of days visiting my brother-in-law and sister then drove back to Danville and returned the trailer. The truck ran really well and had been hot rodded a bit with period parts. The flathead was now a Cragar Overhead, which meant it had lots of power and the transmission had been replaced with one from a 1939 Ford which made it much easier to shift. The tires and rims had also been replaced with Kelsey Hayes rims and 600 X 16 radial tires. 1956 Ford steering had replaced the old 7 tooth steering box and a Borg Warner Overdrive had been adapted into the driveline. I had discussed all this with the owner before I had made the trip to Rio Rico.

CHAPTER 63

Max and I go to Portland

THE MAIN REASON I HAD purchased the truck, was to drive it to Portland Oregon for a National meeting of the Model A Club in 2004. I asked my grandson Max to go with me and he said he'd like to go. I have a doctor friend who also drives a Model A and he was to meet us along the way and we'd drive up and back together. Dr. Swann lives on a ranch near Plymouth, CA. It is about two hours driving time from my home and is just below Hwy 49 in the gold country of CA. With our arrangements made, Max and I left before daylight.

We met Dr. Neal Swann at the intersection of Hwy 12 and Hwy 29, which is near Napa in the wine country. Neal said he needed to find a gas station and asked us to follow him, and we both filled up. Then we followed him up over Cobb Mountain, since he had never been there before, and he felt like this was an excellent opportunity to venture that way. It was beautiful driving through the timber north of Calistoga then over by Clear Lake and eventually out onto Highway 101 for the trip north, a few miles south of Ukiah. I told Neal we were hungry and he took us on a bladder endurance test to a spot near Rio Dell that he thought had the greatest hamburgers in the world. It was closed, but we did find a restroom open and were told of a restaurant just a few miles away that fed us. Max and I needed a lot to fill us up and they came through.

This part of the drive, from Garberville to Rio Dell had us following the scenic Eel River, through the Avenue of the Giants. That is the part of Hwy 101 that takes you from the interior of the state out to the coast and is one of many unforgettable drives in California. There are some of the biggest trees in the United States saved here and we drove right beside many of them.

Then we drove to Crescent City and spent the night in a motel. We had traveled about 400 miles and were pretty tired. We did manage another meal and then had a good night's rest. The next morning, after breakfast, we went on up the coast into Oregon and the beauty of its coast with every turn presenting another post-card photo opportunity. At just a bit past Lincoln City, we turned east on Hwy 18 toward McMinnville and Portland. This part of the drive is through forested land that gives way to lush farmland and greenery everywhere, even in the suburbs of the big city of Portland. We arrived in the afternoon at the Nation Meet headquarters at the Red Lion and checked into our hotel rooms. The day's drive had been on a winding road, but was less than 350 miles. We were tired and hungry, but that went away with a good meal in a restaurant that we found not too far from the hotel. There were several hundred cars there by nightfall and more to come the next morning.

The following morning we got up and went to the breakfast buffet in the hotel, checked out all the cars, met a few friends from our club and others from prior meets. We took part in several things, one being a "fix the problem" sort of test. We had to replace some plugs, time the car and get it running. Another thing we did was in Neal's heavy car, we took part in a "Gravity Drag Race' where we started at the top of a hill, no engine and rolled down the incline and around a curve at the bottom. We watched some that seemed to have no brake drag at all, as they seemed to fly down the hill.

My 29 Ford and Dr. Swann's Sedan on the Oregon Coast

That night I called my brother Walter in Salem. He and his current wife, Nancy, came over and had dinner with us. That was the first she and I had met and she seemed a good fit for him, but who knows how these things will turn out? We went to our favorite restaurant, which was the one we had been to the night before and we had a great time together. Then we all walked around and looked at the several hundred Model A's in the parking lots, before they had to return to Salem.

The next day we went out to McMinnville in Neal's car and went to the air museum there. We saw the "Spruce Goose," a huge plane built and flown once by Howard Hughes. There are lots of airplanes in the building and one of them was a Stagger Wing Beach, that looked similar to the one Bill Woods flew over the Toll Gate. On closer inspection, I found it to be the exact same plane, the Lear jet of its day. Of course Lear jets probably aren't a big deal now, but at that time in 2004, they were still considered pretty snazzy planes.

When we left, I called my niece Katy Adams. She lives in Beaverton and I asked her if she would be able to come meet us someplace for lunch. She said she would and knew a nice spot close by where she told us to wait for her. She sometimes runs a bit late, but this time was there pretty close to the appointed time and told us to follow her. We did and it turned out the spot close by was her house and we had a wonderful meal that she prepared, along with a nice visit with several of her kids and her husband.

The next day Neal's wife and daughter had joined us. We all took a drive out to Mt. Hood and went to some amusement park on the side of the hills there. It was beautiful, but warm. In going up the mountain, Neal's car eventually came to a halt beside the road and Max and I went to investigate. He told me his condenser gets hot after 12 miles of uphill and he has to wait for it to cool down, then it is increments of two miles from then on until the next long downhill where things can cool back down. Max asked me, "What happens if I squirt a little water on it?" We told him to try it. He had a little cooling bottle that would squirt water into an air-stream aimed wherever, so he gave it a try on the exposed end of the condenser. Neal could immediately start the car again and away we went to the park, which was less than two miles away.

Once there, Max and Jolene, Neal's daughter, did a ride on the zip line and they also did a sort of a coaster ride down a bobsled run, which looked to be a lot of fun. There was some sort of a large picnic lunch and some other activities to entertain us, Later we drove back to the Red Lion. That night I took Max and we went to the President's Dinner. The President's of the local club's can bring a guest, so we went to a grand dinner on a deck overlooking the Columbia River. I was President of our club at the time.

We had enjoyed the trip and the little truck had performed admirably. We decided that the next day we would leave Portland before the rush hour started and that we would again follow Neal south. This time we would take Interstate 5, instead of going the coast. We had thought we should drive to Ashland, Oregon and put up for the night, and then we would get up early and drive over the Ashland summit into California before it got too hot. So off we went and stopped down the road after a couple of hours for breakfast. Both cars were running quite well and though it was warm, it wasn't hot and we didn't anticipate any problems.

But then we did have a problem with our plan. The problem was that we were running along so well that we got to Ashland at about noon, not in the late afternoon, where it may have made sense to lay over and try the mountain in the early morning, so we decided to go for it, and perhaps stop in Weed or Reading, We drove up the Ashland grade and after 12 miles Neal's car rolled to a stop in the right hand lane, which is the truck lane with no place to pull off the road. Max and I also stopped in the truck lane. Max did his squirt the condenser thing and Neal's car started and away he went. I tried to start mine and found that I had no power to the points. I had to roll back down the truck lane until we found a place to pull off the road. That was a good half-mile below where we had stopped, but we could get well off to the side and safely check out my ignition problem. I had also become aware that my electric fan wasn't working, so I pulled the seat back loose to reveal the fuse panel that I knew to be there.

Sure enough a fuse had burned out when we were stopped and as soon as I replaced it we got back underway up the grade. Right at the top of the grade we saw Neal walking toward us. I slowed down and yelled for him to jump on the running board and we kept the truck running up the hill. He told us his car was okay, he had just started to miss us and was walking back to see what had happened to us. After a few hundred yards I slowed by his car and he jumped off and I watched as he got it going and pulled in behind us.

We stopped at the top of the next long downgrade and made plans to go eat in Weed. Both cars were doing fine now and we had a lot of daylight ahead of us, so maybe we would go to Reading after we had our late lunch. So we went into Weed and had a good lunch, enjoyed the coolness inside the restaurant and talked about how hot the Valley would be, but we'd go down there anyway, it was just a bit after 2 PM. We would find a room and go through the Valley in the morning, that should be pleasant and we'd be home by early afternoon.

David and his 29 Ford Pickup, with Mt. Shasta

We drove down off the base of Mt. Shasta and past Lake Shasta and as we got to Reading I just knew Neal wasn't going to stop, so I kept on going also, following and hoping that he'd stop in Red Bluff. That we did and I told him there was a good motel close by. He told me, "There's nothing like sleeping in your own bed," so I agreed to his challenge, and we pushed on. It was about 108 degrees outside by then, which was getting toward four in the PM. Max had bought us both the biggest drink he could find and I had made a prop to hold the front window open at the bottom a bit to allow at a breeze to blow through the cab.

When we got to where the road split to Highways 505 and 5, Max and I took 505 and waved our goodbye to Neal, as he continued along Hwy 5 to Sacramento and eventually he'd be back in Plymouth near to the same time we would arrive in Danville, barring either of us having some trouble.

At about Vacaville I noticed the truck wandering a bit and it was a bit of trouble to keep it going straight, but not real bad, so I just slowed down a bit and stayed well to the right, so I could get off the highway if I had to. We made it home before nine that night and Max's mother came and got him. We had enjoyed a real adventure in survival from the heat, but other than the last 200 miles or so it hadn't been bad.

The following day I examined the steering and found that the steering arm on the driver's side had worked loose in the past and someone had tightened it and welded the nuts onto the bolts that held it in place. After it began to work again, it had worn the holes a bit and now it was loose and needed to be replaced, which I did and got a little better arm and built it up so it couldn't pull through the holes like the last one did. That cured the problem. Driving that boxy little truck with the extra heat from the overhead conversion wasn't something I wanted to do again on a long trip; We had driven over 630 miles in that last day, about 150 miles of that total in 108 degree heat.

A couple of years went by and I sold the little pickup truck to a gentleman in Shafter, California. It was just what he wanted and I saw pictures of it at a couple of events he took it to. He had experimented with changing back and forth between the 16-inch wheels that were on it and the 21-inch wheels that were on it when it was assembled at the Ford Plant in 1929. Both sets of wheels made it a cute truck, though it probably performed better with the 16-inch wheels and the radial tires. I often wish I hadn't sold it, as is the case with most of the old cars I have owned.

At this time I still have the Roadster, a 1931 Deluxe coupe, I recently purchased, and a Deluxe Delivery that is being painted by my son-in-law. So I can't have them all, some rotation is good.

CHAPTER 64

Addison Texas Trip

How Not to Start a Trip

IN JUNE OF 2008, THERE was a joint meet of the two National Model A
Clubs. I decided to go and set about making plans and reservations followed by putting our Roadster in condition for such a trip. This is a trip
of over 1700 miles, if you include a few little side trips along the way. I

checked everything I could think of and put together a bunch of spare parts to take with me, just in case. Then I took off all the wheels and drums, checked and adjusted the brake linings and bubble balanced my wheels, greased the entire car and topped up everything. I put it all back together and was ready to go. Full of anticipation for a great ride I left at 5:00 AM to drive to Barstow, CA, where I would meet up with a group that would travel together to Addison.

I drove off merrily on my way and at about ten miles down the road the car began to shake violently as I topped the crossover from I-680 to I-580. This is quite a tall overcrossing and as I slowed, trying to picture what was going on, the left front wheel rolled off, passing me and jumped the guardrail and disappeared down to the freeway lanes below me. I have hydraulic brakes on the roadster and hadn't been alert enough to notice if the tire and wheel still had the drum attached or not so I was afraid to step on the brakes. I just pointed the car to the side of the overpass and let it roll to a stop. As that happened the left front corner of the car settled gently to the ground and there was no scraping sound, so I knew the drum was still on the hub. Just a shower of sparks as the drum skimmed over the rough pavement.

After it stopped I put on my hazard lights and got out to examine the situation. The left front was setting on the pavement, (see the picture above,) and everything appeared fine, except there was no tire or wheel to be seen and I couldn't see any lug nuts. My car is a six- wheeled roadster, so that meant I had two spare tires, held on with three lug nuts each. Simple enough; take a spare and put it on the car using the three lug nuts that hold it in place and steal two more from the remaining spare mount. There you go, the problem is solved, so drive on.

Well it seemed simple enough, but I found that I couldn't get my jack under the axle to raise the car. I could lift it a bit, but alone there was no way I could get the jack in place. I had a cell phone and woke my lovely bride up to tell her where a shorter jack was and why I needed it. She was there shortly, as was the California Highway Patrol. The CHP went looking for my errant tire and wheel, with the promise that when they found it they would chase me down and return it to me. To this day, no one admits to knowing where it is.

With the shorter jack, and Nelda's help, I got the axle on top of the shorter jack and jacked the car up a bit so I could get the bigger jack in place and install the tire. Then I had a choice, cancel and call it quits, or go for it. I decided to go for it. Nelda agreed that this didn't have to ruin my plans and wished me well. I checked all the remaining lug nuts and found them to be tight. Why I had tightened only three wheels, I'll never know, but it is imbedded in my mind to check at least the four on the ground often from now on.

We parted ways and I drove on over the Altamont Pass and into the San Joaquin Valley at Tracy, and took the highway to Modesto, where I joined Hwy 99, then headed toward Bakersfield. By then the sun had come up and the fields and orchards looked lovely in the early light. On my way I passed some guy in a Chevy Camaro that had caught fire and burned right to the roadbed, so I didn't feel I had the worst of luck. My car had four good tires on the road, was running well and there was a spare on the passenger side in case I needed one, plus I had extra water and oil in a rack on the running board, parts under the seat and ...well I just couldn't remember what I had done with most of the spare parts I had set out to take with be, but I had a nagging ache in my stomach that told me they were still on the bench in my garage, a couple of hundred miles behind me when I finally stopped and checked. Oh well, the show must go on now.

I stopped for breakfast along the way and bought fuel. The price of gasoline had gone from about $1.89 to over four dollars per gallon, from the time I signed up for this trip and the time I got on the road. In Bakersfield, I fueled up again and made sure all the tires were good, water to the top and oil level where it belonged. Then I drove over the Tehachapi's to Mojave and off across the desert toward Barstow. I had to stop for the light at Kramer Junction and the poor little car began to miss something terrible as I pulled through the intersection, with trucks and cars backed up behind me. I nursed it along and eventually it seemed to be better and gained enough speed that I didn't feel that I was a hazard to navigation, so I kept going to Barstow, not daring to pull off onto the shoulder and check what may be wrong, as what shoulder there was, looked to be a sand trap. This part of the trip is sagebrush, cactus and desert plants that all are fairly well spaced apart. The soil appears to be mostly pebbles and sand, little dirt.

As I left the highway to enter Barstow the engine died and I couldn't restart it. I rolled into some shade under an overpass and examined the points. They were almost totally closed so I eyeballed a bit and separated them to what looked to me to be about twenty thousandths and then drove fairly well on into town and found our motel. I had driven 388 miles and I was sort of proud of myself, and my little car. I went into the motel and met some of the other travelers on our trip. Some of them had problems also, so I didn't feel singled out for misfortune.

We were to be in Barstow two nights to allow us all to gather and get to know each other. There was a tour of the Harvey House, which is the railroad museum in town. It also features a lot of Hwy 66 pictures and history of one of the largest migrations of people in modern times the "Dust Bowl." Folks from the Dust Bowl came west from their devastated farms and lives to seek a new beginning in California, during the 1930's and then into the 1940's, as workers were needed for the war effort. If you wish, read *Grapes of Wrath*, by John Steinbeck, for a colorful picture of that event.

I found that there were about 30 cars of us going on this trip, lead by the publisher of *The Model A Times*, John La Voy. A couple of the participants were talking about their troubles and one fellow in a pretty little red pickup felt he would have to cancel because he was losing so much water he felt he just couldn't go on. His wife would be really upset with him, he told me, as she had told him to get his radiator fixed before he left. We found that his trouble was that the water was just being pumped out the overflow and onto the ground. Another fellow, Denny Specker told him he had a cure and he should try it before he gave up. The cure was a device that turned the old radiator system into a somewhat more modern version, in that it provided a way to pressurize his radiator to about 2.5 psi and that would also keep the water in the radiator. We installed it and he never added another drop of water all the way to Addison.

Another fellow was about to drive to Los Angeles to get a generator. I told him I had a spare in my car, under the seat, he was welcome to try it and see if that cured his problem. He installed it and I kept my fingers crossed because I hadn't tested it. I had won it in a raffle and the member that put it in there had said it was from our clubs spare parts that they used to call their "First Aid Kit." He started his car and the amps went right up so we knew it to be okay. He bought a replacement in Addison and I still have it. I wasn't concerned much with my car as I had gapped the points and gone to a parts house and bought another spare set and a condenser, just in case.

After our stay in Barstow, another couple and I decided that we would get under way across the Mojave early in the morning and beat the heat to Needles, and then take Hwy 66 up to Oatman, AZ and explore there, before driving on to Williams, our next nights stop. They had a nice little coupe and were pulling a trailer, so the next morning we had the motel breakfast and headed out just after sunup. The road was fairly good, empty of cars at that hour and somewhat cooler than any other time I had been over that stretch recently. At Golden Shores we pulled into a gas station and filled up.

Then when I tried to leave, the little roadster seemed to be happy to stay by the Colorado River and protested mightily as I herded it up the road to Oatman. We stopped there and did some minor tinkering to see if we could improve the performance. We also watched as we and other tourist fed the wild burros that now make Oatman a feeding stop on their rounds. All the stores sell carrots for that purpose. We got a cold Coke and then left for Kingman, where we planned to have lunch.

The roadster ran pretty darn well all the way to Hwy 40, just a couple of miles from Kingman. When I stopped for the intersection, the engine died and I couldn't get it started. Help arrived from all sides and all types of tinkering and advice took place, eventually it was determined by someone that the connection tang on my rotor had broken off, so that was replaced and I limped the car into Kingman and we all had lunch while it cooled off. My traveling companion, Alex Jenke, took my carburetor apart and cleaned it and we got under way again. After a few miles of bucking and snorting I called for our tow vehicle to pick me up. We loaded the car onto the trailer and it was towed into Williams, where it started right up and ran quite well around the motel lot and out into the town streets.

The next morning, a new friend, Dave Uhlig, said he would ride with me to the Grand Canyon and between us we should be able to diagnose what was ailing my machine. Another friend, Steve Lewis was following us closely. He was also in a roadster. We drove blissfully along for an hour and a little more and travelled about 55 of the 60 miles to the South Rim with no problems at all. Then troubles started again and the car bucked and protested against my efforts. We made it to the parking lot, barely, and let the car cool down as we toured the canyon overlook and took a few pictures.

After an hour or two, we went back to the cars and we started it up and all three of us listened for a minute or two, and then decided to shut it off and change out the manifold gasket. We put a new one on and it still leaked so we shut it off and doubled up the gaskets, two new ones now made it quiet. Steve rode back with me and we drove back to Williams with no more problems. That evening, Steve rebuilt the carburetor for me with a kit he had and we tightened all the connections to the amp meter. One of the posts on the amp meter was loose and that was fixed.

The following morning I followed Steve and Dave and we drove to Flagstaff up the hill from Williams and the car ran fine. We stopped in Flagstaff and filled the tanks and when I tried to leave, the popping and backfiring commenced with a vengeance. I turned the mixture control out a few turns and danged if it didn't pick up speed and quit misbehaving. I was happy to have found something that I could do that seemed to work.

We drove to Gallup, after a side trip through the Painted Desert and the Petrified Forest. We settled in for the night. Steve and Dave had me come join them for pizza in their room and we discussed the changes in my car. Backing the mixture control out shouldn't have had that effect on the running, and none of us could explain it, but it worked, so I would do what worked.

The following morning we got under way fine and I followed Steve's car to just a few miles west of Albuquerque, where all of us waited until all the Model A's were gathered beside the road, and then we got a police escort to take us into Los Lunas, New Mexico. The escort took us straight to the central park in town. There the Chamber of Commerce and the local club, Poco Quatros, ("slow fours") hosted a barbeque for us. All kinds of good food and drink, a local gathering of old cars to make a sizable car show, and all our Model A's lined up for the locals to see what had invaded their town.

We left there after a few hours and I had real fears of pulling the grade east of Albuquerque. It was past 2 PM and quite warm. I found that I did okay, slower than most, and it did seem sadly underpowered. Denny Specker passed me in his Phaeton, like I was parked. His car had a lot more wind drag and was probably a couple of hundred pounds heavier than my car. Also they were two people, while I was alone. There was construction on the highway also, so I really breathed a sigh of relief when I topped the grade and found myself in Moriarty. I knew of no more real steep hills between there and Dallas, TX.

We stopped late in the afternoon for a sandwich and to fill up. A lady cautioned us that there was a tornado warning for the eastern part of the state and she advised us to find a room where we were until that warning was lifted. We looked ahead and there were some clouds, but after a bit we decided none of us Californians had really seen a tornado, so we pushed on to Tucumcari, which was our stop for the night.

The following morning I took off on my own and drove to Amarillo early. I had called Nelda's cousin, Margaret Miller, and invited her to join me for breakfast. She told me she would, but didn't quite know where to go, so I should meet her at her house and she would ask her son to join us at some good spot. So I drove to her house and as I parked, I could smell ham and eggs, biscuits and gravy and all of the things she had fixed for breakfast, so I knew we weren't going anywhere. Her son, Mike came about that moment and I went in and enjoyed a wonderful home cooked meal. My first in a week and it was very welcome.

After that I drove to Quanah, Texas, named for Quanah Parker, the last Comanche Chief. That was our last stop before Addison and it was just 209 miles more to our meeting spot. I bought gasoline at a local station for less than four dollars a gallon, first time in the entire trip. Then I found the motel and awaited the rest of our group to appear. My car was running well and I was happy to report that when I called Nelda that night. I also asked her to call Roger Griffith and have him bring a Carburetor and a Distributor to the club meeting that night and she could UPS it to me at her cousin's house in Hurst.

The following day I followed Steve and Dave as we got into the outskirts of the Dallas-Fort Worth area. I had seen on a map that Addison is to the North of Dallas. Steve had a GPS and so I decided to follow them and stick close so I didn't get lost in the maze of roads and crossings. We started to pull into a gas station close to our destination and I saw that their car was having trouble. I parked and we pushed it to a spot where we were out of the way and determined that the float in his carburetor had sunk and so gas was running out all over the ground. He had a spare float and shortly we were under way again and found our motels. I was a block away from the host hotel, but the parking lot was full of Model A's, so I had plenty of folks to visit with if I got bored.

I enjoyed the meet and explored around the area as well. I took a bus tour to the area where Kennedy was killed and through the Dallas Book Depository, saw the window that Oswald fired his rifle from and heard the lead investigator tell his story again about that whole sad day. He sounded convinced that Oswald acted alone and that there had been no conspiracy and no cover-up. I always suspected that if he wasn't alone in the assassination, then again, Lady Bird might have had a hand in it. I didn't bring that to his attention.

After a couple of days, Nelda flew in and her cousin brought her out to the motel, along with the spare parts, and we had a nice dinner at the Claim Jumper, next to the motel. The next morning was a big tour out to the Texas Speedway and we got to take our cars in and drive a lap or two. That was a ball and after as we exited the speedway, my car backfired so loudly, people were seeking cover. I was embarrassed and we hurried out of there and went to her cousin's for the night.

When the meet was over we drove to Clinton, Oklahoma and spent the night there. Nelda had a cousin from Oklahoma City, who came over and joined us for dinner and a tour of the Hwy 66 Museum in Clinton. That was a great treat for all of us and I was pleased that he could come join us.

The following morning we had a trip to Fairview, Oklahoma where the family of one of our fellow tour members had a place that does some machine work for money and for fun they rebuild racecars, steam tractors, and the wife makes quilts. We were adequately fed also with a huge breakfast and all sorts of goodies that the ladies had cooked up for us. I tried to find someone to give some money to help cover our costs, but they weren't having it that way.

Fairview, Oklahoma

Fairview, Oklahoma

That afternoon we drove to Garden City, Kansas, having been joined by a man and his daughter from Massachusetts. They joined us for a meal and we found he would be going with us to California. His wife was to join him the following day and the daughter would fly home. They had a very nice station wagon that had a large warning triangle on the rear of it, indicating a slow moving vehicle.

We drove to Canon City, CO and Nelda and I wanted to go onto a high bridge over Royal Gorge, just a bit out of town, so I drove through town and started up a rather steep incline and there was no way the car was going to go up there, so we turned around and went back to our motel. I decided that I would put the parts on that Nelda had provided, so I took off my distributor and carburetor. As I did that the rain began to fall and suddenly I was drenched, but had finished before I quit for the day.

The next morning we left early and followed another fellow in a truck he had made up out of a bunch of spare parts. It was a beautiful little roadster pickup, with a four-cylinder engine from a Chevy II in it. My car now ran fine and pulled the hill that it refused to climb the afternoon before. We passed over the top of Monarch Pass, 11,312 feet. Nelda and I had lunch in a restaurant in Gunnison, CO. Then went through a museum and joined up with the group in the evening in Grand Junction. While there I noticed that my water pump was dripping a bit. I tried to tighten the packing and remembered this was one of the new "leak-less" ones without any packing to tighten. The parts truck was just going somewhere and I got another spare from him and put it on.

The next morning Nelda and I left for Delta, Utah. We hadn't gone far when the water pump made a loud screeching sound and I pulled over and removed it, putting another spare in its place. The parts guy showed up as I was putting the hood back on and he stopped and within a few minutes we were again on our way. We got to Delta and the pump I had put on was leaking badly so I put on a demonstration of how to change a water pump in 15 minutes, and put my old "leak-less" one back on. It only leaked when the car was sitting without the engine running and I had two gallons of water in jugs on the running board, so I determined that I would add water as needed and forget about the leak.

The next day we drove to Ely, NV and took the train ride out to the huge copper mine at Ruth. We had never seen anything like it before and were well pleased that we had taken the tour. On the ride back the train passed the back of a bordello and one of the girls was out there waving frantically for us to come on down. We didn't. We went back to our room in the casino and played the slots until we got bored, then went to bed.

The following morning Nelda and I drove over to Fallon, NV. My brother, Perry had spent a few years there and loved the pace of life there. We drove through town a couple of times and found that our motel/casino was about in the center of town. There was a good restaurant not far away and that was where we had our dinner and then went to the casino and spent a bit of time there before getting back to our room. We had decided that the following day we would drive on home so we said our goodbye's to all of the new friends we could find, and got a good night's sleep. It was July 4, but no gunfire like in the big cities in California which had become a way of life in Oakland on the 4th and Christmas Eve. This had the Firemen staying inside as much as possible to avoid the bullets raining down outside.

The following morning we were off early, we had breakfast at Heidi's, a restaurant in Carson City and were home in Danville by early afternoon. It had been a wonderful time and we had met some really nice folks along the way.

Now here's the real answer to why my car went into such protests, and what I could have done to repair that problem. My car has an alternator on it. The original Model A electrical system was recharged by a generator. I had never thought of anything being wrong at, or near the alternator, and I guess none of my friends did either. I had felt that the problem was heat getting to the condenser and causing it to malfunction, or dirt in the fuel system. Maybe even an electrical leak somewhere in the ignition system.

Not long ago, April of 2014, I began to experience the same problems I had been having on the aforementioned trip. At one point there was a lunch at a restaurant just two blocks from my house. The members met a few miles away and drove here, I didn't try to take the Model A and they told me to go get it when we got home, surely I could bring it two blocks, so I tried and couldn't get it to run. While we were doing the tire kicking after lunch, a couple of friends said, "Let's go fix your car."

So we three met in my garage and discussed where to begin, as we all looked over the engine, with the hood up. One guy began to wiggle wires and found that the wire to the alternator was very loose at its connection to the alternator. We took it off and crimped it tightly and then put the connection back together. The engine started and ran perfectly.

I have a clear distributor cap on the distributor and when the car was mis-firing, I found that as I revved it up, the first thing to happen was that number two cylinder would quit firing, then if I revved it up a little more number one also quit firing and the engine began to backfire, just as it had all along the trip to Addison. With the wire to the alternator fixed that no longer occurred. I am sure, had I crimped the connector the first time it misfired, my whole trip to Addison would have been much better, than not loading all my spare parts and tightening all of the lug nuts would have made for a much more relaxing trip.

CHAPTER 65

Eugene, Walter and David
Take A Trip to Idaho

ONE DAY IN THE LATE summer, about 2000, my brother Walter called me and expressed an interest in going to the Toll Gate. I told him that I had been there several times and that the buildings were all gone, but that I knew there were some remains of the upper house on Coyote Mountain and that the same was true of the Shearer house. I told him that I would meet him there. He said he would really like to go and that he would drive over from Salem to meet me in Boise. I told him to pick a day and that we would do it. I also said I felt we should invite Eugene to go with us. So we decided on a date and a place to stay in Boise. I called Eugene and told him what our plans were and that we wanted him to go with us. He thought that it would be wonderful for the three of us to go there together and re-live some of our younger days. So we had a day and place to meet and all we had to do was get there.

Eugene and I left early one morning and drove off before sunup. It is about 630 miles, so that figures to be about 10 hours driving time. So we figured that we would get to Boise in the afternoon, after all our meal and gasoline stops. The weather cooperated and the roads were in excellent condition for the most part. We made several stops for coffee, toilet and gasoline breaks and had an enjoyable ride, arriving about 3 or so in the afternoon.

We tried to call Walt, couldn't find him and wondered if he had done another of his "stand me up" tricks. We found that to not be the case, he was in our motel of choice and taking a nap. The guy at the desk didn't understand our version of English and was looking for a Mr. Walter, or some such. We got together and went somewhere close by for a bite of dinner and talked over our plans for the coming days. I had contacted Rex Jensen's daughter, Marion James, and made arrangements to have her meet us also for a few hours before we left the state. I told Walter and Eugene that we would do that after we were through around Boise and the Toll Gate as she lived in Melba near our grandfather's farm. Eugene and Walter had met her father and mother, but we all doubted they had any contact with Marion, so we wanted to do whatever she wanted to do with the time we would have with her.

After dinner, we took a ride out to Cartwright Road and drove as far as the Mason place, which was a few miles short of being at the Toll Gate, but we all had fun remembering the road and where the mailbox had been, where Ben Garrett had lived and where Walt and Eugene had walked down toward Pierce Park instead of staying on Cartwright Road. We also drove by the Idanha Hotel and on Harrison Blvd., just to jar our memories. Then we went back to our motel and I called Earl Ourada to tell him that we were in town and would like to visit with him some the following day. He told us to come on out anytime and make ourselves at home until he got there, which would be in the afternoon, as he and his friend Pat Larsen, would be making the rounds of the valley food banks that he takes eggs to and trades for greens to feed his hens. I believe we were expecting to see him around two or three o'clock in the afternoon. So with that done, we went to bed and waited the coming day.

The next morning we all got together and discussed where to have a good breakfast. We drove a bit and didn't see anything that struck our fancy so at some point we asked a gentleman where he would suggest. His answer was, "Not in this town. The best breakfast around here is the Star Café."

I asked him if that was in the town of Star and he told me it was. Star is a bit west of Eagle and all we had to do was to follow State Street west and when we got into Star it would be on our left. So off we went to Star. None of us had ever been there before, but it proved to be worth the trip and we had a marvelous breakfast at a reasonable price.

After our breakfast we went up Hwy 55 to Spring Valley and saw that one of the old big red barns had been replaced by modern looking one, but the old ranch house looks just the same, including the bunk house that was just ten steps to the north of it. Colin Mac Leod, Jr.'s brick house, just south of the ranch house, is still there and looked to me to have not been altered since it was built.

We did some more sightseeing in the Dry Creek area, then meandered back to Boise and cleaned up a bit in preparation for our visit to the Toll Gate and to Earl Ourada's ranch. We changed into some good walking shoes also as we didn't know just how we would get to the Toll Gate, but figured we may as well be ready to walk the distance, if it came to that. Then we drove out to Earl's and waited a bit for him to return from his rounds. That didn't happen for a bit so Walter and Eugene took off walking toward Camel Rock and I settled into the seat of the combine to await Earl's return.

I think that I waited close to an hour before Earl and Pat got back. We said all of our "Hello's," and such. Then he asked about Eugene and Walter. I told him they were about to the Toll Gate by now, so he and I got in his truck and drove over to meet them, by way of "Old Power Line Road." That seemed funny to me as when I had lived there, the only power lines I knew of were on the north side of Dry Creek, a good six miles away. But now there had been power lines through the north side of the Toll Gate and going past the Ourada's for so long that the road was called, "Old Power Line Road." Maybe there is a "New Power line Road," but if there is, Earl didn't mention it.

We got together with Walter and Eugene near the Spring House at the Toll Gate. They both were studying it and trying to figure it out in their minds. It is the only real remains of any building there, and it is just four crumbling stonewalls now, and a floor, beneath about three feet of greenish water, where that nice cool milk cellar had been. The only other sign of life there was the remains of the well that was just west of the commissary. That is still a round hole, about four feet in diameter, lined with rocks and that year it was fairly well full of water. A fence had been built around it to keep the livestock from venturing into it.

We kicked dirt, dry cow patties and some weeds, while we all got to know more about Earl, and he about us. Then he told us that his sister-in-law, Vreni (pronounced Franny) Ourada, Philip's wife, had asked him to go to the orchard and pick some plums for her. We got into the truck and he drove us up to the orchard. We all picked some plums and filled a couple of bags Then Earl told us that his kids had been there a week or so ago and there was a bear with them, also picking plums, so they hadn't gotten all they wanted. It may have had cubs and bears are nothing to mess with when they are raising cubs.

We took our load of plums and Earl drove us back to his house. When we got there, Pat, Vreni and Philip were all there to meet us and Earl told us they had all planned that we would stay and have dinner with them. So what could we do? No more asking me three times. Once did the trick and we told them we'd be delighted to share a meal with them.

Earl told us that first he had to feed his cattle, and wondered if we'd like to go. We all jumped at the chance and got back into his truck. The bed had a lot of loaves of bread in it. Big unsliced loaves, and Eugene and Walt were to toss the loaves out to the cattle as we drove into the field. This was fun to watch; the cows saw the pickup coming and immediately gave chase. They knew it was full of food. I got a few pictures and we tried to make sure each animal got at least one loaf before we left. Earl got out and hand fed the bull his loaf. Earl told us, "I want to always be on good terms with him."

One look at the bull's size and the horns and you would understand. Earl gave him a loaf and the patted him a bit while he held it drooping down on both sides of his huge mouth. Not the brightest looking animal, but I know it is a clever devil inside. He has all those heifers to himself and his master catering to him at every opportunity. But then again, without him there would be no calves, so why not? He has earned his keep.

We got back to his house and the dinner was ready. Grace was said, as was the custom in the Ourada's house since my first visit, and well before. We had a lovely meal and talked well into the evening before we went back to our rooms in Boise. It was refreshing to all of our memories to have spent the time in the places we had been as little kids and with the people that had so vividly touched our lives at that young age.

The next morning we went back to the Star Café and had our breakfast. We had taken all our things and had checked out of the motel, so I called Marion and we went to her house just out north of Melba. She had asked her sister, Crystal, to come and meet us also. They met us with open arms and asked what we would like to do. I told them we wanted to see our grandfather's place and I thought it would be grand to go over to Swan Falls and then look at the holdings their father had held in his corner of Idaho.

Marion had a van with lots of room, so off we went to Swan Falls and a tour of much of Canyon County. She told us that her father, Rex Jensen, had dreamed of owning property from Donnelly to the Snake River and before he had died, he had accomplished nearly that. Not adjoining places, but many of them within sight of each other. She had taken over ownership, after his death, of much of it and showed us several places that she still held and had rented out. She took us by our grandfather's farm just west of Melba and then took us to see her folk's graves.

We had a burger in Melba and went back to her home. There she told us a lot of the history of her father and mother and how her dad had been asked by Mr. Wrigley to come to Catalina Island and run his sheep business, Rex had looked into it and decided he would rather run his own business in Idaho, so her folks had returned to the Melba area and started their own little empire. The home Marion lived in now wasn't the little shack behind her dad's house that I remembered, but a large Victorian-style ranch house that her son had built for her. I understood he was a building contractor and had built a lot of homes near the Payette Lakes and possibly elsewhere. This house was lovely and quite large, with views to the east out over her fields.

Trees of several varieties were surrounding her house and they were in need of trimming. Eugene saw this and said he would come back and do that for her. She showed us around the grounds, the roses her mother had raised and such, but we didn't go into her father and mother's house. She seemed skittish about going over there and I got out of her that her daughter had died there and now her drunken-son-in law lived there. That place was a mess with garbage and trash all down the driveway. The grandchildren, a boy and a girl, lived with Marion and she didn't have anything to do with their dad.

Chrystal left and went home to Boise and we all went to Melba to pick up some pizza for dinner, which we brought back to Marion's house. As we were getting ready to go in, Walter said he had to leave now and wouldn't be coming into the house. He would just be on his way. That was real sudden and a surprise to all of us. We had been invited to have dinner and spend the night. I thought that we would leave the next morning for a leisurely journey to our homes. But Walter insisted and seemed in some distress to get out of there, so we said out goodbyes and he was on his way. Eugene and I had pizza and visited more with Marion and the grandkids. Later in the evening we all went to bed.

Eugene and I left after a quick breakfast the following morning and drove along the Snake River from about Murphy to Marsing, where we turned onto the main highway and headed for Winnemucca. Just as we got to the outskirts of Winnemucca, Walter pulled in behind us. He had been waiting alongside the road for us. We pulled over and talked a bit and decided that we would have a lunch in Winnemucca.

Walter didn't tell us then, but we found that he had been treated for prostate cancer and he had suffered some bleeding while we had been out to pick up the pizza in Melba and so he had ducked out to hide that from us. He had wanted to talk some, so he had waited for us all morning, having spent the night in Winnemucca. So we had our breakfast and then drove on toward Lovelock and I began to wonder just what was really on Walter's mind, so I passed him and told him to follow Eugene, and me into a gas station in Lovelock. I told Eugene to go ride with him to Reno and see if he would open up about what was really on his mind.

When we got to Reno, Walter pulled over and Eugene got into my car and we continued home to California while Walter took 395 and headed north, back to his home in Salem. He hadn't really disclosed anything to Eugene and we didn't know why he hadn't stayed in Melba with us. Only later did I find the real reason and he told me that shortly after he left us, heading north, the generator on his Jaguar went out and he had the devil of a time getting it replaced. It took him another day to get home from where his car troubles started, which should have not been more than a six hour drive.

CHAPTER 66

The Beginnings of "Deep Stuff" (I Learn More about Angus and Nellie)

OVER THE YEARS I HAVE remained in touch with Earl Ourada and his family. He lived in Idaho and had gone to school with me there, though Earl was several grades ahead of me. He raised hay, turkeys and cattle on the 800 acres he bought from his father. Nelda and I would drop by on visits to Idaho and we got to know his children, and they ours. As the years passed we found that this was a wonderful reach into my past and I took my brothers Walter and Eugene to his ranch for a wonderful meal with Earl and his brother Phillip, along with Pat Larsen and Vreni Ourada, Phillip's wife. We were invited back for a "No Cow Day." Earl used to have a roundup every year and after he sold off his cattle the participants in the roundup told him they would miss the get together. He gave that some thought and came up with "No Cow Day." Just show up and have a party, so they all thought that a great idea. Nelda and I, along with our family, were invited.

At the first No Cow Day we attended I had a great time. I met several people that I had known while I lived up there and many that I had heard of but may have never met. I also found that there was a great lady, Celeste Rush, at the party. She was interested in information on my aunt Nellie as she and her friend, Lyn Winer, were contemplating writing a book about her. We exchanged email addresses and I continued to visit everyone I could find time to talk with. My brother Eugene and his wife spent a lot of time with Celeste and found that she and Lyn had heard a lot of stories of this quaint older lady often found running about half-nude or nude. Sometimes Nellie would be telling stories from her travels abroad or living in Washington, DC. This had really gotten them curious about the truth of it all and when they had talked with enough people that knew her, they decided to put her story together and separate the truth from fantasy as much as possible. When Celeste met Eugene and me she found we really did know things to help her and Lyn in their novel endeavor.

When we returned to California, I started exchanging emails with these ladies.

These proved to be a real inspiration for me to try to recall as much as I could and put it into print for them. I found that a lot of what I had to tell required for me to make a sketch to help clarify what information I was trying to convey. Sometimes the words alone just couldn't get the job done. I have had only the introduction to art as training so some of my attempts seemed to me to be very poor, but the information seemed to be getting passed along.

There were other trips to Idaho for No Cow Days and for a Centennial celebration of the Ourada ranch having been in the same family for 100 years. Nelda and I went to Celeste's house and met with several people that would be an interesting part of the book. These same people were of great interest to me as one was Pete Echanove, whose father had been my first employer. He had marvelous stories to tell and we met Lyn and her husband Ken, as well as Celeste's husband, Carl. We also met again most of the surviving Ourada family and some of the Stiff's, who were from the family of Earl's mother, Gladys. Also I got to meet face to face with Tom Blessenger, whose father was the Tom Blessenger that lived at the Toll Gate. Now I was really hooked on seeing the book to completion and learning as much about my aunt as I could.

The ladies supplied me with a lot of questions and I worked diligently to supply them with proper answers. Much of what they asked I knew the answers to, but some of it I had to dig for in Nellie's photo album, old letters and my own research into our family history. I had saved all of the contents of anything of Nellie's that had been entrusted to my care and that included marriage license, old passport, letters from people she knew, letters from my mother and a few of her collection of business cards from acquaintances. Looking these people up on the inter-net has validated a lot of what she had told me of the ties they had to her and to history. Sharing that information and the research Lyn and Celeste has given me an even greater knowledge of Nellie throughout her life.

Since I was learning so much about Nellie, I got interested more than ever in finding out more about the Mac Pherson's, Mac Donald, and the Mac Leod's, all of whom had touched my life as I grew up. I asked Colin Mac Leod III if he had any history of his family and was sorry to hear that he didn't. He also didn't express any interest in exploring that with me. I got the feeling he didn't like me asking, so I didn't pursue it with him anymore. Angus had told me of his brother that was killed in the runaway of his team and how he had frozen to death. I didn't remember Angus ever telling me about the whereabouts of his brother Donald, though he had pointed out his homestead to all of us as we went to the orchard to pick plums. Angus and Colin Sr. could speak Gaelic and I enjoyed listening to them, or when Angus would sing Gaelic songs, but I didn't know just where they were from. So I decided to do some research there also.

I tried by finding a map of Scotland and finding the county of Ross. I remembered we used to get the Ross-Shire Journal from his sister Margaret. She would send over a packet of half a dozen or so quite often. Then I tried to find where they lived and that came to me in quite an accidental way, in which it will take me five paragraphs to clarify.

My neighbor Bob Comella had a son, Jay, who had gone to several colleges to play rugby. One of Jay's friends, Iain Thomson, taught rugby at Chico State, here in California. He and his brother David were both from

Scotland. I happened to work for Bob, on an addition to another friend, David Holiday's house, where David Thomson was helping us. (Three David's on that job.) We got to know each other a little, and later I met Iain and saw David again at Bob Comella's house, while there to visit shortly after Bob had heart surgery. I recall meeting Iain then also, but am not remembering much about that meeting, as at that moment in time, Bob was a real worry to me, having just returned from his open-heart surgery.

Then there came 9/11 and all that commotion in all of our lives. Out of that came my first look at Rolling Stone Magazine and on the cover was Jay Comella, standing on "the pile"*13 at Ground Zero. Inside was a list of the FDNY firefighters killed during 9/11, including one I had met at Comella's, Andy Fredericks. Also inside was the story of why Jay was on the cover, he had been in NYC to visit some firemen and was just going to Manhattan as the planes struck the towers. He remained there working to recover the victims for a couple of weeks. After that he returned to the Oakland Fire Department, where he was employed. Along with some others, and they put together a memorial golf tournament to aid the family of Andy Fredericks.

I went to one of the tournaments and won a week at a hunting lodge in Scotland as part of the fund-raiser. I'm not saying I was that great of a golfer, I won this at a silent auction. The hunting lodge was on Loch Shin, near Lairg, Southerland, Scotland. Jay and I talked about the lodge and he also found a lady that is the records keeper for births, deaths and marriages for the Highland Council. She found some of Angus's family history for me and I found he was born in Ardgay. I asked Jay if he knew where that was and he told me he had been there the day before. I found that it was only a few miles from the hunting lodge where we would be staying.

Armed with the above information, I soon learned that Angus was born at Lubconich House, near the Manse at Croick Church, which is eleven

---

13 The "pile" was the name for the rubble from the Twin Towers that had to be gone through painstakingly to retrieve any remains of the thousands of people killed there, including hundreds of Police and Fire would-be rescuers killed in the collapse.

miles south of Ardgay, out in the country. I searched the internet and found out that a manse is a home provided for the minister of a church and that it may be miles from the church. But I was getting really close. I also found that a Wilma Mac Kenzie was searching for relatives, in the states, of Duncan Mac Pherson, with the further explanation that one of his sons had frozen to death in Caldwell, Idaho after a driving accident. I found this to be a dead end site and we left for our Scotland visit shortly after.

I had won a one-week stay at Sallachy Estate, near Lairg, Southerland, Scotland. The lodge sits overlooking Loch Shin and will sleep 19 adults. Nelda and I decided we would invite our family and some friends to join us for that week. I made arrangements for our time to be a week in August.

I wrote emails to Pat Smith and her son Roy, inviting them to come for the week at Sallachy with us. I also invited my own family members and determined that the Mc Bride's would not be able to go on this trip. I in-vited Dave and Betty Haliday to go with us also. He is of Scottish ancestry, so I guessed he would enjoy it there. This gave us about thirteen of us that would be there for most of the week, including Tom and Dolores Comella who would meet us at the Lodge.

I also searched the Internet for anything I could find about Angus Mac Pherson. My best source was Jay Comella. He put me in touch with Heather Butling. She was the records keeper for the Highland Council and for twenty-five Pounds, which amounted to about forty dollars; she did a search of the births, deaths and marriages in the Highlands for me. She found that Angus had been born in Ardgay. She also told me that Angus had probably been born at home and registered when someone went to town, nearest one being Ardgay. He had lived in Lubconich House, which was across the road from the Mansk of Croick Church.

I went to Jay to find out where Ardgay was and he told me he had been there the day before. It is just down river from Loch Shin. I looked at the map and found the road from Ardgay went to Croick Church and then farther off to the west and became a dirt path. I found, online, the

Webmaster for Croick Church. My map of the UK showed several build-ings near Croick Church. I became determined to go there.

Jay Comella and the manager of the Sallachy Estate, Iain Thomson became good friends while playing rugby in California together. Jay is the son of my friend, Bob Comella. Bob and Jay live across the street from me, and a short time before we were to be in Scotland, Iain and his family came to visit Jay. We helped to find car seats for their children and pumped them for information about what to expect, and anything we could think of to enhance our stay. They told us to just ask Jay if I had any other questions. Jay told us to shop at Tesco in Inverness, take a shortcut to the Lodge off the A9 through Alness and made a list of things he thought we might enjoy seeing while at the lodge.

CHAPTER 67

Scotland Trip in 2010

OUR DAUGHTER JANETTE, NELDA AND I flew over to London and were met by a friend of our friend, Pat Smith. He took us to Pat's place in Lower Shorne, where we had a wonderful time with her and her son Roy and his family. We stayed at Pats' for three fun-filled days. She drove us to several places of interest, Chartwell, Rochester, Ightem Mote, Leed's Castle and Chatham for a visit to the Dickens Center. We had a dinner with Roy and his wife, Sarah, at their home for a very nice time with all of them. The last day we went to a restaurant out on a farm with the some of the rest of Pat's family, her daughter Leslie and son-in-law, Bim.

After dinner we boarded a fast train to London that took us near our hotel there. We met up with Rob and Max at the hotel. They took us back out for a pub dinner a few blocks away. They had arrived that morning and had done a few things close by the hotel, getting to know the bus and underground rail system, and making plans for the next day.

That next day took us by rail to Cambridge to see Peter House, one of the oldest colleges there and it was where Max had spent a summer session in school, during his summer break from high school. We punted on the Cam, (rode a small boat on the river Cam) and did an open top bus tour of Cambridge. We went to Peter House and saw what a lovely old place it was. We saw where Max had his meals and looked up at his room's only window, as the staff wouldn't allow us to tour inside. We did a tour of Kings

College and had a meal of fish and chips before returning to London, again on the train.

The next two days we did the tourist things in London, visiting the Tower and riding the open top bus around the towns of London and Windsor. We walked through St James Park, past Buckingham Palace, took a boat tour of the Thames and had an elegant dinner at the home of Simon and Carolyn Morgan, our friends from London, near Kensington Park and Marble Arch.

The train took us to the city of York for two nights, where we did the tours of all the top attractions for a couple of days. We saw Clifford's tower, the Minster, Jorvik, walked the City Wall and ate well most every place we stopped. A lady sold us two tickets to the Tattoo in Edinburgh at face value.

Another train trip brought us close to our hotel in Edinburgh for a three nights stay. Nelda and I went to the Military Tattoo and enjoyed that display of marching skills and the pipes and drums from countries throughout the world. We did tours of the castle, the city by bus, and the Royal Yacht. We also walked very many miles in all three of the cities we had visited so far. All of us seemed quite up to it and we enjoyed every step of the way.

We left Edinburgh on the fourth morning after picking up a rental car at Waverly Station. There we also met our friends, the Hallday's, and we took them up on an offer to transport some of our luggage, as the cars were quite small for five people and all of our things.

When we left the parking lot for the rental car I felt that our car was quite powerless. Then as I approached some busy street, a gentleman on the sidewalk shouted at me, "Pardon sir, but your car is alight." As I stopped, three of my passengers bailed out and left just Rob and me in the car. There was lots traffic so I knew I couldn't just stay there so Rob and I found our way back to the rental office and he went in to complain about our car while I examined the shift pattern and found the problem was mine. I was using the top four gears of a six-speed transmission.

With the lady from the car rental berating me for being unfit to drive, I pulled out of the rental spot, drove up a ramp and turned left onto the street to return to where the rest of our family abandoned ship. Doing so, I cut the corner sharp and took some road obstruction with me for a few feet until the car refused to go any more. Rob jumped out to determine what I had hit, told me to back up while he kicked it loose, then got back in and we left with no further drag. A block or so along the street, Rob told me I was way too close to the parked cars, just as our mirror made contact with the mirror of a parked car. We drove away from there, as we saw no damage to either car. I asked Rob to find "New Street" on our map and he replied that, "I can't see the print on the map." I made a mental note to fire him as my Navigator.

We turned near where the family had evacuated the smoking car and were about to make another turn when Janette yelled at us. Now they all got in the car and I had Janette sit up front to read the map. We slowly drove out of town with subtle warnings from Janette to pull more toward the center of the street. Realize that the driver sits on the right in the UK and the car is driven down the left lanes of the road. It took me a few days to get used to doing that.

We made a bit of a detour on our route to Sallachy and made a pass by St. Andrews, home of the game of golf. We bought a hat and took pictures, then went on to Pitlochry and stopped for ice cream. I think that also settled a lot of nerves. Then we drove on to Inverness and went to a Tesco store to do shopping for groceries. Jay had told us how to find it and that it would be the best place for us to shop.

Next we took the shortcut Jay had told us about, through Alness and over the hills until we could look down upon the Firth of Dornach. (Firth means estuary.) We all felt we had to stop and take pictures of this beautiful country. We then went on to Lairg and refueled the car. Then following a map Ian's seven-year-old son, Roddy, had drawn for us, we drove to the lodge.

At the lodge we reunited with the Haliday's and found that our friend's Tom Comella and his sister Dolores Moffat had arrived a couple of days back and were now moved into Sallachy also. We would have another day before Pat, Roy, Sarah and the two girls arrived. That night we settled into our rooms and toured the large hunting lodge. Iain, his friend Fiona and their three kids came by to make sure we were all well and supplied adequately.

The following day we did a drive to the north coast to the towns of Tongue, Thurso, Mey and over to John O'Groats, which is about as far north as one can get without a boat. We toured Mey Castle and had a full day of it getting back to the lodge in the early evening.

In the following days we toured Dunrobin Castle, saw a wonderful Raptor show, ate fish and chips in Golspie, watched the salmon jump upstream at Shin Falls, then we had a proper Scottish evening meal of haggis and salmon served to us by a local lady and her daughter, followed by dessert of sticky toffee pudding. We also went to an old croft several miles along the loch from the lodge to try our hand at shooting clay pigeons. We made a day trip to Loch Ness, and the Haliday's visited a distillery and went to Ullapool for the best fish and chips in Scotland.

The best time for I had, was the day we went to Croick Church. Just my family did that, and we found the church with no trouble. As we walked around outside in the church graveyard, we came to a memorial stone with all of Angus's siblings listed on it, even the mention of Will having died in Caldwell, Idaho, so we knew it was the correct family. Janette played "Joy to the World,| on the church organ and we wrote down all of the names on the memorial stone.

Past Croick Church, there was a fence with a locked gate, so we could go no further. We did ask a neighbor lady if there was any history, known to her, of the families. She didn't know any, so we left and went back through Ardgay to Bonar Bridge and home to the lodge. To me, that had been quite an emotional day, and very much to be remembered.

Following our stay at the lodge, we left quite early in the morning in order to drop Rob off at the airport in Inverness at 5 AM, so he could fly to London and catch his flight home. Fiona had arraigned this for him. Janette, Max, Nelda and I, were visiting some friends of Janette, that lived in Stirling, Bonnie and David had lived in California and Bonnie had worked with Janette for a couple of years before moving home to Stirling.

After we dropped Rob off, we began to look for someplace to have breakfast. That doesn't come easy on a Sunday morning in the Highlands. We didn't find an eating-place open until we were inside Stirling Castle at almost noon. There we did find a place to eat before we did the castle tour.

In the afternoon we met Bonnie and David. They took us to see the Wallace Memorial, where we climbed the several hundred steps to the top. The view made the climb worth the trip. We also saw William Wallace's sword, a Claymore that is about five feet in length. Definitely a two hand-ed sword. Then Dave and Bonnie led us out to Kippen for a wonderful dinner. We left the next morning and returned the car to Edinburgh in time to catch our train to London.

Dolores and Tom Comella had left us a few days earlier and during our catered dinner, we had found out that Tom was in the hospital in London with pneumonia. Now in London, we had dinner with Carolyn, Dolores and Simon. Tom was still having a rough time with the pneumonia and remained hospitalized. The following morning we flew home. It would be hard to have a better trip than that one, with the exception of Tom's devel-oping pneumonia, but in many ways the next one was better.

CHAPTER 68

Scotland Revisited 2012

FOLLOWING OUR JOURNEY IN 2010, my daughter Janette told me that she felt a fortnight in Sallachy would be a good thing to plan for in a year or two. We decided upon 2012, and I made the arrangements for our stay at Sallachy Estate for the first full two weeks in August. Those that decided they could go this trip were Nelda, myself, Janette Stuart, Rob Mc Arthur, Darlene Mc Bride, Warren Mc Bride, Keith Mc Bride, Caitlin Riverbank,[14] Max Stuart and Arianna Surendran.[15] Not all could travel together as some had work obligations to meet and the Mc Brides wished to spend a night in Culcreath Castle, near Stirling. (It is the ancestral home of the Clan Galbraith, Warren's mother's clan.)

While I was preparing the plans for our last trip in 2010, I had searched the Internet and found that a Wilma Mac Kenzie was looking for descendants of Duncan Mac Pherson.[16]I had not been able to contact her until after that trip, but this time I found her and Angus' great nephew, Willie Ross. I invited them to join us at the Lodge for a stay and they had agreed to join us. Willie Ross found the Proctor of the Southerland Estate, which is where Lubconich House still stands, and the Proctor agreed to take us there. This would be a great trip, I could tell.

---

14 Caitlin Rivenbark is Darlene and Warren's daughter

15 Arianna Surendran was Max Stuart's girl friend, now fiancé'

16 Duncan Mac Pherson was the name of Angus's father and Wilma had included enough detail to make it clear to me, she was looking for that same person.

Janette, Nelda and I flew to Newark, NJ where we had a three hour layover. This broke the flight into two fairly survivable segments and gave us time to have a relaxing meal at the Newark Terminal. We landed in Glasgow in the morning, found our rental car and soon were driving north in hopes of getting to the Isle of Skye before it got too late. Roadwork and a detour caused us to spend the night at the Glengarry Castle Hotel. We did see a lot of lovely country and the ruins of Kulchurn Castle, which Janette and I had enjoyed reading love stories about, shortly before we started this trip

Next morning we were again underway and visited the Eileen Dornan castle, then drove across a bridge onto the Isle of Skye and continued to Dunvegan Castle, which we toured. After that we drove back to Glasgow and spent the night in a hotel near the airport. The next morning we picked up Rob, and asked about his flight. He said it was okay but he was lucky to be here as he had trouble reading the signs and his ticket. New glasses were what he thought was the trouble as well as being tired and excited about the trip. This proved to be tragically not the case.

The four of us drove to the Culcreath Castle and saw where the Mc Brides would be staying, drove past Stirling and stopped in Perth for lunch. We then proceeded on to Fortingall; some claim it to be the birthplace of Pontius Pilate. Glen Lyon is just west of there and we went about half way through the glen to Bridge of Baldie. Somewhere there in the Glen Lyon area is where John Mc Arthur was born in 1742, to Robert Mc Arthur and his wife Janet. John immigrated to the USA in 1772 and that started my family line here. At Bridge of Baldie we found a WWI memorial that listed a John Mc Arthur, as a casualty of that conflict.

Inverness is a beautiful spot on the River Ness, along the shores of the Moray and Beauly Firths. We could find no lodging there and found some in Nairn, a bit east, very near Culloden Moor. The innkeeper of the Aurora Hotel let Janette and Rob each have their own room, at no additional charge. The following morning we toured the Battle Field of Culloden and watched the video presentation and other demonstrations that pretty well described the barbaric ways that man has learned to kill and maim one another. This battle had ended the '45, which was the Jacobite rebellion that had hoped to put Bonnie Prince Charles on the throne of Scotland. There was great loss of life and the Clan way of life was forever changed. Many of the Chiefs were killed or forced into hiding, and their power was gone forever.

From that dreary spot, we drove to the Tesco store, in Inverness and did our grocery shopping for our stay at the Lodge. The drive through Alness and over Ross-shire into Southerland was a thing of beauty, forcing us to stop for pictures of some bridges and the Firth of Dornoch. It was just too pretty to pass up. Actually this was true of the entire trip, from our landing in Glasgow until we flew out of Heathrow in London. I took well over a thousand pictures in about three weeks' time.

We had planned on having a Sunday Roast at the Lairg Hotel. Unfortunately our timing was off and we arrived at 2:30 PM, as they were clearing off the tables and mopping the floors in preparation for dinner to be served starting at 6:00 PM. We made our reservation and went to the lodge.

Our return to the Sallachy Estate was just as awe-inspiring as the first time there in 2010. There was more rain, it was a bit darker generally, but the views were still spectacular. I felt we were, in a sense, returning home, after too long of a stay away. Ducks greeted us as we approached the door of the lodge and I was determined to train them somehow before I left. There was a mother and three of her spring brood alive and well. Off in the distance two drakes kept a watchful eye on our approach. Brown deer were browsing on the hillside outside the windows to the east of the lodge and watched us with curiosity as we arrived, seeing nothing exciting they went back to their meal.

Monday morning I was up at 5:30 to watch the sunrise, but two things prevented that, a bit of mist over the loch and the sun had already risen. Seems Lairg is about on the same latitude as Helsinki, Finland. That means an early sunrise and late sunset in August. Rob was already out training the ducks to eat toast and they caught on quickly.

We drove to Shin Falls to watch the salmon jump. They seemed tired and we saw only a couple of feeble attempts in the twenty minutes we spent there. With that little bit of disappointment we drove toward Ardgay. An early turn found us on the road to Ullapool, known as the best place for fish and chips in Scotland, or so folks around Lairg told us.

The sky had cleared and we saw the mountains in the distance and tried to guess if they were islands or part of the mainland, as it turned out we were seeing both, depending on where we looked. This was a very beautiful site and we took many pictures. We went to the "Chippy" in Ullapool, just a bit off the shore, but with views of Loch Broom.

Janette had done about all the driving today and it was a relaxing time for us. She was doing just fine and I was taking pictures with her camera, as mine wasn't functional at that time. One must put the battery in correctly, I found.

The Mc Brides were doing well. We had contacted them through email and found that they had a problem with American accents and the locals, as did we. There are two castles with similar names, and we all mispronounced Culcreath. The directions took them a couple of hours out of their way, before they found their error. They had a good drive and a fun-filled stay in their room at Culcreath. The following day they would tour Stirling and the Wallace memorial and then go to the lodge.

After I had called Willie Ross the next morning, we drove to Bonar Bridge. He is Angus' great nephew and had made arrangements for us to go to Lubconich House on Friday. He had also recommended we have lunch at the Checkered Flag, in Bonar Bridge. We missed finding the restaurant and after our second try, decided to go to the one we knew, the Caley Café. They have excellent soups and sandwiches, which we had enjoyed on our previous trip.

As we sat down and gave our order, Rob got into a conversation with a nice lady, Ann Worthy, who does water color painting on postal cards. He bought a card and I did also to get to ask her who the Historian might be around the area. She told me Marion Fraser at the Checkered Flag, just across the way, she said as she pointed right where we had just looked twice. After we ate we walked across the street and still had to ask in a shop where the Checkered Flag might be found. "Second door up the hill," was the response.

We found the door this time and walked into a yarn shop. A lady came out and we asked about the Checkered Flag. "Oh dear, this place hasn't been that for years," she said. She was Marion Fraser and I bought a couple of books she had compiled and asked if she knew of Lubconich and the Mac Pherson's. She told me to come back in a couple of days and she would have some of the history written down for me. Also she had a book she would give to me, if she could find it. I eventually got some pages she wrote in longhand, but she couldn't find the book. I asked about a couple of Gaelic phrases I knew of and she didn't hear or they didn't mean anything to her, so I gave that up.

So we went back to the lodge and awaited the Mc Brides. They appeared about 5:00 PM and had a tiring day, but very lovely, all told. They did all their planned tours and were quite happy to now be relaxing at the lodge. We enjoyed a great spaghetti dinner and retired relatively early.

Wednesday morning we all went to Dunrobin Castle in Golspie and did the tour there, then watched a falconry show that was quite nice. We had seen it in 2010 and it was just as good as then. The weather wasn't too hot and there was a hint of rain off and on, yet no real showers. A young lad played the pipes for us and Caitlin thought he was gorgeous in his kilt with its complete regalia. We went back to the Golspie Hotel and found it to be out of business. The next stop was a restaurant just nearby, terrible service, but good food. So slow that Darlene finally grabbed up our money and chased down the waiter to settle the bill.

We drove to Dornach to see the golf course where Warren wanted to play golf. It was along the shore and seems very expensive. Warren was about to give it a pass, when some gent informed him there are really two courses and the other one is much more reasonable. He decided that one will do and went off to explore the town and have a warm drink at the

Castle Hotel. Very nice and we spend some time there, then walked about the town and visited the church, which seemed small until we went inside. Somehow, inside this small building, was a very large church.

I had lost one of my medications and was about to leave for Lairg to see if I could get it when Iain came in and I told him my plan. He told me to go to the "drop in Clinic" that is just past the Lairg Hotel, a couple of blocks, on the road to Goldspie. The doctor will give me the required prescription and come back to the pharmacy across the road from the hotel. I did that and it worked just as Iain had told me. No cost for any of it. I protested that, "I was the one who lost the medicine, why should the good people of the UK have to pay for my stupidity?" The pharmacist told me, "It is the British Obama care. No one pays."

Iain's wife, Dr. Fiona Fraser, Iains' sister and both family's kids were at the lodge when I get back. Keith was mixing well with all the children and they were running about having a swell time. We visited for a good while and then decided it was time to drive to Durness, via Tongue, to explore Smoo Cave. It was a good drive to Tongue and we felt the name Altnaharra, a small village we passed through, was like something out of Arabian Nights. Lots of laughter was had over our attempts to pronounce the Gaelic signs along the way.

It was a pretty drive, a bit overcast, yet no wind or rain and we stopped a couple of times for a rest and pictures. Along the far north coast of Scotland there is a real mix of geology. There will be a spot that obviously is where many rocky islands pounded together to become an almost barren rocky shoreline and out to sea a mile or so will be a low island, covered in green grasses that are tall, telling the world there is lots of top soil over there and a whole different eco-system.

We arrived in Durness and walked down the trail to Smoo Cave. We took the tour, which was the last one of the day. The guide took us in a Zodiac boat for a little way into the cave, over a pond, past a high waterfall, and then we got out onto a path that took us deeper into the cavern. There were signs of ancient boat repair where we started and even signs of human activity farther in. We ended our venture in at a little pond and the guide told us of his attempts to scuba dive that little pond and determine how big the cavern really is. So far he has been a few hundred yards past where we were, all underwater, so he isn't sure if the cavern again opens out of the water or not. It was a very interesting tour for all of us. We bid the guide farewell and went into Durness to eat.

Finding something to eat became a problem, the restaurant we chose was closed until about 6:00 PM, so our decision was to check out some of the hotels on the trip back to Lairg. Surely they would have afternoon meals available. We stopped a couple of times and were told that the meal would be available past 6:00 PM. Once again we found ourselves at the Lairg Hotel for a fine meal and to watch the beautiful sunset, at 9:15. It had been another wonderful day in the Highlands.

Friday was our day to go to Lubconich. Iain has loaned me his truck, Willy Ross would meet us at Croick Church with his Land Rover, Alistair Southerland, the proctor of the property Lubconich is part of, would also bring a truck. I didn't know what vehicle the Mac Kenzie's would have, but we all would get to Lubconich somehow.

We met at Croick church about 10, Willie wasn't yet there but by the time we had all been properly introduced, he and a friend showed up. We had now all met Wilma and James Mac Kenzie, Willy Ross and his friend, Anna, Alistair Southerland and his son Neal. We managed to all get into the vehicles and drove about six miles on a dirt track to Lubconich. No rain, not cold, but there were a few clouds and a bit of mist toward the top of the hills.

We arrived at Lubconich and I got a lump in my throat. I did really wish that Angus could have made this trip with us. The house was in great condition, all windows intact and obviously it had been well cared for. The house was constructed of stone and had been stucco coated on the outside. At some point a bathroom had been added adjacent to the front entry. Two dormers had been added to the front roof section of the second story, making the building appear fairly modern. I am guessing that it was constructed in the early 1700s, but no one seems to know for sure.

Inside, the house was divided into three rooms on the ground floor. An oil stove was a recent addition, in the kitchen, as well as electrical lights and outlets, there were no power line to the house, electricity had been furnished by a generator powered by a diesel engine, Neal told us. There was a small entry hall that had stairs leading to two rooms above. These rooms were separate by a duplicate of the entry hall, which may have served as a place for Angus' mother and his sisters, to sew. All the walls had been wood clad on the inside of the house, the stairs were wood and the heat was from fireplaces downstairs. No heat was provided up stairs. This obviously was a home of some crofter who had done pretty well for himself.

Out behind the house was a stone pen for the livestock. Behind that was a quite long barn that appeared to me, have once been the original croft house, with its attached barn as had been the practice in earlier times. It was divided into a horse barn on one end, haymow in the middle and cow barn on the other end. I suspect that the cow barn was the original barn and the rest of the structure had been the original croft.

Alistair showed us that there were also the remains of a little shed that had been made of loosely stacked stones, no mortar used. This, he told us, was for the family cart.

We all returned to Croick Church and Alistair bid us farewell. The rest of us visited the church and the graveyard. Willy pointed out a good many of his Ross relatives that were buried there, as well as Mac Pherson's and many other relatives of the Ross and Mac Pherson Clans. Then we went to Bonar Bridge for lunch.

I rode with Willy Ross and someone else drove Iain's truck back to the lodge. As we neared the lodge I saw Iain out by the road. We stopped and I introduced Willy Ross to Iain Thomson. Iain had torn down the Ross Cottage, numbered the stones, (which became the office of his home) and put it back up with each stone cleaned and replaced in its exact original location, except that now the bottom stones rest on a concrete foundation. Then Iain built a substantial home for himself adjoining the old building, from matching stones. Iain showed Willy the rest of the house and the two of them had a great visit. Willy had been born in the Ross Cottage and raised on the estate.

Eventually Willy and I joined the others at the lodge and after much talk, and picture sharing, the ladies announced that dinner was served. Darlene and Janette had made a large pan of lasagna, and a salad, along with breads and anything else one may want.

Willy's wife, Angela had come to join us and his friend from school, Anna, had gone home. I was confused, I had thought Anna to be the wife or live in girl friend of Willy's and hadn't hear the explanation that she had lived about three miles past Lubconich, with her grandmother at some earlier time. After dinner, wine, a bit of whisky and much talk and laughter, we went to bed, it was very late.

Saturday we were fed a great breakfast of scrambled eggs, potatoes, bacon, sausage, toast and jellies, with coffee, teas, milk and juices to drink. This our two daughters had put together. About 11 the Ross' and the Mac Kenzie's went their separate ways, heading home after lengthy and somewhat emotional goodbyes. We were tired but still had a full day ahead of us. We went Shin Falls and played pee-wee golf and had lunch. Then Nelda, Rob Janette and I drove to Lairg and took a walk around town. Then we went back to the lodge, rested and had leftovers for dinner.

We visited Tain[17] on Sunday after dropping Rob and Warren off to play golf at the course in Bonar Bridge. We had a Sunday Roast at the hotel. Then walked the town and found that it had the date 1066 prominently displayed on a park gate, we are sure that the town had been founded by William the Conqueror, when he became King of England in that year. We went back and retrieved our two golfers. They had a good time even though they had borrowed clubs and were on a strange course. Rob was not a "by the rules golfer," but Warren was. They had decided to just have a good time, which they did.

At Sallachy, we found that our friend from London, Simon Morgan had arrived on his Ducati 1200 cc motorcycle. He was at Iain's having a

---

17 Willy and Angela Ross live on the edge of Tain

drink with another friend also, that same Jay Comella that has made such a profound difference in our stays in Scotland previously, with his local knowledge and being well aware of our needs and preferences. Eventually they all come over to the lodge for dinner and to watch the closing program of the Olympic Games, in London. I went to bed early as I intended to get up at 5 for some picture of the sunrise. This I did, however Janette was the one who took the best photos.

Monday, Janette, Rob and I drove to the bus depot in Inverness to pick up the last of our travelers, Max and Arianna. We made the connection and having done a small bit of grocery shopping, we drive back to Sallachy, with a short stop in Bonar Bridge to feed Max. He is a big boy and needs his food, so this was a good stop for him. The Mc Brides had gone to Ullapool and Simon had followed them on his motorcycle.

Tuesday morning Simon was off to London. He had hoped to see a friend in Stirling first, but I found they didn't connect, so he drove the Ducati straight through to London. Our plans were to go to Mey Castle and see the North Coast some more. Weather was not cooperating and by the time we got to Helmsdale, the rain and fog were making traffic into a solid string of cars, barely doing 25 MPH. We made a pit stop in Wick and the traffic and fog had let up some. We continued up the A9 toward John O'Groats and stopped for a bar lunch in a hotel near Duncansby Head. After lunch we took the road over to Duncansby Head and tried to find some puffins on the towering cliffs.

Duncansby Head has sheer cliffs that are surely over a hundred feet from the top to the seas that constantly are pounding on their base. The cliff looks like it is made of bricks by a magic hand that somehow piled them layer on layer, but they aren't bricks. They are made of rock, which has eroded with thousands of pockets and small shelves having been formed. In many of those are the nests of seabirds and the sky is filled with birds coming and going, taking care of their chicks. The puffins had flown the nests and were many miles west on the Outer Hebrides Islands by the time of our visit. Wind was blowing and the rain was cold, so our visit there was cut a bit shorter than we had hoped. On we went, to John O'Groats, just a few miles away.

The mist was so heavy that we couldn't see the Orkney Islands at John O'Groats. We got our pictures taken with the road sign reading 5276 miles to San Francisco. Next we drove to Mey Castle and did a tour there and visited the kiddy zoo. Still the weather was a bit brisk and the mist was too heavy to see the Orkney's. We drove past Peedy Puckles,[18] through Castletown, and into Thurso, stopped at a Tesco for a few groceries and got Max a sandwich to ward off starvation, then a fairly decent drive back to Sallachy. There had been a shower every now and then, but no low fog and not a lot of traffic. I was glad to quit driving though when we got to the lodge.

Wednesday we went back to Dunrobin Castle so Max and Arianna could see the falconry show. We again met Ann Worthy and hubby in the Coffee Bothy in Golspie, just by coincidence they were there also. Thursday the Mc Brides took their two kids to Fort William. They had booked a ride from there to Mallaig and back on a "Harry Potter" train. Such fun for the kids, Keith was then reading the Harry Potter series. Thursday, Friday and Saturday, we spent pretty close by the lodge, a trip or two to Tain and Bonar Bridge being the big travels. Mc Bides had their overnight in Ft. William and had rejoined us. Max and Arianna had ridden Iain's Quad out past the lodge several miles to where we had gone shooting in 2010.

Saturday night we all went to Iain's for a big dinner they put on for us. They had bought many types of foods to serve us. We had haggis, langoustine lobster, steaks, salmon and venison, all served with the appropriate dishes accompanying them. There were a multitude of beverages and desserts also. Jay Comella was in charge of the barbeque and did a marvelous job. They had also invited another couple from near Bonar Bridge and their daughters. This made a wonderful gathering of the clans.

We had been out shooting clay pigeons out over the loch just below Iain's before dinner and the midgies ate us up. No one did well with the shooting, but all took a turn, even Caitlin and Keith. I don't think we hit

---

18 Peedy Puckles was a gift shop near the exit road from Mey Castle. Janette loved the name.

anything very often and the midgies eventually drove us all away and into the house. It was different after we had our dinner, the midgies let up some. Iain sent three floating lanterns out across the loch. They are much like a small hot air balloon and have a little fuel cup to keep them airborne for three or four minutes. That was a wonderful sight to see the three lanterns strung out over the loch, then one at a time the fire quit and they just disappeared into the loch. This was truly a night that we all will remember always. We still speak of it often.

Sunday morning we were off early for York. Max and Arianna went to Inverness with Jay and Fiona, caught the train to Glasgow, then they flew home from there in time for Max to go back to work. The rest of us spent three nights in York, and then we took the train to London for three nights. While in York we did the tourist stops again and rode the open top bus on a city tour. The Train Museum was a great stop for all of us. It is one of the largest train museums in the world. We also took a ride on the York Wheel, another large Ferris wheel. Warren treated us to a riverboat ride down the river Ouse to the home of the Archbishop of York. We couldn't do more than look at the outside of that stately home, but it was interesting to see the wealth of the head of the local church in ancient times.

In London we met Pat Smith, her daughter Leslie and Leslie's daughters and their kids, for lunch at Caluccio's Restaurant in St. Pancras Station. We all had a fine lunch, then said our goodbyes and found our way to the Holiday Inn near Marble Arch. This was like being in the Middle East. Every corner had a bunch of men sitting outside the restaurants, in their pajamas, smoking hookah pipes. There was also a fair share of London's beggars around the streets. We met up with our friends, Simon and Carolyn, while having dinner at a Thai restaurant and had another wonderful visit. We put the finishing touches on our plans to go to Hampton Court Palace with them.

The following day we journeyed around London on foot and by bus. We split up so the Mc Brides could go to the Tower and we went our way to go where we hadn't been before. We had lunch at the club Simon and

Carolyn belong to. Bruno, their Boxer dog was able to join us, as we ate outside in a covered patio. It was a very nice place and we were able to tour a good portion of the building as well.

The following day we all went to Carolyn and Simon's house on the Beverston Mews and saw all the work they had done to remodel it. It wasn't finished yet, but the work was far enough along for us to understand how it would look and function when it is finally finished. It will then be one of their truly fine remodel jobs. Another one that impressed us was a Carriage House in Rhinebeck, New York. Both were totally remodeled, Rhinebeck was 7500 square feet and London was 1500. The cost was about the same for both jobs, hard for me to fathom.

Our next to last full day in London, Carolyn and Simon acquired Zip Cars,[19]and took all of us to Hampton Court Palace.[20] It was as beautiful as Nelda and I had recalled it, from our visit there in 1978. The grounds were covered in flowers and the trees were all neatly trimmed, making anywhere one chose to look, a spectacular scene. We all toured the Palace and agreed to meet in the entry courtyard some hours later. Some of us read slower than others and with a group the size of ours it was not worth the effort to try to keep them all together.

I cannot describe Hampton Court Palace as it should be described. I will give you a bit of how I viewed it. It was a large palace built over the course of several years and several monarchs. It is basically a large square building that has a large open courtyard in the middle of it. The portion that is the oldest is the farthest from the river Thames. The newer part is closest to the river and both are connected by large buildings that connect the old and new in such a way that they seem to melt together, from the inside. When one is out in the gardens it is quite easy to see the difference

---

19 Zip Cars are part of a rental scheme that makes cars available throughout London. The ones we used had to accommodate six people each, which is more than the average British sedan normally, will hold.

20 Hampton Court Palace was built by Cardinal Woolsey and given to Henry the Eighth, upon Woolsey's death. There was suspicion of foul play, but no one has said how it played out, that I have heard.

from old and new, but from the inside it is well disguised. As with all grand houses, castles and palaces that we toured in the UK, there is a fine chapel built into the old section. There are two Roman emperors carved into the casing of the entry doors of the old portion, Hadrian on the left and Trajan on the right.

We did the tour and rode a horse-drawn wagon around the grounds. The Palace is about a mile back from the Thames and the grounds go to the river. They are well manicured and there are places to sit in the shade and we found some snacks to keep our hunger down. We all gathered in the courtyard and noticed that there is a fountain that in the day of Henry VIII would have been flowing wine, not water. There are wooden carvings of drunks leaning on a nearby wall and laying beside the fountain.

Our last day of this trip was spent tidying up loose ends, last minute cab and train arrangements to get to Heathrow, checking on flights and confirming times of everything, gate numbers and requesting that Janette's husband Mark meet us and take us to our homes. The Mc Brides had a friend do the same for them and we all arrived safely home. It had been another wonderful experience for our whole family.

Epilogue

OUR LAST DAYS IN SCOTLAND had us concerned for Rob's health. He had complained of a loss of memory and some headaches. He was talked into calling ahead and making an appointment with his doctor for the day following our arrival home. He went to that appointment and then to several others and eventually to UCSF Hospital in San Francisco. He was diagnosed with a brain tumor. We had the best of doctors and a family full of love and concern all doing our best to make him well. It was not to be. We found the tumor had destroyed the very brain of our beautiful little boy and there was no magic treatment to fix it.

We all met with the doctors and determined that we would have him come to live out his remaining days at our home in Danville, where we let him have his dog beside his bed and with the help of a nurse occasionally and our daughters, at least one of them there every night with us, we kept him as comfortable as we could. On December 15, 2012, he simply quit breathing and went peacefully away to his reward. His last words were, "Beautiful." Though mute, blind and paralyzed, my girls and Nelda had described a bouquet of flowers to him and he said "Beautiful."[21]

---

21 " Beautiful" was the name of a theatrical performance put on several months later by Carol King. She was Rob's favorite entertainer and Nelda and I along with our two girls, went to see the production. The tickets were complimentary and the staff welcomed us to the show. The girls had made them aware that Rob was a fan and his last word, "Beautiful."

Made in the USA
San Bernardino, CA
23 July 2016